The Restaurant Marketing Bible

ANDREW WOOD

Copyright © 2019 Andrew Wood
All rights reserved. No portion of this book may be reproduced, stored in a retrieval system, or transmitted in any form or by any means – electronic, mechanical, photocopy, recording, scanning, or other – except for brief quotation in reviews or articles, without the prior written permission of the author.

Printed in the United States of America

First Printing, 2019

ISBN: 9781700023636

www.AndrewWoodInc.com

Table of CONTENTS

	INTRODUCTION	1
1	Don't Fall for These Restaurant Marketing Myths	4
2	Developing a Legendary USP	17
3	Your Creation Myth	33
4	Creating the Right Look and Feel…While Creating an Emotional Bond with Your Guests…and Turning Them into Your Own Social-Media Marketing Army	43
5	What's the One Item on the Menu You Have Just Got to Eat?	81
6	Building the Perfect Website	111
7	Creating Legendary Landing Pages	129
8	Data Collection	145
9	Legendary Email Marketing	188
10	Social Media—Facebook	219

11	Building Buzz and Brand by Blogging	244
12	Facebook Ads	253
13	How to Write Legendary Headlines for All Your Marketing	270
14	The Art of Selling Ice to Eskimos	291
15	Irresistible Offers and Iron-Clad Guarantees—Your Secret Weapon in the Battle for Massive Response	306
16	Designing Legendary Ads, Collateral, Sales Letters, and Direct Mail That Work!	319
17	Meetings, Groups, and Special Events	347
18	Legendary Sales—Get Ready to Maximize Sales	361
19	Selling Private Events, Banquets and Catering	377
20	Legendary Closing	397
21	Boosting Your Profits by Selling More Wine	409
22	Building a Referral Machine for Your Restaurant	417
23	Developing Legendary Service and a Guest-Friendly Culture	436
	Epilogue	456
	About Andrew Wood	459

INTRODUCTION

I spend six months a year traveling the world. This also means I spend six months a year eating out in restaurants. I generally prefer a local place to the hotel restaurant, although there are many fine hotel restaurants these days. In the last few years, I have visited restaurants in United States, Canada, Scotland, England, France, Wales, Switzerland, Germany, Austria, Belgium, Singapore, Thailand, Spain, Portugal, Holland, Italy, Dominican Republic, Jamaica, Morocco, South Africa, Panama, Bali, Australia and Dubai.

Add this vast first-hand restaurant experience to over twenty years in which my company Legendary Marketing has been a world leader in golf, resort, and destination marketing, and I could easily claim to have more experience than all but a handful on the planet. That's before I mention that we managed several properties ranging from a 38-room hotel to a 168-room resort, all of which had restaurants.

My wife ran a restaurant for over ten years and we both waited tables for five. My son and daughter at this moment are both in training to be restaurant managers and my daughter is looking at buying one. I have seen the business from almost every angle: the good, the bad, and mad chefs throwing knives.

While I pick up new and innovative restaurant marketing ideas all over the world, the vast majority of restaurant marketing that I see, from the individual entrepreneur to the multinational chains, is poor and ineffective. They get caught up in style over substance, branding rather than results, and mediocre multichannel marketing without actually acing a single one!

A simple change in marketing strategy can have a major impact on your income. Dramatic results can be gained in simple ways like tightening up the effectiveness of the response you get from your existing efforts. Three percent here, five percent there can add up to huge increases in business, and these often cost little to nothing to execute.

It's exciting stuff, so let's get started...

"One cannot think well, love well, sleep well, if one has not dined well." **—Virginia Woolf**

CHAPTER 1

Don't Fall for These Restaurant Marketing Myths

One of the major reasons why most restaurants don't market effectively is that they are under the influence of marketing myths. Who knows how these misleading ideas got started, but many of them have been around for decades. Before you start any marketing program, you first need to "clear the decks" of these marketing misconceptions.

In this chapter, you will discover:

- ✓ the secrets of successful restaurant marketing (an overview; later chapters will provide the details),
- ✓ what the biggest myths in marketing really are,
- ✓ why long copy works better than short copy,
- ✓ why, if everyone likes your ad, the ad is probably worthless,
- ✓ how to avoid being seduced by the law of large numbers, and
- ✓ why copying your competitors is a bad idea.

Andrew Wood

UNDERSTANDING WHY MOST RESTAURANT MARKETING FAILS

Before I get into the "meat" of how to massively improve the effectiveness of your restaurant's marketing, it's important to take time to debunk some of the common myths about marketing. This is a very important step because on your journey to marketing success, managers, owners, spouses, board members, waiters, bartenders and cooks will question you at every turn. They will question your strategy. They'll tell you that you must do this or that because that is what your competitors are doing. They'll beg you to discount, will disagree with your long copy, and advise you on graphics, colors, and media at every opportunity.

There is no place for myth or personal prejudice in a comprehensive, results-driven, marketing system.

Most opinions are wrong!

Everyone has an opinion about marketing. Rarely, however, are those opinions based on facts. Instead they are almost always based on personal preferences for colors or styles, or based on myths that have been handed down for decades from others and repeated so many times that they are now wrongly considered to be fact by 99 percent of people. Most important, since the people judging your marketing are rarely the same as those you are actually trying to attract, their opinions on anything are basically worthless! Worthless because their opinions are based not on marketing science but are based on their own social, economic, and psychological preferences, not those of the people you are trying to attract!

Unless you are willing to drop your personal preferences and debunk years of marketing misinformation in favor of proven marketing science, you cannot accomplish your goals of achieving Legendary Marketing at your restaurant.

The following pages include the biggest myths and inhibitors to marketing success. Read them, understand them, believe them, and take them as gospel. Share them with your owner, boss, manager, spouse, or whoever else is most likely to sabotage your efforts. Get them to understand the science of effective marketing before you attempt to market, so that everyone is on the same page, moving in the same direction.

AN ESSENTIAL CRASH COURSE IN MARKETING MYTHS

1. People don't read any more.

Myth.

The biggest myth in marketing is that *people don't read any more* or at least they won't read lots of copy. The truth is, in fact, the opposite. In almost every case, long copy will out pull short copy. Yes, in today's world people's attention spans are short, especially for things in which they have little to no interest.

The key factor is interest.

If people don't care about your vegan menu, kids menu or *He Man Burger,* they won't read anything, long or short. If prospects are specifically interested in what you have to offer, and if you provide information in a compelling fashion, they will read it. The more you tell them, the more they'll trust you and the more interested they'll get in experiencing your restaurant.

Send me a magazine or email on horses, and I'll pass it to my wife without glancing at a single page. Send me a magazine or email on cars, and I'll give it a quick flip through. Send me a magazine on sports cars, and it will get a little more of my attention as I flip through every page, scanning for something that catches my eye. But send me a magazine on Ferraris, and I will take it to bed with me and read it cover to cover, word by word—every article and every relevant ad. The difference in how I read these different magazines is my level of interest in the subject matter. If I am interested in a topic, I want to know as much as possible. If I am not interested, I don't want to know anything. Your customers are no different. They will pay attention to what interests them and will ignore what does not. They want more of what interests them and less of what does not.

This holds true for websites, landing pages, emails, videos, and any other form of marketing.

2. The more the people who like your ad, website, landing page, email or video, the better your marketing!

Myth.

Design your marketing to create *response,* not to please your owner, your staff, or your wife.

Graphic designers are not marketers. In fact, in many cases they have the opposite effect.

Web designers are not marketers.

And, if truth be told, most ad agencies are not marketers. A nice way of explaining this is that most ad agencies are bored with simple approaches that work. Or they are so busy that they tend to produce generic ads. A more cynical way of explaining the failure of many ads produced by ad agencies is that the agencies are more interested in competing for awards and inflating their egos with their clever designs than they are in making money for their clients.

No matter what people say about being "open minded," they (as we all do) judge you on their preconceived notions about marketing and with their personal preferences for design, text, and style. They may know something; they may know nothing. But make no mistake about it, 99 percent of the time they judge your work based on what they like or think they know about marketing, not on what will actually work!

The key to great marketing is not to design ads, websites, and mail campaigns that people like. It is to design marketing that motivates targeted prospects to take the action you want.

Your target market is very likely a small percentage of the entire population. Your ideal prospects are a certain age, have certain hobbies, wants, needs, passions and favorite foods.

Some of the best restaurant marketing my company has ever produced has never seen the light of day because it does not meet the criteria of the person paying the bills. I call it the Everyone-Loves-My-Ad Syndrome!

Just because everyone loves your ad, website, landing page, or video doesn't mean that the phone will ring, people will click, or that anyone will buy your offer.

You should design your marketing campaigns specifically for the people who you think will buy.

You should test different ads, landing pages, and email headlines based on *response*. It doesn't matter whether you like the ad, your wife likes the ad, or anyone on your staff likes the ad. What matters is whether or not the people you want to buy respond to the ad.

Guests buy only two things: benefits and solutions. They do not buy features. They do not buy because of your logo, because your picture happens to be in the ad, or because you have been in business for twenty years. They only care about what your restaurant can do for them.

Do you have clearly unique or superior food?

Is it a better value than the competition?

Is it a great place to meet people?

Can they get in and out fast for lunch?

Is it a good place for a business meeting?

Will your amenities or location enhance their ability to relax and have fun?

Before you hire anyone to design an ad campaign, educate yourself.

Read a good marketing book. Discover the real principles of marketing from a true leader in the field, not from someone who happens to run a small design company down the street and thinks he or she knows something about marketing. Read *Ogilvy on Advertising*—Ogilvy built the biggest ad agency in the world from scratch. In its pages you will discover many things you never knew, like why long copy always sells better than short copy. Or get the classic book *Scientific Advertising* by Claude Hopkins, or Al Reis and Jack Trout's classic book *Positioning*. Or one of Dr. Rick Crandall's books on marketing services. In books like these you will discover that the real secrets of marketing are not what most people think they are—in fact, very often they are the opposite.

The number one goal of a good ad, website, landing page, email, social post, sales letter, or brochure is to connect with a specific targeted reader and motivate that reader to action.

In the case of an ad for a vegan restaurant that means not just any reader. Not your husband who loves big steaks, or son who is fourteen and lives on McDonald's—you need vegans. Your ad should be written and designed only for him or her, not anyone else. What anyone but that targeted reader thinks of your copy or design does not matter one iota. In fact, if lots of unqualified people look at the ad and like it, it's an almost sure sign that the ad is not speaking to your target audience in an emotional and personal enough way to be effective. It's almost like "they" should be the only ones who get it.

It's no different when targeting any other type of food that some people love—for example, Mexican, Indian or sushi—and others do not.

3. Reaching ten thousand people via social media or on a portal website is typically more effective in generating revenue than mailing to five hundred people whom you know for a fact have a strong interest in your type of restaurant and live in your

market area.

Myth.

Thousands of ad salespeople make a living by seducing restaurants with large numbers.

Successful marketing is, and always will be, about reaching targeted prospects.

Target prospects are those who have the characteristics of your best customers. For example, they might prefer your style of food, be in the right age bracket, live within a specific geographic area, or be in the right income bracket. A targeted mailing list of a thousand prospects would be 70 percent cheaper and about 1,000 percent more effective than mass advertising on a website to one hundred thousand people. But that small number throws people off. They think bigger is better. In fact, *targeted* is better! That means you should use targeted mailings, targeted emails, targeted landing pages, and doubling or tripling the response from the people you already have in your database.

Most people just don't get it. They think the numbers are too small. Huge circulation numbers or traffic numbers seduce them when they should be focused on the *quality* of the leads they get, not the *quantity*.

4. You don't want to exclude or offend anyone with your marketing.

Myth.

Actually, that's exactly what you want to do—exclude all those people who aren't good prospects, so you don't waste any more time or money chasing them. When I say offend, I don't mean you stand up and insult them. Think of it more in terms of how a Republican might react to a Democrat's comments.

For example: If you are a steak house in the Northern woods, you might run an ad that says something like:

Around here the only thing sushi is good for is bait!

This might be a nice provocative headline to appeal to macho hunters who inhabit the area. Sure, some women or Japanese might take offense, but the number of macho guys you excite by this headline will more than make up for the furor of a few people who are obviously not your true target market. In fact, if people make a fuss about your ad, you will get free publicity with the target market that matters to you.

You have to take a stand. The more targeted your position is to your true market, the more effective your marketing will be, even at the expense of excluding or even irritating some potential customers.

5. If all your competitors are doing it, you have to do it too just to compete.

Myth.

You do not have to advertise in the local web portal, Yelp, or the restaurant directory, just because fifty of your favorite competitors do. In fact, it's plain stupid to do so. Nor do you need to discount because they do. The less you act like your competition, the quicker you will define your own position in the marketplace.

Those are the five big myths we come up against again and again. Don't let your marketing decisions be influenced by these dangerous beliefs.

TOP TWENTY REASONS WHY MOST RESTAURANT MARKETING FAILS

In the next few pages I'm going to save you hundreds of thousands of dollars and years of trial and error by detailing exactly why most restaurants fail to reach their marketing goals. This is not subjective; this is not our opinion. It is based on over thirty years of research into the science of marketing and the analysis of several thousand clients. (Some of these twenty reasons also relate to the five major myths I just covered. That's okay; this is a full list.)

Here are the top twenty reasons why most restaurants' marketing efforts fail. Read them, believe them, and resolve not to do them.

1. **They don't collect enough data from guests,** potential diners, names, emails, phone numbers, and so forth—before, during, and after contact. Building a huge database of prospects is the most important job there is at any restaurant that wants to rapidly increase income. The person with the biggest database always wins, and the deeper that data goes, the better. Only one or two restaurants in a hundred make an effort to get my email address, which I always gladly give.

2. **They don't do enough with the data they do collect.**

    They are scared to overuse their data. As a result, many don't use it enough, failing to maximize the potential of their email lists and social-media following.

3. **Their websites are ineffective.**

    That is to say, websites are generally set up as electronic brochures, not as sales machines, data collection machines or long-term customer-bonding hubs.

4. **They do not track their promotional campaigns effectively**, so they have no exact way of knowing which promotions were effective.

    This is not easy even with today's technology, as what triggers a reservation could be multiple engagements with multiple messages, but most don't do enough to track even the basics.

5. **They run campaigns that people say "look good"** rather than ones that actually get the phone to ring or the customer to click. Too many effective campaigns are killed by people who know

nothing about marketing and a great deal about what they personally "like," what their competitors do, or what they "think" constitutes good marketing.

6. **There are no written sales process or scripting or training of the people answering the phones or at the greeter's station.** You tend to get the best results from the things you focus on the most. Few of the restaurants I have worked with had any formal sales training in place at all. In the off hours it was a lottery as to who picked up the phone—you might reach the hostess, chef, new waiter or bookkeeper. Even a few hours' training and some simple scripts can have a dramatic effect on your bottom line.

7. **Follow-up to all requests is not automated** or systemized, so follow-up is generally poor.

8. **They do almost the same marketing as all their competitors;** they are afraid to risk being different. It astonishes me how many restaurants' ads or emails look identical and how many use the same media and approach as their fifty closest competitors. Instead you should do everything in your power to stand out.

9. **Websites, brochures, ads, emails, and sales letters are written in** boring, generic corporate-speak and wouldn't motivate a drunk to leave his seat to get a free beer. They have cute headlines, pretty pictures, and *impotent* copy.

10. **They discount prices to get more business rather than look for ways to add more value.** Adding value even to something as simple as an email is harder than discounting, so most restaurants just don't do it.

11. **Their budgets are based on a percentage of gross** or a number someone handed down from head office instead of being based on the goals they are trying to meet. In other words, the goals are pure fantasy with no consideration whatsoever of the number of leads and sales they need to generate.

12. **They do nothing to set themselves clearly apart from other restaurants in their marketplace.**

    Yet these restaurants still say things like "We have the best food and great customer service"...Yeah, yeah, yeah. "Tell it to the judge," as my kids used to say!

13. **Their service is really about 80 percent worse than they think it is.**

    They have no system in place for measuring service and they never run extensive customer surveys so they never really know how good or bad their service truly is!

14. **They fail to thank their customers** with letters, cards, and small gifts, as is done in almost all other professional businesses.

15. **They confuse "loyalty" programs with discount programs.**

    Loyalty is earned, not bought.

16. **They don't understand social media.**

    Just because you have a social-media account and know how to post does not make you a social-media expert. Almost none of the thousands of restaurants I have worked with can articulate their social-media strategies. This is not surprising because they don't have one.

17. **They don't capitalize on the website automation that's available to help them maximize their operations.**

    Too many restaurants are using a website provided by their POS company or reservation engine that is not the best-in-class technology by a long shot.

18. **They do not set clear marketing goals or review marketing results on a weekly or monthly basis.**

    Few restaurants know how many leads they need in each category or how many prospects it takes to get a sale.

19. **They do not do enough A/B testing of offers.**

A/B testing is where you vary one characteristic of your ad (for example, the headline), and then send half the group the ad with one headline and the other half gets the ad with a different headline. It has never been easier to test headlines, copy, graphics, and offers to see what works best rather than guessing yet few restaurants do it religiously.

20. **They keep doing what they have always done** because it's easier than changing to a more systematic sales and marketing approach that would actually work.

Meanwhile their market shares and margins are sinking fast.

SUMMARY

Now you have the key information and reasons why most restaurants don't get where they want to go. You are ready to do things differently and get the corresponding successful result.

"There is no sincerer love than the love of food."
— **George Bernard Shaw**

CHAPTER 2

Developing a Legendary USP

How important is a Unique Selling Proposition (USP)? So important that without a great one your business will always be an "also-ran."

The USP was first described more than sixty years ago in the classic book by Rosser Reeves, *Reality in Advertising*. While given much lip service, the concept of USP is seldom understood or operationalized well. Reeves said that your USP must meet three criteria to be complete and powerful:

- It must say to your customer, "Buy this and you will receive this specific benefit."
- Your USP must be one that your competition does not, or cannot, offer.
- It must be strong enough to attract new guests to you.

Your USP is the basis for your marketing and advertising efforts. It is the unique advantage you use to sell your *restaurants*.

Your USP should be so strong and memorable that it will both distinguish you from other restaurants and attract new business. It should also be memorable enough to generate word of mouth to drive referrals. It is not a meaningless slogan like "Charlestown's best-kept secret" or "a London tradition." It must offer a clear benefit to the guest.

In this chapter, you will discover:

- ✓ why your USP is so important to lower your costs and increase your income,
- ✓ why most restaurants have no USP,
- ✓ how to develop possible USPs,
- ✓ how to gather input for your USP development,
- ✓ formulas for possible USPs,
- ✓ sample USPs,
- ✓ how to test your USP for effectiveness, and
- ✓ how to best use your USP.

LEGENDARY USP

No matter who you are or where you are located, your reputation precedes you in your market. The more positive and solid your reputation for whatever your USP is, the easier it will be for you get customers. More people will seek you out, be willing to pay you more money, and will happily refer you to others.

While some restaurants have taken decades to build their legacies and reputations, others have done it much faster. In today's world of the Internet, email, social media, and targeted blogs for every audience, the opportunity to build a reputation quickly has never been greater. The challenge is to accurately define your USP—the essence of what you offer that is superior and unique.

DON'T BE A "ME-TOO" RESTAURANT

Many owners or managers have never heard of a USP. And while a select few instinctively emphasize their uniqueness, most have done nothing to set themselves apart in the marketplace.

The importance of accepting this challenge to differentiate yourself from your competition is that without a USP you can waste thousands of dollars marketing the features of your restaurant—features that many others also have, or that no one cares about. You will be another me-too restaurant with "good food and great service."

By taking the USP challenge, you will, with a few words and concepts, set yourself apart from your competition. You will find yourself more focused and your message more on target, while attracting a far greater number of the right type of customers.

Let me give you a few clear examples of what I mean. Pebble Beach sells a once-in-a-lifetime experience, not a round of golf. A Hyundai dealer and a Rolls Royce dealer both sell cars, but they are hardly in the same business. A Hyundai dealer sells transportation; a Rolls dealer sells luxury. A Timex dealer sells watches that tell time; a Rolex dealer sells jewelry and status.

Most restaurants don't have a USP that is strong enough so they never build a strong marketing program on a secure foundation. Instead they bounce from idea to idea without a consistent theme. In fact, I've had clients who proudly showed me the twenty different ads they had run over the last five years—each touting something different! This approach wastes lots of time, lots of money, and a great deal of effort.

For you to attract the maximum number of prime clients in your market, you must determine exactly whom you are trying to reach and what message from you will resonate with them. Then you must shape your performance to deliver this unique experience.

"RESTRICTING" YOUR MARKET

You might argue that if you focus on one USP, you will limit your market, but, that, my friends, is the very idea. You focus your market on the people who value the one thing you can do best. Then you harp on it for all you are worth and develop your own niche market within a much broader category.

It turns out that this new focus doesn't limit you as much as it attracts more customers. Your USP also produces a tagline on your business card, a slogan on the bottom of your ads, and is attached to your name like a double-barreled surname.

Without a position around which to build your marketing, you are just another commodity that no one thinks is special. With a strong USP, you lower your marketing costs, increase word of mouth, focus your efforts to do a better job for your guests, and increase your income.

What comes to mind when you hear Domino's Pizza? "Domino's delivers in thirty minutes or less." That was their unique selling proposition and it fueled one of the most rapid business success stories ever. Domino's wasn't really selling pizza, what they were selling was fast delivery. There are hundreds of different chains around the country that sell pizza. But when you think of Domino's, you think of their thirty-minute delivery guarantee. You might be interested to know that those ads haven't run since the early 1990s, ever since a driver was killed trying to get his pizza delivered on time. Yet the thirty-minutes-or-less perception remains because that thirty-minute USP was so strong!

WHAT DO YOU WANT YOUR REPUTATION TO SAY?

The first step in building a legendary reputation is to determine how you want people in the marketplace to perceive you. Your USP will be the basis for getting your marketing message across and building your reputation. It will be what they remember about you and pass on to others. It will be the foundation on which all your marketing is based, from your website to your customer-service training.

In contrast, if you try to advertise yourself as all things to all people, they will think you're a "Jack of all trades and a master of none." A strong USP doesn't limit you; it opens up your options!

Throughout this discussion, I will continually emphasize that you must pick one USP and stick to it. However, if you have distinctly different audiences, it is possible to have different USPs for each audience.

HOW TO DEVELOP YOUR USP

There are several factors to consider when creating your USP. The best way to start is to gather input from your staff and guests. If possible, get your staff together and ask them as a group to come up with individual words or phrases that define you. Make a list of at least ten to twenty key words or statements. Do the same thing with your customers, either in a group (like the board) or individually. Ways to ask about a USP include the following phrases:

- Our guests tell us that what they like best about us is _____.

- We are the only one in our area that does _____.

- We are the best restaurant in the area because _____.

- The thing we are proudest of is _____.

- We're better than anyone else at _____.

- The thing people remember us for is _____.

- The most unusual thing about us is _____.

If you heard people talking behind your back about your restaurant, what strengths of yours would you want them to be mentioning? What is it about your restaurant that people use to describe you (the quality of the food, the history, the status, the exclusivity, the value, the pricing, the attentive customer service, the scenery, the ambiance)? Specifically, what is it that you do better than anybody else, or what is it that you have that no one else can offer?

Try to avoid generic answers like quality or service because everyone says these things. You can't be everything to everyone. You should therefore select one main perception that you want to convey in your marketplace, and back it up with a couple of subsidiary points.

Take some time to carefully consider the questions and write down your answers. Even "silly" answers can sometimes stimulate useful material. For instance, if you have a nickname it may suggest a USP.

The answers to these questions often will involve a physical attribute of your restaurant. But they could also involve your people, your general location, your price or value, your service, and so on.

After you have collected information, develop variations and combinations and narrow the list down to three or four of the very best possibilities. Once they have been defined, these answers should be synthesized into a possible defining statement. This may take you a while, and that's okay. This is much too important a decision to rush, but make sure you follow through and come up with just a single sentence, preferably one that offers a clear benefit to the customer.

Focus on one key trait.

Another concept closely related to USP is positioning. Positioning focuses a bit more on you compared to the competition, not on your uniqueness. For our purposes here, however, both positioning and branding mean the same thing as USP.

You will only be remembered in one key area, with perhaps a couple of sub-thoughts at most. Once you choose that area, you must use as it as your central focus in making future decisions. This means focusing on one particular area and spending less time and effort on others.

It's very important that you decide what your image should be. If you try to be everything to everybody, it won't work. And once you have developed your reputation label, it's nearly impossible to shed it. Good or bad, your reputation ultimately will depend on a few words, so choose the statement that represents yourself wisely. It will stick with you for a long time.

SOME COMPONENTS OF USPs

Here are some other ideas to get your creative juices flowing.

Andrew Wood

Preempting the truth for your USP

While it's better if the USP you design is something nobody else can claim, it's not essential. You can choose to highlight some aspect that your competitors may also possess but have failed to exploit. By being first, you lay claim to the particular benefit that you're promoting. Jack Trout and Al Ries, the originators of the term positioning, call this "preempting the truth."

Miller Brewing Company built its business on "lite beer," but they didn't invent the category. Coors did that more than a decade earlier. But Coors failed to position its beer as a light beer, and lost out to Miller (who exploited the position to the tune of hundreds of millions). You don't have to invent it; you merely have to claim it!

The word "probably" diminishes your USP but can make you seem more honest. But "Probably. The Best Barbeque Ribs in the World" were for sure the best in Patong, Thailand (not that I tried the second-best place ☺).

Seriously confused! Swiss Palm Beach Restaurant's sign says "Italian, French & Thai" under the name. Do one thing and do it well, do not try to be everything to everyone!

Standing out from the crowd

Let's say that you are one of ten restaurants on your strip of the beach. You're better than some, not as good as others. How are you going to make your mark?

First, look at what your competitors are doing—what do they specialize in? Take a look at their websites, brochures, print ads, billboards, and any other literature you can find to determine what positions they are claiming. Fortunately for you, in most cases there will be nothing significant. However, their random claims may give you a few ideas and help you spot their weaknesses.

Maybe you can claim to be the lobster specialist? The shrimp specialist or the only steak house in a line of fish restaurants!

Here's a couple of outside the industry examples to get your creative juices flowing ...

When I lived in southern California, I used to ski in Big Bear where I had the choice of two resorts. Both were more or less on the same mountain and one was ten dollars a day more than the other was. Where would you ski? I skied Snow Summit, the more expensive of the two.

Why? Because they limited ticket sales and had a ten-minute lift line guarantee. If you were not on a lift in ten minutes, they gave you a ticket for another day free. It never happened. The two or three times I tried the cheaper place, Bear Mountain, I waited as long as thirty minutes to get up the mountain—no thanks!

Let's say your restaurant is the worst of the ten aforementioned competitors. What then? Don't market food as your key feature. Market something else. When the new GM of the New Jersey Nets basketball team took over in the mid-nineties, he had on his hands the very worst team in the NBA. Not only did they have a terrible winning record, but the players also had bad attitudes and the few fans who did show up hated them. So how did the new GM manage to go from a stadium that was not even half full to selling out every game in just a few months—while the team continued to play as badly as ever?

Brilliance, that's how! Brilliance and a change in his USP. He stopped trying to sell his team. It was pointless—the Nets were terrible and everyone knew it. He couldn't change the team play without some serious personnel changes and time to work on things. But he could change the USP and turn the team into a profitable business instead of a money pit. Instead of marketing his team, he started to market the stars of the opposition teams!

> Come see Michael Jordan and the Chicago Bulls!

> Shaq and The LA Lakers!

> Larry Bird and the Celtics!

In his favor was the fact that many of the stars he was promoting were nearing the end of their careers, so he added some of that into the mix. *"This might be your last chance to see Jordan play in New Jersey!"*

He bundled the good games into packages of five, tripled the ticket prices for those games, and threw in all the mediocre games for free. He sold out the stadium in a matter of weeks while the Nets continued their mediocre play. But it didn't matter—he was no longer selling his team. He was instead selling the superstars on the opposing teams as the reason to come to the game. Brilliant!

TESTING YOUR USP

Like other parts of your marketing, your USP can be tested. You can use focus groups to compare different USPs. You can use surveys. You can test headlines in emails or landing pages using different USPs. You can test USPs as direct mail or advertising headlines. Just don't fall in love with the first clever idea someone comes up with. As famous advertising man David Ogilvy used to say, "You don't want your ads to win awards for creativity; you want them to make you money."

YOUR USP STRENGTHENS YOUR MARKETING MESSAGE

With a USP in mind, your logo, ads, website, brochures, and other marketing material can all be designed in a very cohesive manner. This is integrated marketing, where your different pieces reinforce a consistent marketing message and convince rather than confuse the customer.

All too often, people bounce from one message to the next, hoping in vain to be everything to everyone. It doesn't work. Stay focused. Develop your campaigns around strong images. Use strong colors that carry the feel of your USP throughout everything you do!

Confused prospects do not make good customers because confusion causes doubt. Doubt leads to fear of making a poor decision, and fear leads to paralysis or procrastination. Use your USP as a roadmap for your marketing materials. When completing any new marketing tool, ask yourself the following simple questions.

Are the graphics and copy congruent with your message?

A client recently brought me a marketing piece in which he claimed to offer both the finest and the cheapest service in town. But you cannot be the cheapest and the best. People simply won't buy that concept. They have been preconditioned to believe that the best of anything is always more expensive. The cheapest may offer good value, but you hurt your credibility, never to regain it, if you also try to claim that you are the best. The best is never the cheapest. On the other side, words claiming that you are the best in town would not be supported by printed material that was cheap looking.

Does it enhance your position in the minds of your customers?

Check if each marketing effort stands out and brands your name clearly and uniquely in the minds of your prospective customers. If it's only as good as anyone else's effort, don't do it.

Stand out and be bold—or save your money and invest it in bonds.

Is your delivery consistent?

With your marketing materials in complete harmony and building on your USP, the next question to ask yourself is how consistent you are in delivering your message. In many cases, business owners develop a winning concept and then become bored with it, thinking that others must surely have tired of the concept as well. So they move on to a different and far less effective concept, just as the other one was taking root in the public consciousness.

In my consulting, I frequently design marketing tools for clients that they instantly proclaim to be the most effective they have ever used. Eight weeks later, they are back on the phone asking me to design new ones, even though the original ones are still pulling far better than anything else they have ever done. I ask them why they want new tools.

They tell me it is because everyone has seen it already. Good marketing can go on working indefinitely. Sure, you might rest them for a few weeks and then bring them out again, or perhaps change the picture, keeping the copy much the same, but the fact remains that a good ad will work far longer than most people have the patience to keep running it!

Consistency is the key to building a long-term image that allows you to dominate your marketplace. Most great marketing campaigns last for years, even decades, as has the Marlboro cowboy, the Energizer Bunny, the twins in Wrigley's Double Mint Gum ads, and Budweiser the King of Beers.

I'm sure that in your town you can think of at least one particular business that has made an impression on you just because they are so consistent, even if their marketing is consistently bad. The Crazy Greek Mattress Shop, the car dealer who always wears a ten-gallon hat on late-night TV, or the attorney who pitches injury law with a cast on his leg. Consistency is no substitute for great marketing, but great marketing done with consistency will produce the best results of all.

BUSINESSES UNCLEAR ON THE CONCEPT

Do you really know what business you're in? Sounds simple, but very often I find that business owners think they are in one business while the customers think it's another business. As Charles Revlon once said, *"In the factory we make perfume, in the stores we sell hope!"* Remember, people buy for their reasons, not yours! You might brew the best coffee in town, but if everyone is coming to you for your donuts it would be better to focus your marketing message on donuts. It doesn't matter if you own a coffee plantation and grow the beans yourself—if your customers are coming for the donuts, it will pay you to go with the flow. Forget what you are trying to sell and focus instead on what your customers are buying.

DIGGING DEEP FOR THE DIFFERENCE THAT MATTERS

What is unique, truly unique, about your restaurant, unique enough amid the common clutter of shared features and benefits to get me to spend my money with you?

What's the difference between one restaurant and another? Often in any given category, not much.

But sometimes even something small is enough to influence a person's purchasing decision.

I frequent one local restaurant with very average food because in my rural setting they are the only one that has a selection of IPA beers.

My wife and I visit another frequently because they have a small selection of vegan items for my wife. Most other local restaurants think a baked potato and broccoli is a good vegan meal.

I visit another with average food because of their great location on Kings Bay.

We visit another for their great cheese plate and there is a pub in the UK I visit only for its amazing antipasto plate.

In California I used to go to a place that guaranteed lunch in 15 minutes or less or your lunch was free. This appealed to workers on their lunch breaks. Although the food was good, they were actually selling the place based on time, not food quality—and the place was packed. They had their act together too because I never did get that free lunch.

These all are simple yet potent examples of positioning yourself as better and different in an incredibly crowded market!

So what USP are you going to build on and champion in your marketplace?

Without it, you are just another business saying how good your service is…they all do that.

AVOIDING THE MUDDLE IN THE MIDDLE

In every market there is a Ferrari and a Chevy, a Rolex and a Timex, a Ritz Carlton and a Motel 6, a Neiman Marcus and a Wal-Mart. The closer you are to the top or the bottom of your market, the easier it is to meet expectations and to price your dishes and event services correctly to maximize profits.

The problem is that most restaurants find themselves in the middle of the market. This muddled area is where they are neither the best nor the worst, neither the most expensive nor the cheapest, neither the newest nor the oldest, neither the quickest nor the slowest.

The middle of the market is by far the most difficult area in which to compete. You should first try to move toward one end or the other by either increasing your service and offerings to increase your price, or by decreasing service and offerings to lower prices and increase volume.

In my experience, the latter is actually the harder of the two to accomplish successfully. In contrast, it's relatively easy to add something that moves you up and differentiates you in the marketplace:

- The restaurant that greets you with a glass of champagne when you check in for your table.

- The bar with a plateful of trendy appetizers (to offset the even trendier prices) that is delivered just as your first drink is almost gone so you stay for a second drink as you eat the food.

- The only valet parking that offers a free car wash while patrons dine.

- You create a new category—a category that you can lead.

Take yourself out of the muddle in the middle by doing something different that allows you to be a leader in your own category. The only business in your category that also offers X—where X is a strong enough factor to create a new, or at least stronger, position within your category.

ONCE YOU COME UP WITH A USP STICK TO IT

I was doing a consulting visit at a private country club somewhere in New Jersey, near Atlantic City. Around lunchtime the owner asked me whether or not I like crab? I said, I did, and he said, "Great! When we're done tonight, I'm going to take you to the best crab place you've ever been. It's the number one crab place in New Jersey. My friend owns this restaurant and it's great for all seafood, but the crab is exceptional." At the end of the day, the owner, his team and I headed out to his friend's restaurant. It was a Friday night and the restaurant was packed, with people lining up out the door. I heard people mutter that the wait was 90 minutes. My client just walked in past hostess and gave a wave to his friend at the back. His friend came out, greeted our group of eight and immediately walked as to a table in the back of the restaurant.

As my client had been telling me all day how great the crab was, just for fun I asked the waitress, "What do you recommend?" To my utter astonishment and with howls of laughter from everyone at the table, the waitress said, "I don't really like seafood so if I were you, I'd try the steak!" I ordered the crab, of course, which was great but when the waitress came back to the table and asked how everything was I said. "You were right; I should have had the steak." She said triumphantly. "I told you." and walked off smiling as the whole table burst out laughing again.

SUMMARY

Trying to be everything to everyone is a sure way not to conquer your market. You must decide on what your core business is and build a USP around what you do best. To define your USP you must answer at least two questions:

- What is the word or statement you want to "own" in the minds of your customers?
- What one thing do you do better than anyone else around?

Once you have answered these questions and decided on a USP, you must stay focused and use your position as a guide to both marketing issues and business decisions.

You must make your marketing congruent with your USP message so it builds and grows in the minds of your customers. Finally you must remain consistent within your marketing message. Resist the temptation to change for change's sake. Once you find a good marketing message, ride it for all it's worth, over and over again, until it's burnt into the collective consciousness of all the prospects in your market.

"My weaknesses have always been food and men — in that order." — **Dolly Parton**

CHAPTER 3

Your Creation Myth

Once you have decided on your USP, it's time to write your restaurant's story. Great stories are the foundation of all great marketing. All the best stories of have some common characteristics: a time, a place, a protagonist, some setbacks and an "aha moment" that was the catalyst to success. Like a great book or movie, the branding of your restaurant will start with a story, *your* story. Some call it a *backstory* or, in many cases, a *creation myth* because over time fact is blended with fiction until no one really knows the truth, but the story lives on. The more engaging that story, the more successful you will be.

Your story answers the basic questions of where it all began. Why you do what you do? You will want to explain how you found your calling and how you developed your talents. Your fans will be interested in your "aha moment" and what challenges you conquered along the way. Once you are happy with your story, tweak it and enhance it so it resonates with your audience in an emotional and empowering way to grow your brand!

Let's start by reviewing a few creation myths of some famous restaurateurs.

Colonel Sanders believed that his little restaurant and motel would remain successful indefinitely, but at age 65 he had to sell it after the new Interstate 75 reduced customer traffic to a trickle. Left only with his savings and disgusted with his $105 a month from Social Security, Sanders did some serious soul searching. After completing an inventory of his talents it become clear to him that the best asset in his inventory was his fried chicken recipe.

He decided to begin to franchise his fried chicken concept in earnest. He traveled the US looking for restaurants who would use his secret recipe. Often sleeping in the back of his car, Sanders visited thousands of restaurants at which he offered to cook his chicken. If the owners liked it, he negotiated franchise rights of four cents a chicken.

It took him offering the deal to hundreds of restaurants before anyone took him up on the offer!

His face and his 12 secret herbs and spices became synonymous with fried chicken. The rest, as they say, is history.

Andrew Wood

Paper cup salesman Ray Kroc was amazed by the efficiency of the McDonald brothers' hamburger stand in San Bernardino, California. Having been in over a thousand kitchens, Kroc believed the McDonald brothers had the best-run operation he had ever seen. It had a very simple menu, cheap prices, and tons of business. Procedures were set up with simple systems that got good results every time. The restaurant was clean, modern, mechanized, and the staff professional and well groomed. Roadside hamburger restaurants were more often than not hangouts for motorcycle gangs and rebellious teenagers, and Kroc saw in McDonald's a better vision for a restaurant. Kroc opened the first McDonald's franchised under his partnership with the McDonald brothers in Des Plaines, Illinois.

A little-known part of the McDonald's story is that the brothers had already sold franchises to other people! But those people didn't carry through all the difficult steps that Ray Kroc had to go through to really get multiple franchises running successfully.

Howard Shultz

Andrew Wood

In 1971, Starbucks was a single store in Seattle's historic Pike Place Market selling the finest fresh-roasted whole bean coffees. In 1981, Howard Schultz (now Starbucks CEO) had first walked into a Starbucks store. From his first cup of Sumatra, Howard was drawn into Starbucks and joined a year later.

In 1983, Howard traveled to Italy and became captivated with Italian coffee bars and the romance of the coffee experience. He had a vision to bring the Italian coffeehouse tradition back to the United States. He wanted Starbucks to be a place for conversation that provided a sense of community—a comfortable place between work and home. He left Starbucks for a short period of time to start his own Il Giornale coffeehouses and returned in August 1987 to purchase Starbucks with the help of local investors. Their mission is to inspire and nurture the human spirit — one person, one cup, and one neighborhood at a time.

Where's the Best Italian Food in NYC?

I was in New York and decided to look online for a great Italian Restaurant. I found Patsy's, which according to their website is a traditional family-owned restaurant located in midtown Manhattan, in operation since 1944 with only three chefs in all that time. Patsy's website has a great story…

Patsy's Italian Restaurant

Patsy's Italian Restaurant has been known for years as the restaurant Frank Sinatra made famous, and in fact, his family still enjoys dining at Patsy's Italian Restaurant whenever they are in town. In addition to Sinatra and family, Patsy's Italian Restaurant has become a favorite with countless stars on both the east and west coasts, who have come to regard Patsy's Italian Restaurant as a mecca of Italian fine dining.

Some of Patsy's Italian Restaurant's high-profile patrons include Michael Bublé, Ben Stiller, Tony Danza, Al Pacino, Placido Domingo, Alec Baldwin, Kim Basinger, Tom Hanks, Madonna, George Clooney, Rappers Heavy "D" and Sean "Puff Daddy" Combs, David Letterman, Oprah Winfrey, Keanu Reeves, Jonathan Demme, Tony Bennett, Don King, Robert De Niro, …(the list goes on).

Just steps from Carnegie Hall, Lincoln Center, and the Theater District, a visit to New York City is not complete without a meal at Patsy's Italian Restaurant. For lunch, dinner, business, or pleasure, Patsy's Italian Restaurant has been serving traditional Italian cuisine at the highest standards and in the warmest atmosphere for well over half a century. Family owned and operated for 71 years, the original Patsy's Italian Restaurant, in its only location, 236 West 56th St in New York City, has been the place for homestyle Neapolitan Italian food that has been enjoyed for generations.

Stories Matter

Even if you are the local take-away pizza joint and your most famous customer is a high-school quarterback or local soccer star, your story is important. Showing the people behind the business makes it more real, human, interesting and likable.

You are in town for one night and read the following two descriptions. Everything else being equal, where are you going to eat?

Franks Pizza
Serving great homemade pizza, pasta, meatballs and subs since 1978.

Romeo's Pizza and the Secret Sauce
It has been said that men have died for the recipe and I don't doubt it. Since my grandfather came from Sicily in 1927, our family has been in the restaurant business in Buffalo. While people rave about our pasta, meatballs and subs, Mama Gandini's secret pizza sauce has always been at the heart of our success. You're gonna love it, or we'll send the boys round!

The ten elements of a great restaurant creation story

There are ten key elements to a great restaurant creation story. While some miss a few, you will find these elements in almost all. Think how your story can be enhanced using this formula. Some are simple descriptions, but they help clarify who you are in people's minds.

Andrew Wood

1. **Location:** Where did it all begin, once upon a time?

2. **A problem needs to be solved:** No sushi restaurant in town. No Chicago-style pizza, vegan or Indian. No fine dining, al fresco or lakeside dining. No pizza and beer location next to the ball fields. What void does your restaurant fill?

3. **Protagonist:** Existing options are poor; you are going to change that. Who are you?

4. **Aha moment:** That moment when you discovered it was all going to work as the planets align. The day an ex-priest from Florence walked into the restaurant and became your chef.

5. **A dream is dreamed:** A goal is set, a position taken. We must have Chicago pizza here in small-town Florida.

6. **Talent development:** Perhaps you were a great chef but not so good with the business and had to develop those talents. Perhaps it was the other way around you knew how to run business but burnt every order in the kitchen. But whatever talent you lacked, you sought out a mentor, training, experience and conquered your deficiencies.

7. **Challenges must be overcome:** Short on funds, but burning with passion. Or perhaps you had many failed attempts to hit on the right menu combination, the right recipes or the right theme.

8. **Setbacks occur:** There was a flood; we were closed for six weeks, almost for good but…

9. **The regroup, retry and persist:** But we opened again and our loyal customers saw us through, even donating to help us rebuild.

10. **Success:** Today we are the most successful restaurant in town and give back to our community by donating food to the local homeless shelter every week.

Berns' Steak House

The Restaurant Marketing Bible

In Tampa there is one restaurant everyone knows, even if they haven't been there yet—the famed Bern's Steak House. They carry 400,000 bottles of wine—50,000 on site and another 350,000 in a warehouse nearby. Before you dine, you can take a tour of the wine cellars (they have bottles of sherry going back 200 years) and the kitchen. They also have their own farm where they grow many of the vegetables. Let's take a look at how their story fits nicely into the formula I just gave you.

Location
In 1951, newlyweds Bern and Gert Laxer planned to move from New York City to California, but they first wanted to visit Bern's aunt in Tampa.

Problem
During their time in Tampa, Bern and Gert ran out of money so they decided to call Tampa home. Bern found work in advertising while also freelance writing a garden newsletter called *Garden Notes* in his spare time.

Protagonist
In 1953, the Laxers bought a small luncheonette called The Gator Juice Bar that served orange juice, coffee, and cold sandwiches at lunch time. After several months, the Laxers added cold breakfast and opened earlier in order to accommodate more diners.

Aha Moment
Acknowledging their success, the Laxers purchased the Beer Haven bar in what was then a small strip shopping center and moved their operation to 1208 South Howard Avenue. After a "historical" meeting with 10–20 investors, Bern and Gert began their new endeavor in what is now the Bordeaux Room of Bern's Steak House.

Challenges and setbacks
Not long after opening the bar, the Laxers learned that the man who sold them the Beer Haven had done so without permission from the landlord,

and the landlord threatened to not renew their lease due to his disapproval of alcohol sales.

Re-group and persist
Bern and Gert agreed to go back into the food business and became a restaurant once again. The Laxers labored seven days a week, Bern as the cook and dishwasher and Gert as waitress, hostess, and second dishwasher, as they served breakfast, lunch, and dinner, and served beer and coffee in between meal service.

Success
As time marched on, Bern and Gert gradually bought adjoining shops and grew Bern's from one to eight dining rooms and from 40 to 350 guest seats. Finally, the world-famous Harry Waugh Dessert Room was built in 1985 using redwood wine casks to create 48 private rooms where guests to this day enjoy nearly 50 desserts, wines, ports, sherries, and Madeiras.

Today son David carries on the tradition and runs Bern's Steak House.

Using this formula as a guide write your story, tweak it, enhance it, edit it until you get it perfect. Write out a long copy version of a page or more for your website, then edit the story down to a paragraph to use in bite size situations.

"He was a bold man that first ate an Oyster."
— Jonathan Swift

CHAPTER 4

Creating the Right Look and Feel... While Creating an Emotional Bond with Your Guests...and Turning Them into Your Own Social-Media Marketing Army

How can you make an average restaurant stand out without an expensive remodel? How can you create an experience guests remember for all the right reasons, even with average staff? How can you make price irrelevant, within your category, to the majority of your guests?

There is an answer to all these questions, and it boils down to just one word—passion. The passion to create an experience that differs in many subtle ways from all others in your category. Whimsical ways that bring a smile to your guests' faces and have them reaching for that cell phone photo quicker than they would cash a winning lotto ticket!

With a few simple moves your restaurant can create its own social-media marketing army. Just imagine if you had hundreds, perhaps thousands of people a month promoting your restaurant for you! How much easier and profitable would your life be?

In this chapter you will learn:

- ✓ why passion, not price, is your unbeatable marketing edge,
- ✓ how to create a marketing army from the ranks of your guests,
- ✓ the "one thing" you need to do to wow your guests,
- ✓ how to go from ordinary to extraordinary, and
- ✓ creative ways to create simple Kodak moments.

Is it really all about price?

For most businesses, including restaurants, discounting seems to be the first choice, the line of least resistance in trying to attract more customers to their doors. There are far more productive ways to attract and retain loyal customers while turning them into social-media evangelists for your cause.

Let me ask you a few questions:

Do you always buy…

- the cheapest product or service,
- the best-made product,
- heck, even the best-value product?

No, no and no!

Your favorite restaurant is not always the least expensive or even the one with the five-star food!

If everyone bought the cheapest product, we would all be driving Nissan Versas (currently the cheapest car in the US at less than $15,000), eating at McDonald's or Taco Bell, wearing Timex watches, and staying at Motel 6, Premier Inn, Formula 1, or Etap, depending on our geographic location.

Price is just one of a many different factors that go through a prospect's mind before committing to the majority of his or her purchases. Yet it seems to be the only factor that most businesses are capable of focusing on. This myopia costs them dearly each and every minute they are in business.

Your favorite restaurant is not always the least expensive or even the one with the five-star food!

Amazingly cool Italian restaurant in Valencia, Spain.

The Reasons People Return Again and Again to a Specific Business Are Complex and More Emotional than Rational

Think for a moment of your own "go to" restaurant (aside from your own!), maybe not the one you go to for really special occasions, but the one you find yourself at most frequently. The chances are it is neither the best nor worst in town, neither the most expensive nor the cheapest. You like the food, but it's more than just the food. Perhaps it's the view, the special ambience, or the fact that they stock your favorite beer or wine. Maybe they treat you like you're special, or you know the server or owner, or parking is easy. If you really dissect your decision, you will find a large number of reasons, both conscious and unconscious, that go into making your choice.

Your go-to restaurant has an edge over the competition when it comes to your eating-out decision-making.

I want to show you how your restaurant can be the go-to business in your sector.

Many of my examples will not be exactly right for you.

That's okay.

My goal is to get your creative mind flowing. Take the core concepts and adapt the ideas and examples I give you and then tweak them to custom fit your restaurant's circumstances. Many of these concepts will not only make your guests' experiences substantially more attractive, but they will also enhance your employees' experiences (which in many cases may be just as important).

Just open your mind to the possibilities…

Andrew Wood

Your favorite restaurant is not always the one with the best food!

How to Stand Out from the Crowd in a Very Crowded Market

Before I tell you how to do exactly what the headline suggests, let me ask you a question:

What outstanding feature do you think of when you think of these three US flagship airlines?

- American
- Delta
- United

Which one really stands out head and shoulders above the rest as the best? Sorry, but it was trick question. All three airlines have poor service and have little or nothing (other than a few routes) that differentiates them from each other. I have personal horror stories from each. And, these days, when individuals can gain a worldwide audience online, heaven help the company that disrespects a demanding and tech-savvy customer.

(See YouTube for a quite hilarious video shaming United Airlines for mistreating and breaking a passenger's guitar and not reimbursing him for it. Google "United Break Guitars." Cost to United: more than thirteen million views of negative publicity—and that was long before they dragged a guy kicking and screaming off a flight!)

If I added Southwest to the mix, you might have come up with something different:

At the very least, I am sure most of you who live in the United States know that on Southwest, at the time of writing:

- "BAGS FLY FREE,"
- tickets are much more flexible,

- personnel are much more fun,
- their frequent flyer program is much easier to understand and has no blackout dates.

Southwest is also perceived as having cheaper ticket prices, although that is very often not the case.

Which airline is the only one of the four not to have gone bankrupt?

And to actually have made an operating profit the vast majority of its existence? Yes, that would be Southwest. People understand that Southwest is a different type of airline. That is what drives their success!

The same can be said of Virgin Atlantic on which I fly often. They have a great emotional bonding package. In first class they have lie-down beds and a martini bar you can sit at. They have good food, nice wines, and a great clubhouse at Heathrow when you land. There you can take a shower, get your suit pressed, scarf down a full English breakfast, and be on your way refreshed and ready for action!

On the way out, they have an awesome lounge and spa. It is in a totally different league then flying first class on a US carrier.

What's the Average Customer Experience Like in the Restaurant Industry?

Now let's look at the restaurant industry. Let's take half a dozen restaurants in the same category as yours in a town near you. What makes one demonstratively different from the next?

Usually **absolutely nothing** at every touchpoint. (Touchpoints are the various places at which a customer interacts with a business.)

- Ads, brochures and sales letters are average.
- Parking lot is average.
- Website is average or often below.
- Waiting areas are average.

- Emails are average.
- Physical location is average.
- Bathrooms are average.
- Displays are average.
- Menus are average.
- Food is average.
- Furniture is average.
- Look, feel, sounds, smells are average.
- Social-media engagement is average.
- Service is "awesome"—just kidding; it's average too—very, very average!

In fact, the total sum of the entire experience at most restaurants (within specific price categories) is alarmingly average, and they just struggle along trying to maintain the status quo.

Profound Breakthrough—It's Not All about Your Main Product

In the golf and resort industry where I do a lot of consulting, way too much emphasis is put solely on the golf course, which, for better or worse, is usually about where it's going to be without spending millions in improvements. Or the emphasis is on invisible "service" or on creating a golfing "experience" that in most places exists only as a word in their outdated brochures.

I, and many of my friends, have had some of our most memorable days ever at some sheep-infested golf club in the Scottish Highlands, with awful weather, a colorful caddie, and a wee dram of local whisky afterward as we warmed ourselves around a fire in the pub.

The total sum of club membership, a nice day out at your local daily-fee course or a weekend away at a golf resort includes far more than just the quality of the golf course. Some of it is tangible some of it is not, but the "emotional experience" the customer gets, from wherever it comes, is what will either bring them back or not. And it's the same for your restaurant.

The More You Do to Make Every Step of Your Restaurant Experience Memorable for All the Right Reasons, the More Chance that They Will Choose You!

That does not mean spending a ton of money. That does not mean pretending your restaurant is something that it is not. What it does mean is that you have to think out of the traditional, conservative box. It means transforming your operation into something different in its category. This requires a simple paradigm shift in the way you think and operate.

At many of the seminars I give, I ask the audience members what business they think are in. The top three answers are always:

- The service business
- The people business
- And, of course, the hospitality business

What few people realize is that the answer to this critical question fundamentally changes how an operation is marketed, sold, and run, and therefore changes the experience it provides to the customer.

A customer shows up at a golf resort, ultimately for the one key factor few ever mention. They are there to be entertained by the course, range, staff, food, drink, and the experience the club provides by allowing the members to interact with people of similar interests.

Food is the vehicle by which a restaurant entertains its guests. The more entertaining you make your marketing, emails, websites, letters, social-media posts, special events, menu descriptions, plating, and just the everyday experience of eating a meal out, the more value they will deliver. Therefore, the more people they will attract, and the longer they will flourish.

If customers are not entertained, they will look for their entertainment not just at other restaurants but also at the mall, bowling alley, movies, and a million other places. Understanding that their competition is not just other restaurants but every other form of entertainment makes a profound difference to how you approach the creation of value at your restaurants—and few really get it.

Now here's the important thing—this concept works for every type of business, albeit in slightly different ways. You are competing for your customers' attention, emotions, time, and money.

From Very Ordinary to Extraordinary in Just a Few Hours!

Recently I was in the United Kingdom for the summer and the friend I was visiting, golf professional Mark Wood gave me an awesome four-hour golf lesson. In return I took him out for dinner at a local hotel that also had a cool gastro pub attached.

Two months later, I was back in the area again for a lesson, and he suggested we go somewhere else for dinner. I said, "No, let's go to the same place we did last time."

He was not sure where we had gone two months earlier, and I couldn't remember the name of the place. But I did want to go back there…

"Why?" you may ask.

Because the food was awesome? No, but it was good.

Because it was cheap? No, it was reasonable, but certainly not cheap.

Because it was the closest place we could have eaten? No.

What was the real reason why I went back and spent another eighty or ninety dollars at this place? The men's toilet!

Weird, eh?

So, a few months later I was in Las Vegas, at the Sports Bar in the

Vegas Hilton. Great big screen, average prices, poor food, and not much choice in beers.

But the men's restroom... incomparable!

The next time I go back to Vegas with new friends, the Sports Bar bathroom will be one of the first places we stop at—well, after fueling up at the bar.

Now, before you think I have some kind of strange toilet fetish (for the record, I do not), let me bring you up to speed on two key marketing concepts that should be at the forefront of your mind.

The Unbeatable Marketing Edge

The power of passion was recognized years ago by the famous advertising guru David Ogilvy.

As mentioned earlier, he found that the key to success for any company was its ability to create an emotional bond with its customers that went far beyond what the company was actually selling.

To paraphrase Ogilvy's words slightly:

"A company competing on the basis of price can always be undercut. A company competing on the basis of uniqueness can always be copied. A company competing on the basis of a technical advantage can always be caught. A company competing on the basis of value can always be matched. But a company with passion cannot be touched."

The long-term success of your restaurant will be determined not so much by the product and service you provide, but by the emotional bond you create with your customers. Those restaurants that fail to create such a bond, a feeling of something greater than the food they happen to be selling, will not be able to compete at the top for any length of time.

The "Experience" Factor

We are, and have been for at least the last decade, living in the experience economy. *Auto Week* magazine now lists over fifty places where, for a couple of thousand bucks, you can learn to drive like Lewis Hamilton or Jeff Gordon in real race cars at Silverstone or Daytona. Talk about an experience for the average red-blooded male!

For about the same price you can pilot a MIG fighter in mock combat, float across the Serengeti in a hot air balloon at sunset searching for wildebeests, or attend Rock Star summer band camp.

In Orlando, a world leader in the experience economy, you can dine at:

- Jimmy Buffet's Margaritaville
- Toothsome Chocolate Emporium
- Rain Forest Café
- Planet Hollywood
- Pirates Dinner Adventure
- Capone's Dinner and Show
- Medieval Times
- Or a number of themed restaurants at Disney World Resort or Universal Orlando Resort depending on what type of memorabilia or ambience you are looking for in your dining experience.

People are spending more money than ever on adventure vacations and theme-enhanced cruises and tours. Let's not forget Paris, New York, Egypt, and Venice in Las Vegas!

People want—no, demand—more than just a vanilla experience in almost every business.

I have a marketing strategy I call the ONE Strategy. It's a simple strategy that will have an untold positive effective on your business if you embrace it wholeheartedly.

The strategy is simply this…

Make ONE Thing at Every Touchpoint of Your Restaurant Memorable to Your Guests—So Memorable that They Market for You!

Just have one little thing that you do better than any of your competitors, something that makes your customers smile, remember you, and talk about you when they leave. And more importantly take a picture of and share, promoting your restaurant worldwide hundreds, perhaps thousands of times, per week.

Creating that "Kodak Moment" for Your Restaurant

Photography company Kodak had a long-running and very successful advertising campaign inviting users to capture that special "Kodak moment" on film and remember it forever.

These days, with digital cameras and smart phones, people take more pictures than ever. Not only do they take more pictures, but they also share them faster and further afield with the power of social media.

You need to figure out creative ways to get people to take pictures of your restaurant and share the photos with their thousands of social-media friends, thus providing you with instant and powerful free advertising.

Let's start in a place that most people, well at least most men, wouldn't even think of as an experience:

The toilets. Imagine if you could make your toilets so cool that people would come to your restaurant and bring others just to see them, regardless of your other attractions.

In large cities, many department stores actually attract customers because people know they will get clean, safe, comfortable restrooms if they go to a particular store, albeit on the tenth floor! (And, people infer that if bathrooms are well taken care of, the rest of the business is also well-run—and clean.)

Getting customers from your restrooms sounds crazy, right?

But it's not; if you can ace it in the bathroom, just think how easy it will be to ace it in other much more attractive and interesting parts of your operation...

Here is the men's restroom in the Bell Inn I was telling you about, in the United Kingdom.

Restrooms that Draw Customers and Light Up Your Social Media

Pictured above is the men's room at the Las Vegas Hilton sports bar. There are about twenty different images in all, each as funny as the next.

Priceless.

Now if you were going to Las Vegas with the "boys," you just might want to take a friend or two into the Hilton sports bar just to see the restrooms.

There are hundreds of sports bars in town, but why not go to one where you watch the games on giant screens, drink, gamble, and can have a laugh while you pee?

If it's that easy to make your men's toilet experience so unique and memorable, just imagine how much easier it is to make your window display, bar, menu, uniforms, waiting room, parking lot, lobby area, advertising, social media, or follow-up memorable.

Enhancing your current restrooms could be as simple as pinning something entertaining to the wall of the men's room: a simple poster in a frame, a special notice, or a wall of jokes. It could be sports memorabilia from a local team. I even know of a bar that has flat-screen TVs over the urinals. Perhaps it's nothing more than a funky color scheme or some cool tiles. It doesn't have to cost a lot; it just has to be different and memorable.

Then again, you could take it up a notch or two and really stand out.

When I was a kid, the local department store had the nicest, cleanest restrooms in town, and that was a real draw. They were located at the very back on the fourth floor, in their restaurant so you had to walk through the entire store to get there.

Did that increase their sales? You bet it did—pretty much everyone in town ended up there at some point.

Andrew Wood

I took this photo at Jimmy Dean's Bar and Night Club in Prague. Not to everyone's taste I am sure, but it was memorable!

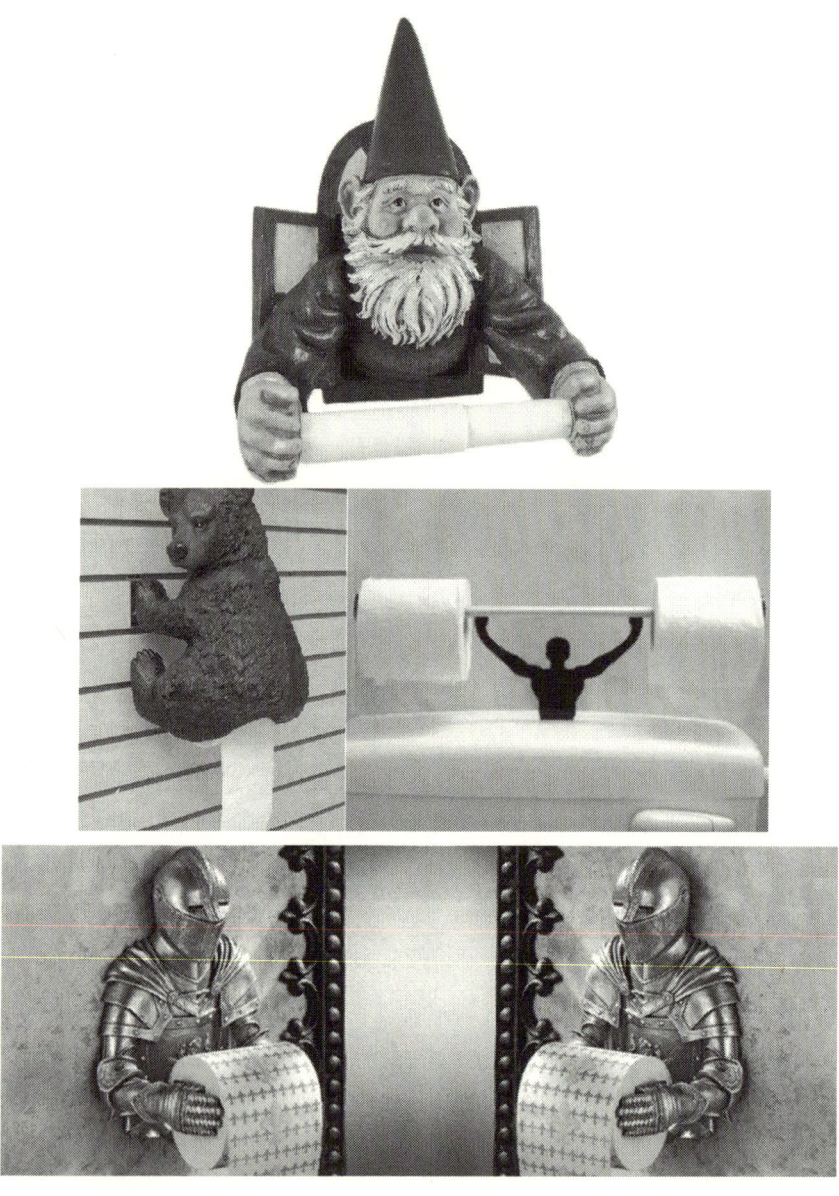

Keeping the "Mo" Going in Your Bathroom

Now if you have gone to all the trouble of making your toilets cool, you shouldn't have a standard stainless steel holder and hard white toilet paper to ruin the positive experience, should you?

How about some unusual toilet paper or some cool holders that might match your business?

Is your crowd into art, music or money?

Go ahead and have a little fun you'll be amazed at the response the simplest little change can make!

So, what's the ONE thing you could do to make your restrooms memorable—so memorable that people want to come back and bring their friends?

CREATIVE FIXTURES THEY'VE NEVER SEEN

Let's Keep It Clean

Okay, so with toilets out of the way, it's time to wash our hands. Let's not ruin the good will and positive feelings we have already generated from our first efforts by giving you customers a white sink with ordinary metal taps!

Instead, let's continue to engage them, amaze them and entertain them with some cool taps that color the water blue, red or even pink as it comes out of the spout!

All it takes is a cool tap to change ordinary into extraordinary!

Andrew Wood

Perfect for a sushi bar but would be a cool addition to any business.

It could be as simple as having a restroom with a running waterscape on the wall or unusual mini-waterfall faucets like my old club in California had. My kids thought they were awesome they came up with any excuse to use the bathrooms just so they could wash their hands under the cool taps! Beyond taps look at the washbasins themselves—there are a million ways to get more creative and be memorable!

Have you ever been in a high-end restaurant where someone has come back to the table and said you need to go in there just to look? That's the response you are looking for!

Take the restrooms in, say, a Barnes and Noble bookshop—NOT! Barnes and Noble goes to great effort to create a nice atmosphere almost like home in the main space with chairs, a coffee shop and music. Then you go in to their bathrooms and it's basic with no effort at all. A bookstore should be a mine of creativity!

In any place where you sell drinks, your bathroom is a huge opportunity to make a statement about your business. Imagine a convenience store or a gas station that had amazing restrooms like the ones I have shared with you. Don't you think that alone would improve their business? Once people in the area know that it's super clean and super cool, that's going to be the place they stop, not the one on the other side of the street!

All it takes is a little out-of-the-box effort!

The Restaurant Marketing Bible

Love this one.

Andrew Wood

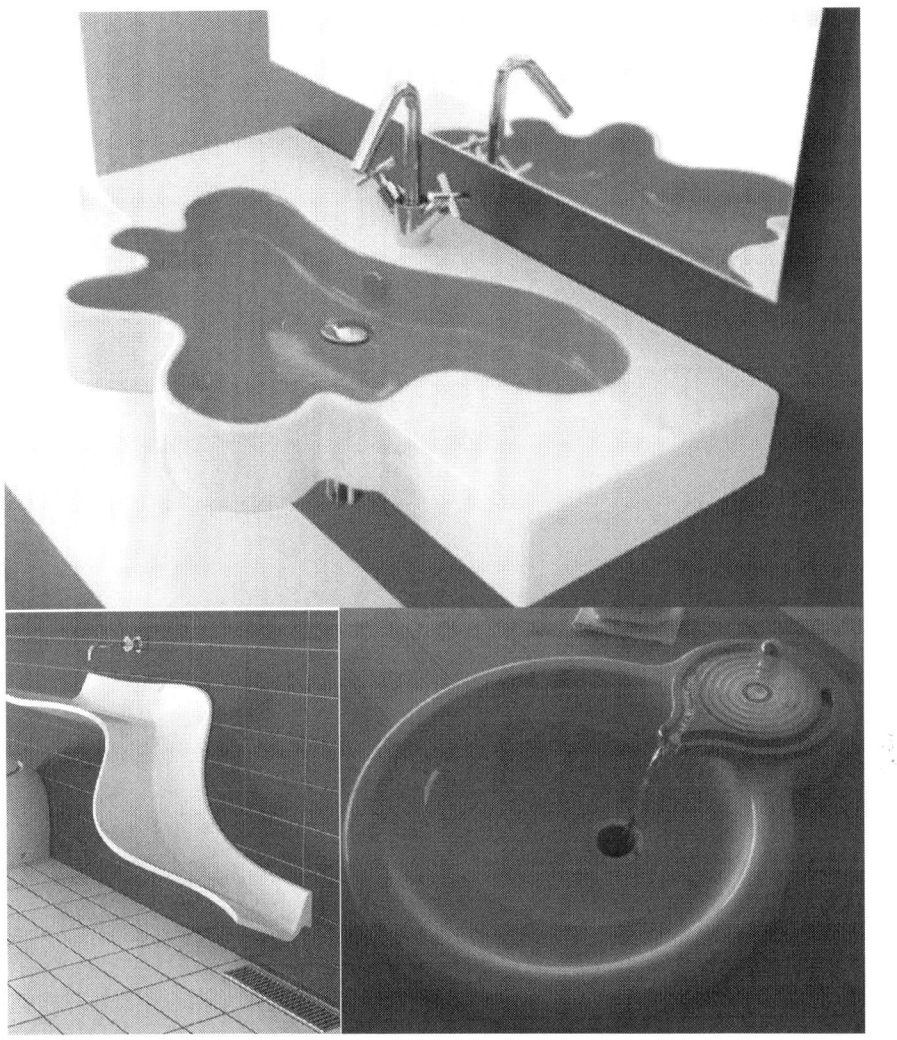

Imagine being in a restroom and being confronted with anyone one of these washbasins!

What would you think?

Adding some aftershave, hand cream, or sun block in large dispensers puts you a further cut above.

It all counts when it comes to building the experience and making your business memorable in as many places as possible, not just the places you think you should stand out.

For People to Buy, They Have to Feel They Are in the Right Place

I'll tell you a funny and very revealing story (although not all that funny at the time) from my days in the karate business about the importance of the right furniture. It's one that helped me understand the importance everything plays in both sales and the emotional experience you provide to your potential customers.

You'd think furniture would be unconnected to the buying experience (unless you're selling furniture), but it's not. Furniture is part of the very complicated experience that is the decision-making process of the human mind.

Andrew Wood

When I first opened my small karate school, I went big—a $900 Chinese desk with carvings, two carved dragon chairs at $450 each (one is pictured on the pervious page), a large Chinese painting and an Oriental screen.

After a really great first year, my studio was broken into and both chairs were stolen. I replaced them with normal cheap office chairs and thought little about it except for wanting to catch the thieves who stole my chairs and putting a few karate moves on them.

To my complete surprise, a lot of the parents and students noticed and asked, "What happened to the dragon chairs?"

When I told them they had been stolen, nearly everyone asked if I would be replacing them. I had really not thought about it, as I didn't realize that they really mattered all that much to my business and replacing them would be expensive.

Sure enough, over the next few days it was confirmed they really did matter, as more than one student told me they had signed up because of the furniture. We looked a cut above the other schools with their cheap desks and metal chairs and because of that they were willing to pay more and sign up with me!

It was a very interesting lesson in human psychology and one that plays out in all kinds of sales situations regardless of the professional, industrial or retail nature of the actual customer interaction.

In restaurants, chairs can be more important, or interestingly varied, than in most businesses.

Feel like you ought to be sitting in this chair and being pampered? Good—because so will anyone else who sees it! If this chair is in your waiting area under a sign with your restaurant's name, think of how many people will share photos with a member of their party sitting in it.

Andrew Wood

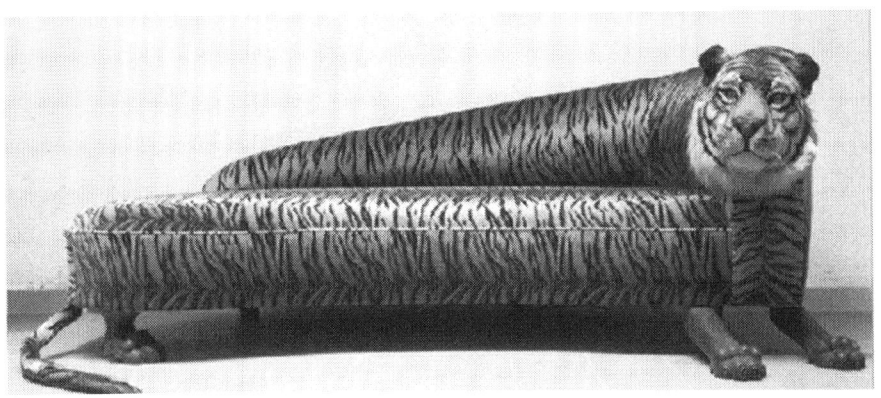

If you saw one of these sofas in a restaurant lobby anywhere, wouldn't you want to sit on it? Might you get a picture of yourself or your party on it? Would you share that picture on your social media and tell people where you found it (thereby promoting that restaurant for free)? I know I would have my iPhone® out in a New York minute!

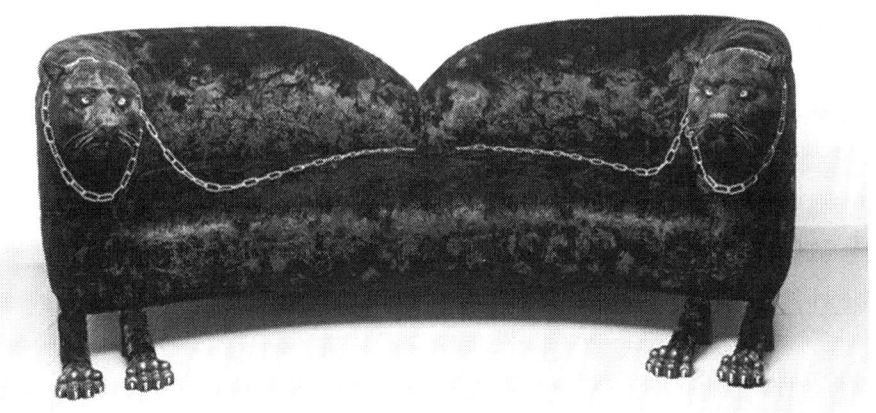

Start with One Interesting Piece

Once again, you don't have to refurnish your whole restaurant to make it memorable. Maybe start with one or two really cool looking chairs in your lobby, the type that people want to sit on as soon as they walk in the door—like the throne.

There is a bar in Tampa with an oversized throne. Sooner or later everyone wanders over and gets a picture of themselves sitting on it, and no doubt many share their pictures and their location with hundreds of their best friends on social media!

We are not just talking chairs here. Tables, coffee tables, card tables, pool tables, lights—everything counts when it comes to being memorable. Start small and work up!

The positive effect of creating this emotional excitement with furniture works just as well on your employees as it does on your customers. Just look at the work environment of high-tech companies like Google. Fun is a major part of their approach and that's a big reason why people love working for Google.

What ONE thing could you do to enhance the emotional connection your customers have with your restaurant through your lobby furniture?

Maybe none of these particular ideas will work at your restaurant. **It doesn't matter.** The point here is to think out of the box—don't think corporate, pretend you work for Disney or Virgin and are charged with enhancing every single area of your restaurant experience. And I do mean every single area.

Theme Restaurants Connect with Customers on Multiple Levels

Theme restaurants combine menus, food, uniforms, furniture, service, and many of the other attributes we have already discussed to create a unique ambience.

My personal favorite was in West Palm Beach, Florida for over twenty-five years until they expanded the airport. The 391st Bomber Group was a restaurant located on the site of Palm Beach International Airport. If you Google it you will see hundreds of people writing about how great it was and how special it was to many people for so many years.

As you approached the parking lot, you passed under a barrier with a sentry post and an old army jeep. The main building had been created to look like a bombed-out French farmhouse complete with shell holes in some of the walls.

Out back, two huge World War II bombers sat on the tarmac at the edge of the airfield. The bathrooms were done from floor to ceiling in sandbags, and piped-in speeches from Churchill and other famous war heroes played. The waitresses were dressed in Red Cross uniforms and the waiters were dressed as airmen. In the bar, there was a dance floor. Early in the evening, they played music from the 1940s. Each hour, the music advanced a decade until the current dance tunes hit around 11:00 p.m.

To top it all off, they provided headphones so you could listen to the actual pilots of real incoming planes talk with the tower. Everything there created the perfect illusion that you had in fact, gone back in time. The food was great too, but that was secondary to the actual experience of the place.

The 391 Bomber Group Clubhouse at the Royal Obidos Golf Club in Obidos, Portugal, the last designed by the Legendary "Seve."

A trio of theme restaurants in Las Vegas—everyone a winner!

You must remember this...Yours truly at the piano at Rick's Café in Casablanca. Yes, there really is one.

Home of the Twenty-Dollar Hamburger

The Hard Rock Cafe, the All Star Cafe, Planet Hollywood, The Harley Cafe, The NASCAR Cafe, and hundreds of other theme restaurants all sell hamburgers for ten or twenty dollars—not because the food is special but because the places are special. The experience for the rock fan, race fan, or sports fan seeing the actual sunglasses Elvis, Jeff Gordon, or Andre Agassi wore is what counts; the food is secondary.

Sam Snead's Tavern

There are several Sam Snead Taverns dotted about the country. Decent menu, decent food, but awesome memorabilia and a great atmosphere as it attracts—guess what? Golfers! Worth checking out for some ideas.

Not Your Average Joe's

In Sedona, Arizona, I came across an Italian restaurant called Not Your Average Joe's (apparently a chain now). The walls are lined with pictures of famous athletes named Joe—like Joe Montana, Joe Lewis, Joe DiMaggio, and so on. Once again, a simple concept turned a fairly ordinary Italian restaurant into a place that I've talked about to hundreds of people, even though it was closed the day I was there.

Your Surroundings Create Powerful Feelings and Emotions

Too many restaurants are stuck with an awkward design mishmash from the decorating attempts of six different managers, three decorators, two talented mistresses, and the ex-wife, strung out through three decades of trends and not seriously looked at since the Reagan administration. Colors are dated, furniture is dated, pictures are faded, and the overall feel, instead of being relaxing, exciting, or productive, is instead just sad.

The more your décor, furniture, uniforms, music, colors, lighting, or menus connect, the more that feeling connects with your customers and your staff. The more it resonates with people, the more memorable it will be and the more they will want their family and friends to join them there.

Make an Impression with Your Music

What's the first thing you think of when you think of restaurants and music? Elevator music or Seventies-lite? Maybe some big band or a little Elvis? If your music hasn't been updated, it doesn't have to be that way, especially if you want to connect with people in their thirties or forties. Music should not be an afterthought because it can be powerful mood alterer.

Background music is a key element to the success of any restaurant, but few realize how the music is chosen or why it's being played. If you've ever walked into a retail store and wondered why certain music is playing, there is, in fact, some rhyme and reason to the selection.

In fact, scientists have studied the effects of music on customers in various retail settings. A 2003 study published in the journal *Environment and Behavior* found that customers spent more when classical music was played versus no music or pop music. However, there is also research that shows people perceive restaurants that play classical music as expensive, which is not something all restaurants want to do. A study on *"The Effect of Music Tempo on Consumer Behaviour in a Restaurant"* found that slow music caused restaurant patrons to linger longer and buy more.

Another study found people perceive shorter wait time if music they like is playing.

A study at a restaurant in Australia found that the amount of the average check varied by type of music played with no music ($17.12), easy listening ($19.67), classical ($20.20), pop ($21.01), and jazz ($21.82). An interesting side finding was that when classical music was played, the after-11 pm crowd disappeared.

As any music fan will testify, listening to a particular style or piece of music can alter a mood. While music is typically enjoyed for leisure purposes, smart retail-business owners are also aware of how the atmosphere within their stores can influence their customers' spending habits. Research has shown that consumers shop, drink, or eat longer and make more purchases when they're exposed to music.

Of course, it's important to make the music match the preferences of your target customers. For instance, if you're selling upscale dining, the best choice is probably classical or jazz. A modern urban theme would have to be upbeat. People don't stay as long when music is fast-paced, but that's perfect for a fast-food place or any restaurant that wants to move customers along.

You obviously need to choose music that will best describe or complement your restaurant. If you are in Texas at a bar that attracts mainly blue-collar workers, maybe it is country music. If you are in Scotland and attract lots of tourists, perhaps some folk music lauding the charms of Bonnie Prince Charlie.

Keep the melody in the background. Consider music an ambience enhancer, not the focal point of the mood you're trying to create. "Customers shouldn't really be aware of the music you're playing," says Kurt Mortensen, an expert on motivational psychology and author of *Persuasion IQ*. "The music shouldn't be overpowering. Rather it should be merely an atmospheric presence." Don't get too lively. Beat matters as much as volume. "To some extent, slower-paced music may make people feel calmer, and they may spend more time in your business," says Lars Perner, assistant professor of clinical marketing at the University of

Southern California's Marshall School of Business.

In a fine dining restaurant it is best to opt for soft, ambient, slow music that will make customers want to stay longer, chat with other diners, order more wine, and so on. Another helpful tip is to opt for music that will best describe the image you want to project to your clients. Should you want your diners to perceive your restaurant as youthful, energetic, and lively, play upbeat music to convey that.

Make an Impression with Your Scent

Scent is very important in many businesses—like selling homes, for instance.

"When [buyers] walk into a house, they smell it before they actually see anything in that house, because they breathe the air. So they are actually getting an impression, whether it's conscious or subconscious, of your home—just by the way it smells," says Rick Ruffolo, senior vice president of brand, marketing, and innovation for Yankee Candle Company. That's why real-estate agents often suggest baking cookies or brewing a pot of coffee prior to a home showing.

Impress Your Customers and Your Staff With a Remodel

In most businesses, if you don't consistently re-invent yourself, you are in big trouble. Restaurants and nightclubs are the most extreme examples. A hot restaurant or club is a license to print money for three or maybe four years, then the bubble busts and a new place across town suddenly becomes the "in" place.

While inexperienced club owners ride the tide to the very end until crashing in bankruptcy, astute club owners do just the opposite. They reap the rewards while the going is good then close the club for several months as business starts to show a pattern of decline,

Then they remodel, rename, and re-open the club and make a killing all over again. But it's not just clubs, restaurants and bars that can benefit from this strategy—almost any business can.

The majority of businesses wait far too long in their business cycle before thinking about a revamp.

What can you revamp quickly and easily?

- Paint is cheap. What can you paint?
- Moving furniture around (my wife's favorite pastime) creates a new look and feel without spending any money.
- The same is true of swapping out or moving around wall art.
- Remove faded beer signs, broken lamps, unused furniture and other clutter that accumulates over time. The rule of thumb is simple—if it looks junky, junk it!
- Adding plants, especially large plants, or even fake plants, can really change the look and feel for not much money.
- If things have stains, clean them or replace them.
- Paint a life-size mural of something connected to your business on a big ugly wall.
- Add a feature to your waiting room.
- Freshen or replace your road sign.
- Improve lighting in your OFFICE.

The interesting thing about remodeling, even if it's only a quick facelift and a new name with some fresh carpet and a lick of paint, is that it almost always attracts new business and allows you to increase sales with existing customers.

What is the "one thing" you can you do to quickly revamp your restaurant and create an exciting, relaxing or productive atmosphere for your business?

"Know you food, know your farmers, and know your kitchen." — **Joel Salatin**

CHAPTER 5

What's the One Item on the Menu You Have Just Got to Eat?

In my last twenty-five years of private golf club memberships, I can count on two hands the times I ate dinner at my club, except for the occasional special event.

It's not that the food was bad, it was just boring.

Their fine dining was the usual steak, chicken, one catch, and pasta. Their casual dining was uninspiring, so we'd drive twenty-five miles to other restaurants to get sushi, Indian, Italian, tapas, or the burger to beat all burgers.

Now more than ever, people don't want boring and uninspiring, they want to try new and exciting food. Maybe it's Turkish or a new spin on Greek, for example. The good news is that even if you ARE boring, all you need is one item that people rave about and it's off to the races – just look at what the fried chicken sandwich did for Popeyes.

The Restaurant Marketing Bible

What's the one item on the menu that has people saying, "You *have* to try the _____"?

It isn't the steak; they can get that anywhere. It most likely isn't the burger either! All it has to be is *one* thing that wows them, like the six-pack of appetizers from a local restaurant in Florida. I took this picture two years ago and shared it on my social networks—long before I ever thought of writing a book—it was that good. We went back several times and took friends.

If you're in the restaurant business, all you need is one killer item, whether it's a unique dish or a dish you do better than anyone else in your geographic area.

If there is nothing on the menu that people can't get anywhere else in town, that's just not good enough. It does not have to be gourmet; it does not have to be expensive; it does not have to be exotic. It just has to be great.

For example:

- A great foot-long Italian sausage served with onions and peppers
- A giant barbecue turkey leg
- An awesome cheese plate
- Jalapeno French fries
- A turkey burger with your signature sauce
- Chocolate soup

It doesn't matter what end of the food chain a business is on, from snack bar to fine dining, all you need is one item that's awesome—one item every server jumps to recommend—the dish every guest is told by existing customers to order.

If you can do two or three awesome dishes, so much the better, but start with one.

If you serve food, challenge your cook or chef to come up with a unique dish. Get servers behind it and go from there. Food is, after all, the way to a man's heart.

Make an Impression with Your Menu

Your printed menu is a very important element of your overall food and beverage success, and you must pay careful attention to it to get it right.

Many places treat their menus as an afterthought. It should not just be a place to list the food items you have decided to serve in any old order with little to no description of the uniqueness of your recipe or preparation. Your menu is your selling tool (in the same vein as a brochure or website), and it needs to be treated with as much care and planning as anything else you do in your business. You can make your menu special regardless of the actual food offered.

Your menu should be an attractive and inviting presentation of the food you have decided to serve. It should be laid out in a logical manner, highlighting the items you particularly want to sell, either because they represent your best achievements or are your highest margin items (or preferably because they are both).

Where Do Customers Look First?

Research shows that most people look to the top-right corner of your menu first. This is a good place to feature one of your most popular menu items.

From there, a customer's eyes generally drift down and to the middle of the menu page. This is a good place to feature your most expensive menu item. Even though many may pass on this particular dish because of the high price, you can put other popular (and fairly expensive) menu items around your most expensive item. The contrast in prices makes people more likely to buy the items you place around your most expensive offering.

Food is the only art form that engages each of the five senses. Explore each one in your menu description.

Your menu description should make a guest's mouth water. Don't be afraid to explain what is in a dish and use ethnic names if they fit. They'll add a bit of authentic flair to the menu description.

For example:

"Chicken Margarita" sounds better than just "chicken topped with spicy tomatoes." You can explain what is in the dish (spicy tomatoes) in the description itself.

Incorporating geography or local history into a menu item name is also a way to make your restaurant menu unique.

"Maine Lobster Roll" sounds inviting, whether you're eating it in Maine or somewhere else, as does "Texas Barbecued Ribs" and "Georgia Peach Pie."

Even a sandwich shop can be memorable.

Food on display is a visual delight.

In the United Kingdom, it's now very common in better restaurants, and even some pubs, to actually state which farm the produce comes from and which butcher made the sausages. (They did look at me funny when I asked which pond the duck came from!)

Even if you are working out of a snack bar by the pool, "Joe's Famous

Burgers with Grandma Mildred's secret sauce" sounds better than just "burger"!

The more of a story you can build into your food, the more of it you will sell:

> When only the best will do. Private Reserve Tenderloins are hand selected from the finest quality beef found anywhere, then naturally aged and carefully trimmed into mouth-watering perfection. These exquisite filets give you the melt-in-your-mouth tenderness and juiciness you crave. Private Reserve Filet Mignons are crafted to give you and your loved ones the ultimate Filet Mignon thrill. Tender, succulent and impressive beyond belief, they'll transport you and your lucky gift recipients to moments of sheer bliss. [Omaha Steaks sales pitch]

Who could resist that?

The type size on your menus should be large enough for people over forty to read, especially when the light is dim. Make sure background designs don't make the type harder to read. The customer shouldn't have to work to read the menu.

You want to intrigue the customer with your menu and your descriptions. If they have more questions, their server should be able to give further information about a dish or recommend a house favorite.

What is the "One Thing" you can you do to enhance your food, menu, or delivery experience?

The Restaurant Marketing Bible

It's not just the food but the way the food is presented that creates the experience. Here, salt-crusted Sea Bass, in Monaco...awesome!

I have never in 30 years had anything but a great experience in Japanese steak houses.

Andrew Wood

Make a Memorable Impression with Your Drinks

Above is a picture of the world-famous Sombrero Margarita at The Margarita Grill. It's their signature drink and people go there from near and far just to have that one drink. They often take snapshots like the one I took and, of course, they share those snapshots on their social-media and travel-review sites—it's that memorable. If all you have is Miller Lite and Bud, you are not creating a unique experience.

Any Bar Can Be Memorable

When I was in my early twenties, we used to go to a hole-in-the-wall bar in Delray Beach. It was twenty miles out of our way and had no ambience, no girls, and no music. What they did have, or at least claimed to have, was a bottle of every beer in the world. Since at that time we didn't have the money to travel the world, my friends and I decided to do the next best thing and drink our way around the world!

Every time we went in, the barman would say, "What country will it be tonight?" Through beer, we traveled to Belgium sampling Trappist monks' beer, to India with their Taj Mahal beer…it was a different country at every bar visit

The Signature Drink

Signature drinks provide fun, unique experiences from drinks that are not offered by the bar or menu of the joint down the street. Having one or two signature drinks will bring customers back with friends to share the experience.

Infusions are one way to make something truly special to your bar. An infusion uses fresh herb or fruits soaked in vodka for three or more days, allowing the flavors to "infuse" in the alcohol. These flavored vodkas can then be used to create unique mojitos (pronounced mo-hee-toes), martinis, and other drinks that can easily become a signature cocktail. Infusions and micro-distilled artisan liquors are number nine on the top twenty trends in the NRA's chef survey.

Another top trend includes culinary cocktails, so another area to consider when planning your menu is what food to serve that goes well with your selected drinks. Small plates and tapas are very popular and offer many wonderful options for food that pairs nicely with wines, beer, and mixed drinks. And remember, drinks are much more profitable than food.

What is your personal favorite specialty drink, the one drink you must try at your local bar?

- José's world-famous Mojito?
- A yard of English ale?
- A stein of German beer?
- Local hard cider?
- Local wine?

Bars find it far easier to sell specialty cocktails if they have a separate drinks menu explaining the way the drinks are made or telling stories of their origin. That costs next to nothing to do and greatly enhances both sales and the customer's experience.

For example:

The History of the Magnificent Mojito

People associate drinking fun and unusual cocktails with parties and relaxed, tropical vacations. A visually appealing and fragrant fun drink is not typically drunk when alone—these kinds of drink imply a social experience. One of my favorites is the mojito (a refreshing concoction of white rum, sugar, sparkling water, lime, and mint). It has been referred to as a Cuban version of a mint julep.

The drink has quite a storied history—though how much of it is true is open to debate. No matter, though. People enjoy a great story, regardless.

There are two versions of the mojito's origin—both of which point to Cuba.

As one story goes, African slaves working in the Cuban sugarcane fields crafted the drink. The African word "mojo" means to place a spell. And the mojito has certainly cast a spell in recent years on millions of mojito drinkers around the world!

The other story has the pirate Sir Richard Drake concocting the first mojito. It was originally supposedly consumed for medicinal purposes (I bet there were a lot of pirates claiming to be sick just to get some of this medicine), and was called "El Draque" (the dragon) after Sir Richard's relative, the explorer Sir Francis Drake. As the pirates went on treasure hunting expeditions throughout the Caribbean, the drink ended up in Cuba, and eventually acquired the name mojito.

Which of these tales is true? I am not sure. Or maybe neither is true. But a great cocktail deserves a great story and the better the story, the more people pass it on and the more people buy.

Now don't these stories make this drink much more of an experience? I want one...You ready?

Memorable Drink Menus Sell More Drinks

Just as with food menus, having the right drinks menu to advertise the drinks that are available will always help any bar sell more drinks.

How many times have you tried a drink you have never had before just because you saw it described in a memorable way on a drinks menu? I know I have had plenty of cocktails I would never have ordered had they not had intriguing descriptions.

As with food, the same rules apply: the more you talk about the ingredients and the special way the drink is made, the more you sell.

How a Cup of Tea Can Change Your Business for the Better

I was having a chat with one of my UK clients about the ONE Strategy and what his signature drink should be. He told me hardly anyone drank alcohol at his place anymore during lunch because of the drunk driving laws. "All they drink is tea." "Okay," I said, "Are your teapots white and boring?"

"Yes," he said.

"Then change them," I said, and googled "cool teapots" right then and there.

I have urged three or four clients with tea-drinking customers to purchase unusual teapots, and the response has been fantastic. Women especially love the whimsical nature of the different pots. They talk about them, wonder which pot they will get today, and take smartphone pics and post them on their social networks…All for twenty or thirty pounds a teapot…Score!

A British phone booth and Doctor Who's time machine as teapots. Priceless!

Andrew Wood

Drinkware Can Also Make a Big Difference to the Overall Customer Experience!

Oversized mugs, funky mugs, cool colors, pilsner glasses, or unusually shaped receptacles like boots or jars all stand out over the typical pint mug or boring white coffee cup!

If you were walking through a city and glanced over and saw this yard of beer (pictured) it would make you want one, right? How could you walk past, this restaurant in Bruges, Belgium, and not? I had two! It was their signature glass and they got me—hook, line and sinker.

How many times have you been in an office and the assistant comes in with a bunch of mismatched mugs and leftover promo items from last year's trade show?

Now imagine the comments you might get from mugs like the ones above. It might even go a long way towards building some rapport!

So match your cups to the environment that you want to create at your restaurant and let the smiles begin!

What's the one thing you can do to enhance the drinking experience in your restaurant?

Andrew Wood

Statues Attract Attention

The more ways you can get people to stop, look, click, and share, the more free buzz you are going to generate for your store, shopping center, or town.

Statues provide great photo opportunities for restaurants wanting to promote themselves.

Making Your Signs Memorable

Your sign will typically be the first impression people have of your business. It is often the first thing they see, so it should always be fresh and in good repair.

Marquee signs, banner signs, and in-house and table-top signage all offer an excellent opportunity to connect with your customers in a memorable way and to generate a positive emotional response.

Removable signage like banners should be changed often to generate new interest as people quickly get used to seeing the same one and start to ignore it.

Go ahead—make people smile, stop them in their tracks and entice them to take a picture of your business and share it.

Humor features in a lot of my examples because it creates a positive response and is more likely to be shared via social media.

A chain of these Charlie Chaplin icons painted on the sidewalk leads people to a restaurant in the Swiss Alps. How do I know? Because we followed them through town to find out what the images would lead to!

Cheeky Burger King franchise laments the passing of his favorite competitor!

Loved Buzz's simple and direct call to action on the Big Island of Hawaii... so we took action!

Really—they've got it!

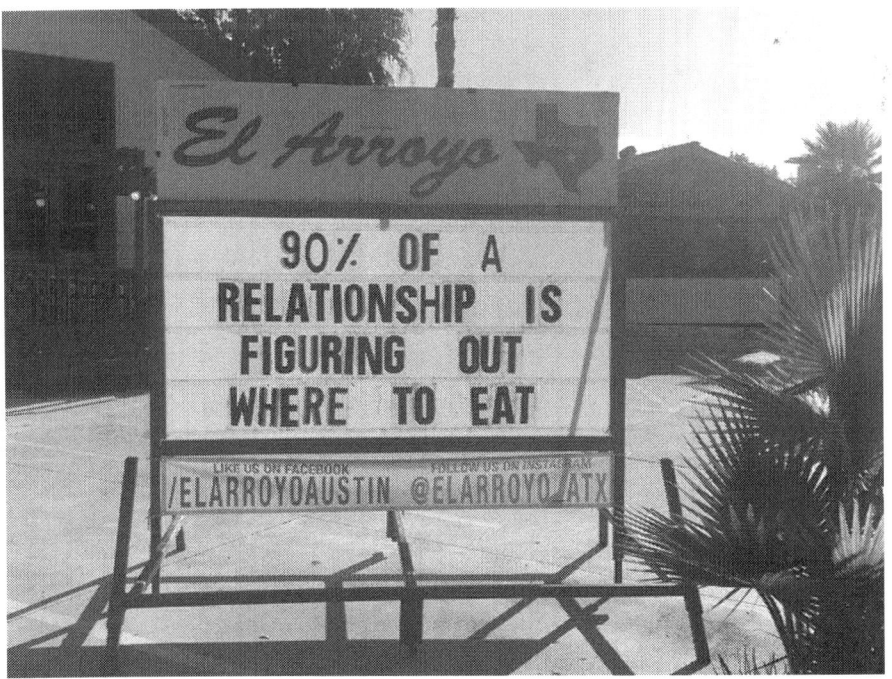

The Restaurant Marketing Bible

Remove or Replace Negative Signage

A great many of the signs I see at restaurants around the world are negative. This creates a poor customer impression. First of all, theses sign are an eyesore. Second, they are annoying and...Third, no one pays any attention to them anyway! Let's start a national campaign to ban useless negative signs in restaurants wherever possible.

At all cost, try to remove negative signage from your premises. I am astonished by the amount of negative signage I see.

- No refunds
- No exchanges
- All sales final
- No food or drink
- No sneakers

At the very least try to reword them to soften the negative impact.

For Example:

"No Checks, Cash Only" could be changed to a softer and more memorable, "In God We Trust, All Others Pay Cash."

There is a positive way and a negative way to influence the behavior of your customers. Which you choose says a lot about the attitude of your business, and negative signs are NEVER the answer!

SUMMARY

We live in an experience economy. Give your guests something to talk about, take pictures of and ultimately do the marketing for you! Wow them with just "One Thing" at every touchpoint at your restaurant and marvel at the difference it can make.

"The secret of success in life is to eat what you like and let the food fight it out inside."
— **Mark Twain**

CHAPTER 6

Building the Perfect Website

WHY YOU MUST HAVE A WORLD-CLASS WEBSITE AND BUILD ALL OF YOUR MARKETING AROUND IT

It's still tough to get some people to realize that your website is the absolute foundation of all your marketing activities. It's better than print, radio, TV, and billboards. In fact, about the only marketing that gives the web a run for its money is direct mail. Since that is about one hundred times more expensive than a website, it pays to focus your attention on the web first.

Think about your website:

- ✓ It is the only employee you have who never calls in sick. It books tables and answers questions twenty-four hours a day. (If your site doesn't do this and more, talk to us.)
- ✓ It's the only marketing you have that can send an instant and personalized response to prospective guests at 3:00 a.m. on a Sunday morning by using preprogrammed auto responders and follow-up letters.

- ✓ It's the only marketing you can do that incrementally lowers your future marketing costs with almost every visit to your website.

There is no more important marketing tool than your website, yet most are content to trade out to amateur designers, their POS company, or the owner's son-in-law rather than make the commitment to a world-class website. Even where restaurants have made substantial investments with ad agencies or web-design companies, a lot miss the mark. While these vendors understand the technology and design aspects, they do not understand the marketing aspects of dynamic websites. Nor do most understand the restaurant market, and those who do, come at it from only an online perspective rather than integrating online marketing with your overall marketing efforts.

Your website cannot just be pretty; it has to be a marketing machine to be an effective tool. 98 percent are not!

In this chapter, you will discover:

- ✓ how your current site measures up,
- ✓ how to design an effective website,
- ✓ what the most important features are,
- ✓ why you should automate as much as possible.

Take this quick test to see how effective your current website is as a marketing tool:

1. Do you have multiple different ways to collect data on your site?

    YES or NO

2. Can you make quick changes to your site anytime you want without calling anyone and without any computer experience necessary?

    YES or NO

3. Can you do email blasts to drive bookings anytime you want with no computer experience needed?

   YES or NO

4. Can prospective customers, make a reservation at your restaurant, or buy products online at your site?

   YES or NO

5. Does your site have compelling copy that asks for action on every page?

   YES or NO

6. Can prospects make meeting, event and wedding requests online at your site and can you preprogram your site with sales letters to automatically follow up on all requests?

   YES or NO

7. Does your site offer a media section where the media can download high-resolution pictures, logos, and fact sheets when they want instant information on your restaurant?

   YES or NO

8. Do you use a monthly newsletter to let people know what is going on at your restaurant?

   YES or NO

If you answered "No" to more than two of these questions, you do not have a marketing machine, you have an average website. It looks pretty, but does little to help you.

THE TWELVE MOST IMPORTANT FACTORS IN BUILDING THE PERFECT WEBSITE

1. Your website must be a data collection machine.

The number one function of your website is to collect information. Only when you have good information from your customers can you meet their needs correctly. This is every bit as true for a local restaurant as a national chain. You must know your customers' wants, needs, and trends before you can fulfill them.

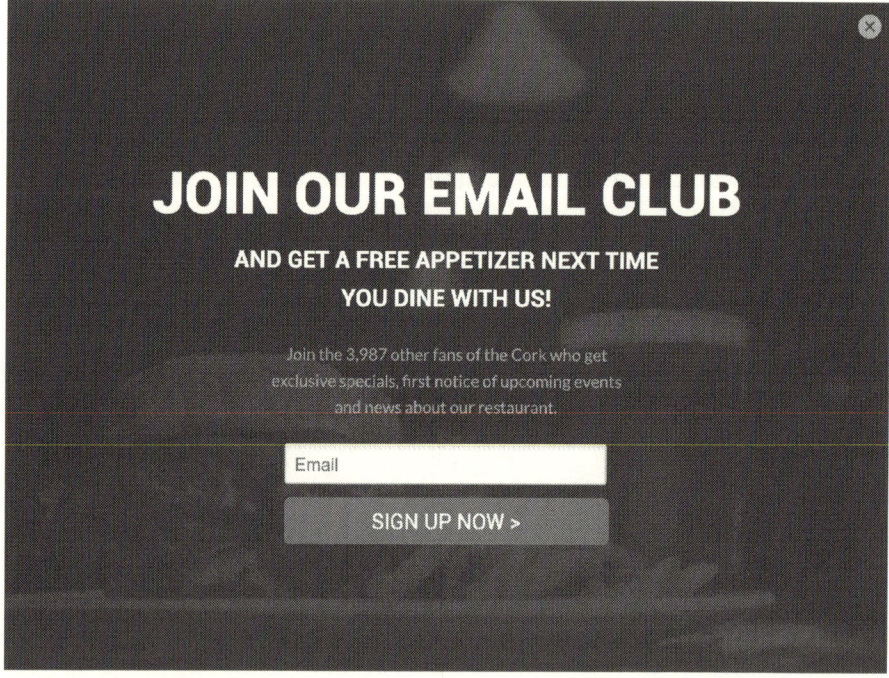

For this reason, you need multiple data collection points incorporated into your site's design. If you just offer a single newsletter sign-up on your site, you are only collecting about 20 percent of your potential email addresses. If you doubt me for a moment, look at your traffic and look at your sign-ups.

Some people are contest people—they respond to a chance to win. Some people are coupon people—they respond to discounts. Give me a chance to download information though, and I will gladly give you my name, address, email, and mother's maiden name!

Everyone has a different motivation so the only way to get maximum response from your site is to build multiple data collection points into your site.

My websites always have no fewer than five different ways to gather data. If your site doesn't, you are really missing the boat.

With the importance of data collection in mind, the key goal of your home page should be to collect data, either through surveys, contests, downloads, request forms, or online bookings. Other pages should also make a strong effort to collect data like group events, weddings, banquets, meetings, and so forth.

2. Detailed information must compel the visitor to action.

The second most important key to web success is to provide lots of information. The biggest complaints of web surfers is finding a site and then not finding the information they were looking for once they get there. Put as much information on your site as you can and let the visitors decide what's important to them.

The more you make your website the center of communication, the more you will gain from it. Post news, schedules, specials, recipes, wine reviews and photos of guests enjoying themselves. When visitors know that the site is updated regularly with the latest information, they will use it. When they show up several times and nothing has changed, they won't be back anytime soon. Have an active blog that you update weekly. Even just a few paragraphs and a photo will make a big difference to your Google rankings. Google loves fresh content.

Each page should be a sales pitch for something.

Each page should be a mini sales pitch to move the prospect to do something. Book a table, reserve a banquet room, inquire about an event, cooking class, wine tasting, or whatever eventual action you want them to take. It should be a complete sales pitch with a beginning, middle, and end—features, benefits, testimonials, and a call to action. Only if each page contains all these elements can it be deemed a great web page—and that's not just one page, it's every page you have that ultimately pushes for a sale.

There is no such thing as too much good information, only too little information or information that is not relevant to making a decision.

3. Your site must be easy to navigate and easy to read.

A visitor to your site should be able to easily move from any page to any other page. Many restaurant sites I have looked at (thousands) break this rule.

Use navigation menus that have a consistent look and location on every page, at the top or left-hand side—don't put any obstacles in your visitors' way.

Do not add so many distraction to your website that it becomes nearly impossible to read the copy or browse through the page. This may sound like a no-brainer, but for some it is not!

I recently viewed a website that had a specials bar across the top, a reservations bar across the bottom, buttons above the logo and navigation bar and due to the sticky navigation (that was impossible to not hover over as you scrolled down), you were left with literally one inch of viewing space – I measured!

Menu design 101

- ✓ Menus on the right don't work well. People naturally look left or up.
- ✓ Menus at the bottom of your site are often below eye level on many computers, meaning there is no menu at all as far as those users are concerned.
- ✓ Don't have more than about eight or nine choices in the main menu. You should use submenus from that point.
- ✓ Sites with twenty or more items in the menu are not user friendly. If you have that many, always used a left-side menu.
- ✓ Make the type style of your menus large enough to read. Bigger is almost always better.
- ✓ White text on a black background is 33 percent harder for the human eye to read. Why make it harder?

4. Your site must allow the visitor to complete a transaction.

There are few things as frustrating as investing time visiting a website only to find once you have made a decision to act that your next step is to call between 9:00 a.m. and 5:00 p.m. to actually book a table. The web is open 24-7, 365 days a year, and a great majority of web surfing is done after normal business hours.

You must have online reservations and the ability to request dates for events and banquets without having to wait until the next day. If you do not, you will lose business. Web surfers will rarely, if ever, take the trouble to print out a form, fill it in, and then mail to you. If you don't offer online booking, your web visitors are likely to go to one of your competitors who do rather than wait to call you in the morning.

5. Auto responders increase your response.

An auto responder lets you preprogram sales letters and follow-up messages that respond immediately to any request generated from your site. For instance, when someone registers on your website for more information on your bridal shower lunches, you can immediately send them a message thanking them and providing your latest offers.

Immediate, consistent follow up increases sales, branding, and income. Best of all, it's automatic and does not rely on anyone on your staff remembering to do it.

Warning: Do not make your auto responses passionless John-Doe follow-ups that generate the excitement of the automatic train voice at the Atlanta airport. Write them like great ads, with compelling headlines, benefits, testimonials, and calls to action. "Thank you for contacting us," doesn't cut it.

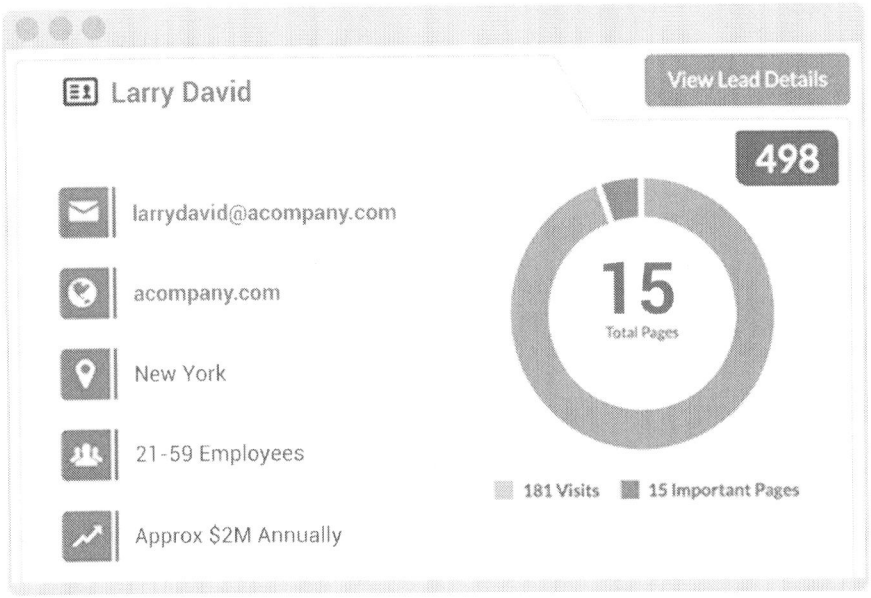

Engage leads at critical points with marketing automation

Marketing automation allows restaurants to streamline, automate, and measure marketing tasks and workflows, so they can increase operational efficiency and grow revenue faster. This will primarily be advantageous to things like catering requests and wedding and group events.

Use marketing automation to create email campaigns to continually engage leads early in the sales process. This will educate prospects and stay on top of their minds as they move their way through the purchase decision. The system will then notify you when leads are ready to buy.

Score leads based on engagement. Increase or decrease scores based on page visits, filled-out forms, content downloads, and the demographic characteristics that fit your sales model. Decrease scores by setting a "decay rate," and automatically nurture leads until they are ready to be dumped.

6. If your site is expected to create business, you must take the search engine rules into account.

Search engine rules and tactics change weekly so writing a definitive piece that remains current is impossible. But whatever the rules are when you build your site, you had better know them.

7. Your site must have excellent e-marketing tools.

This is where the gold lies, in e-marketing. E-marketing is even more effective if you can segment your target markets and make specific offers to those most interested. Almost all programs can do this, but few restaurants go to the trouble. For example, you can email only people who have entered your contest, only women, or only people who live more than 20 miles away.

In fact, you can sort by any category you choose with the touch of a button. This allows you to promote "shrimp night" to the people most interested in seafood dining. Because you target people's real interests, people receive what they are interested in and there are no spam problems. In other words, customers don't unsubscribe when you are sending them the information of most interest to them. Is that how you do your current email marketing? Can you see the advantages of doing it this way?

8. Your site must have excellent reporting tools.

Your site's reporting tools are the mechanism that you will use to evaluate your site's performance and tweak your online offerings. There are four important areas you are going to want to generate reports from:

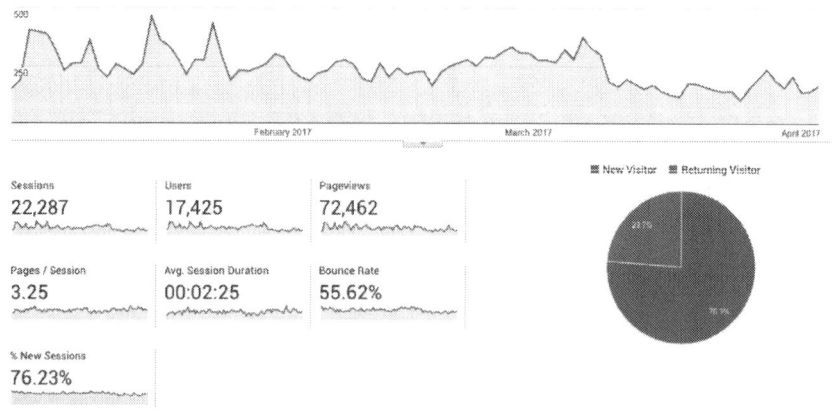

A. Website traffic

Your site should record the following key traffic information and review it monthly—if not weekly.

- ✓ How many visitors did you get?
- ✓ How many pages did the visitor view?
- ✓ What specific pages did they view?
- ✓ How did they find your site?

B. Email results

When you want to track the success of your e-marketing, you need powerful reporting tools on your site for the elements that matter most to making good decisions about your future marketing.

You should be able to quickly and easily find out the statistics you need including:

- ✓ how many emails you sent,
- ✓ how many bounced,
- ✓ how many were opened,
- ✓ how many people clicked through to your site,
- ✓ which links they clicked,
- ✓ how many opened on mobile vs desktop,

The Restaurant Marketing Bible

- ✓ how many people forwarded the email,
- ✓ how many unsubscribed.

In other words, you can tell the results of your emails on almost any dimension, in any time frame after you send them. These reports should also be presented in various graphic formats for quick inspection.

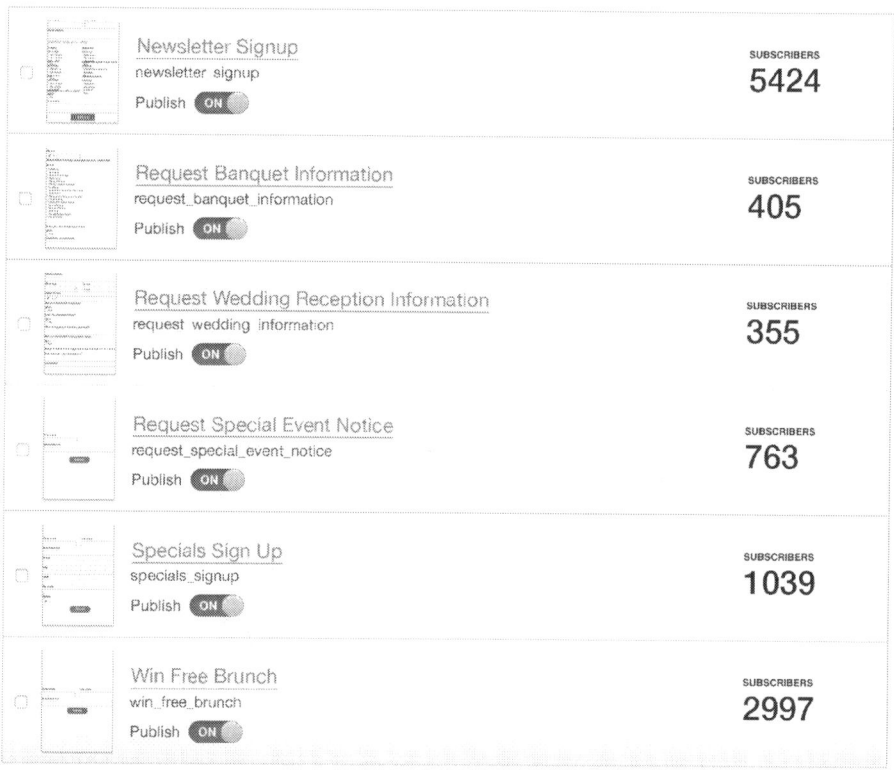

C. Contact point report

Since there are an unlimited number of questions you can ask in surveys or contact points, there are an unlimited number of reports you can run depending on what data are important to your operation. Common reports might include:

- ✓ Guest frequency
- ✓ Guest price points

✓ What other restaurants they frequent

Month	Year	Orders	Payment Amount	Payment Authorized	Payment Received	Sales Tax 1
12 - Dec	2016	37	$3,432.25	$3,432.25	$3,432.25	$107.25
11 - Nov	2016	10	$1,587.15	$1,587.15	$1,587.15	$62.15
10 - Oct	2016	13	$1,528.75	$1,528.75	$1,528.75	$79.75
9 - Sep	2016	35	$4,169.66	$4,169.66	$4,169.66	$193.66
8 - Aug	2016	14	$2,344.00	$2,344.00	$2,344.00	$0.00

D. Transaction reports

If you are running a shopping cart, your backend will log all the transactions and provide numerous reports on customer spending habits.

9. Your site must be easy to manage and update.

This is a big deal because no one wants yesterday's news on the web; that's what newspapers are for. This is critical to your overall success because if your site is not easy to manage and update, your staff will never do it.

Let me repeat that: *If your site is not easy to manage, your staff won't do it.* Add to that a revolving door for the position of "website updater" and you have just washed your entire online investment down the drain. Ah, you say, but our web company updates our site for us. Do they do it on weekends? Do they do it in the evenings? Do they do it immediately after receiving your request? In my experience, probably not.

Make sure you have a feature like this built into your site, so that you are not held hostage to anyone and can quickly get news and information posted on your site to keep it fresh.

10. The site must look good.

Notice how far down the list this rule came. On many people's lists, design comes first. The truth of the matter is that while look, feel, and design elements are important, they are a lot less important than the copy or what your site does on the back end. As long as you follow key guidelines about menus, make your type large enough to read, and have plenty of copy; there is almost an unlimited number of good designs you can come up with.

Here are a few key considerations:

- ✓ Be sure not to confuse the eye; people read from top to bottom and from left to right. Don't mess too much with that pattern.

- ✓ Highlight your four most important products at the very top of your site. For example Book a Table, Special Offers, Upcoming Events and Enter to Win!

- ✓ Avoid reverse type (white on black)—it's 33 percent harder to read.

- ✓ Make sure background colors or shading contrast enough that the text can be read.

- ✓ Pictures in the body copy should always face in so the reader's eye moves toward the copy.

- ✓ The pictures should be big enough to actually see.

- ✓ Make sure your site loads fast. Have you ever waited more than thirty seconds for a page to load? Probably not. And neither will your visitors. Compress all your graphics for faster load times. Assume your website is going to be viewed by the oldest browser on the slowest connection. You don't have complete control over this attribute, but what you can control, you should.

- ✓ Maintain a consistent look and feel. Be conscious of the rest of your printed material when you create your web pages. Be consistent in your graphics; use the same logo that appears on your letterhead and the same kind of color and style that's found on your other business material.

11. The site must be built to grow with you.

Websites go out of date faster than computers. You need to be using website technology that evolves with new technology.

We see many restaurants that spend thousands of dollars on building websites only to find they have to spend thousands more and start from scratch two years down the line because their sites are dated.

12. Be reliable; be protected.

Last, and by no means least, your site should be reliable. The term 24-7 is the colloquialism for expressing the expectation that the web, including your site, should be available twenty-four hours a day, seven days a week.

Add a media section to save time and money

Does your site offer a media section where the media can download high-resolution pictures, logos, and fact sheets when they want instant information about your restaurant? This is a simple example of using your website to save time. By having a media section you increase your chances of getting some free PR. You also don't have to spend time and money shipping out high-resolution pictures or logos to people who want to design brochures and flyers for their events or want to write articles on your restaurant. Simply direct them to click on the picture of their choice and it instantly downloads a high-resolution image to their computer. Now that's instant gratification.

As you can see, there are many factors that make up a great website. Some publicize you to the outside world, others help you better serve your guests. Your website should be more than just a pretty brochure online. It should be the heart of your marketing.

SUMMARY

My discussion above of how to use the web comes from our experience doing hundreds of websites over the last few years. The items discussed above are the key elements you must build into your website if you are to use the web most effectively.

"If more of us valued food and cheer and song above hoarded gold, it would be a merrier world."
— **J.R. R. Tolkien**

CHAPTER 7

Creating Legendary Landing Pages

Landing pages are one of the most important elements of lead generation for your restaurant. According to Marketing Sherpa, landing pages are effective for 94% of B2B and B2C companies and according to a recent marketing benchmarks report by HubSpot, companies see a 55% increase in leads by increasing landing pages from 10 to 15.

In this chapter, you will discover:

- ✓ what exactly a landing page is,
- ✓ why landing pages are so important,
- ✓ why you need to be using them,
- ✓ the six principles of high-converting landing pages, and
- ✓ the various types of landing pages.

What is a landing page?

A landing page is the web page a potential customer arrives at when responding to any of a multitude of forms of advertising.

For example:

- A search-engine result

- Social-media advertising (Facebook, Instagram, Twitter, Pinterest, etc.)
- Banner ad
- Google AdWords or AdSense
- A link in an email
- Print advertising
- TV or radio commercials

The purpose of a landing page is to convince the visitor to convert taking a specific action. This conversion can be anything from collecting an email address to the sale of a special event ticket.

It's not rocket science, more content, offers, and more landing pages equals more opportunities to generate more leads!

The use of landing pages enables you to send prospects to targeted pages and capture leads and convert at a much higher rate than through other means. Visitors are on a landing page for one purpose only: to take action (for example, to complete the lead capture form or make a reservation).

Landing pages are essentially the heart and soul of any effective marketing strategy. These pages are the destinations for your numerous prospects to find out more information on your specific offers—New Year's Eve, Valentine's Day, wine pairings, and so forth. Whether you're looking to generate leads, sell out events, or simply collect data for future sales, your landing pages are where it all happens.

Well-optimized landing pages allow you to take the prospects that you have attracted and convert them into leads. Unless you have a massive stroke of luck and something causes your business to go viral and it launches into the stratosphere, landing pages are your primary means for generating leads for your business and it is absolutely critical that they are *well designed, highly optimized, and relevant* to the wants and needs of your potential prospects.

Why do I need landing pages?

At this point, you may be thinking, "I have a great homepage, why would I need to use landing pages?" Too many people send their advertising, email, or social-media traffic to their homepage. This is a huge missed opportunity, as people quickly get distracted from the main purpose by clicking on unrelated links. There is no point in spending money on advertising if you are not driving traffic to a page created specifically for the people you are targeting. The following are six landing page principles that will help you convert at higher rates and generate more leads than ever before.

Ideally, you should have a landing page for *every* different source of targeted traffic you wish to produce, such as:

- Pay-per-click (PPC) campaigns;
- Promoting new products or special events at your restaurant;
- Advertising in offline media such as TV, radio, and newspapers;
- Contest landing pages;
- Building your email list;
- Targeting a particular type of customer demographic.

Six Principles of High-Converting Landing Pages

1. Message Match

Your ad and landing page must be consistent.

The Restaurant Marketing Bible

Message match is a measure of how well the headline on your landing page matches the call to action in your ad. This consistency is especially true for pay-per-click marketing. A strong match leads to more conversions, as people know they've landed in the right place.

The great thing about message match is that there are only two main things you need accomplish: matching the headline to the call to action and matching the design to the ad (if the ad has a visual component).

Message Match is so important but so many landing pages get it wrong…don't be one of them.

2. Headline and Offer

A few months ago, I read an article in *The New York Times* titled "The Eight-Second Attention Span," that discussed a Microsoft survey of Canadian media consumption and concluded that the average attention span had fallen to eight seconds, down from twelve in the year 2000. We now have a shorter attention span than goldfish!

This is why your headline is so important.

The headline is the first thing people see on your landing page. It should clearly convey your USP while matching the copy in the ad that was clicked.

Great landing page headlines cut right to the chase, are relevant only to the offer at hand, provide the benefits of what you're offering right away, or state the actual offer itself in them. It's best to keep the headline simple and utilize a headline/sub-headline combination.

You typically will want to add a *sense of urgency* to our headlines as well to boost conversions:

- Limited Reservations!
- Act Now!
- First 20 Couples ONLY!

3. Main Image, Video, or Graphic

The purpose of the main image or video is to show your restaurant or food in action so your prospects can picture themselves experiencing your wonderful food and hospitality.

People are visual, so it's no coincidence that landing pages with better images are higher converting than those without. You want your visitors to read the headline, see your image, and understand what they're looking at within those first eight seconds that we discussed in point #2.

Getting the main image, video, or graphic right is another very simple step that a lot of landing pages don't get right—if your product is an ebook, you should include an image of the ebook cover. If you're giving away a free dessert, make sure your main image is a dessert.

4. Benefits

Now that you've got your visitor hooked, it's time to show them your benefits and answer the all-important question—"what's in it for me?"

Not to be confused with features—they only describe your offer—benefits show the value people get from your restaurant.

A large number of people, over 75 percent, are going to scan your landing page rather than read word by word (at least until they find what they want). To capture the attention of visitors who won't read, show your benefits as bullet lists in addition to short paragraphs.

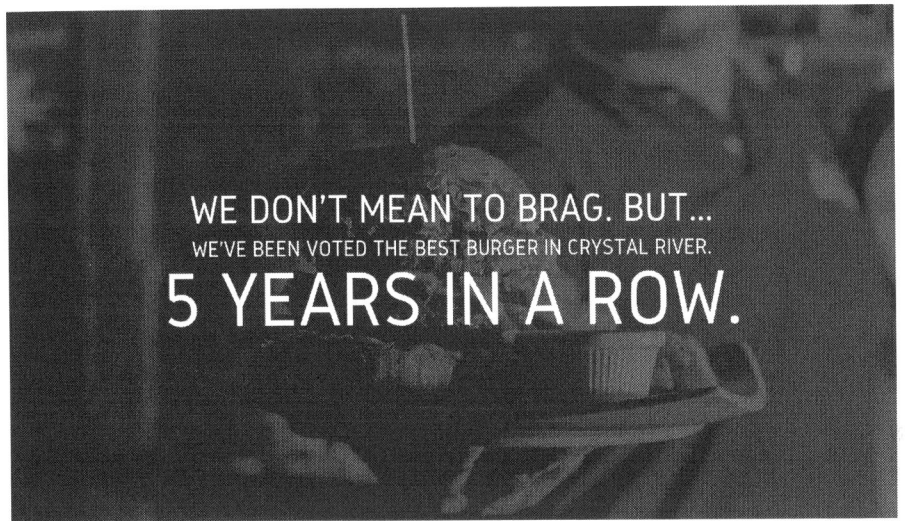

5. Call to Action

Your call to action is the one and only thing you want people to click on your page. It's the big button you're trying to steer attention toward; it's what *every* campaign is built around. "Call now," "click here," "download it now," "share this," and "join now for free" are examples of typical CTAs found on a landing page. You want to use phrases that make the visitor feel like they *need* to take the next step to purchase.

New Year's Eve reservations go fast—book today!

Spurring your prospect to take action is the ultimate goal of the landing page. It is what you want your visitors to do in response to your offer. Like the headline, your CTA should be clear, benefit oriented, and action centric. It should be asking to get clicked.

Since it is the goal of the landing page, it should be easily discoverable—use bright colors to make it stand out and try to avoid simply using the word "submit!"

6. Endorsements or Testimonials

The last principle of a high-converting landing page is endorsements or testimonials, which can be verbal, written, or video.

Powerful testimonials are one of the best ways of building social proof on a landing page. The best testimonials tend to describe the resolution of a specific pain, describing how your offering solved it for them.

These testimonials should be short and to the point, and should ideally include a photo of the person giving the testimonial to make it more authentic. Even better are video testimonials, which are proven to increase conversion rates more than any other type of testimonial. When using testimonials you must be careful; people pick right up on testimonials that appear to be fake (even if they're real) and will immediately discredit your offer.

To recap, the six principles are:

1. Message Match

2. Solid headline and offer

3. Main image, video or graphic that inspires action

4. List your benefits

5. A compelling call to action

6. Include testimonials

It doesn't matter what type of landing page (we'll go over the major ones on the following pages) you're using, following these principles will ensure that you are converting at the highest level possible.

Types of Landing Pages

There are essentially five main types of landing pages:

1. Sales
2. Click-through
3. Lead generation
4. Viral
5. Squeeze

Not all landing pages are created equal. Each type follows a different approach, but each has the same goal—generating clicks, sales, or high-quality leads at high conversion rates.

Sales Landing Pages

A sales page is used to sell a specific event. The purpose of a sales page is to give all the information needed to make a purchase. There are a number of different types of sales pages, but they are generally either short or long form.

Short-form sales pages are used when the value of your product or service is easy to communicate or when the investment is not large.

Long-form sales pages are used when your product or service requires a more in-depth explanation or is a larger investment.

The more you need to explain why your restaurant is worth the price or the commitment, the longer the landing page needs to be. Think about every possible objection your potential customer may have and answer it on the page.

How do I know when to use short-form or long-form sales pages?

You should use short form when:

- potential customers are highly aware of your restaurant,
- your offer or event is straightforward, like buy a ticket to a wine event,
- your offer is low-cost, low-risk or low-commitment.

You should use long form when:

- your offer carries a big price tag,
- your offer is complicated,
- potential customers have low awareness of your restaurant,
- your product or service is high-commitment—for example, a year-long dining club membership.

Click-through Landing Pages

A click-through page is a landing page without a form. A click-through page is most often used to quickly inform your visitor about what you're offering and get them to click through to your product or service.

The goal of click-through landing pages is that when the potential customer clicks through via the call-to-action link or button, they land on your site ready to buy or take your desired action.

Lead-Generation Landing Pages

The main goal of lead-generation pages is to gather information about your visitor that you can use later on to market to your prospect.

The contact forms must be the center of attention, so design your lead-generation pages around them. Copy on lead capture pages must thoroughly explain the product or service so that the visitor becomes emotionally invested in the page and clicks the call-to-action button.

A lead-generation page could be for a:

- contest or sweepstakes;
- free guides for hosting a successful banquet, wedding reception, baby or wedding shower, meeting;
- webinar registration;
- how-to guide;
- newsletter sign-up.

Here are examples of lead generation landing pages:

This landing page together with Facebook ads generated over 2,200 names and emails for a San Diego restaurant in two months.

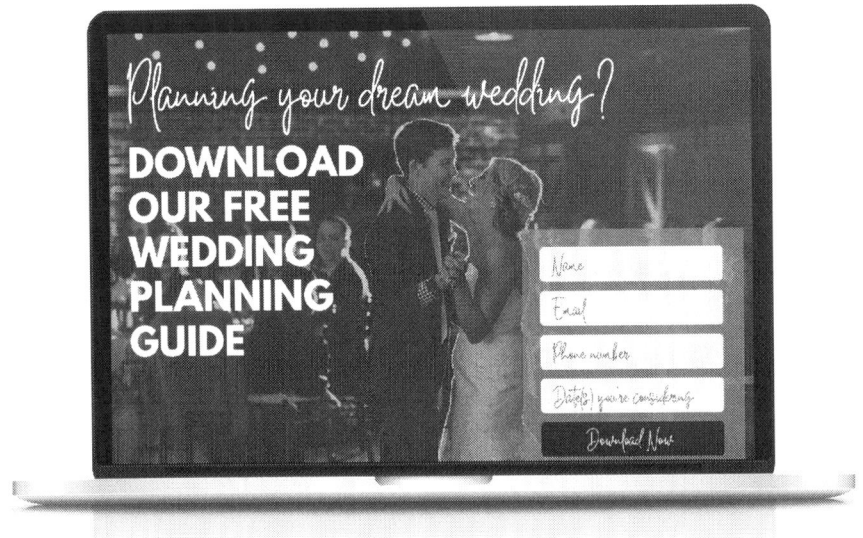

Create landing pages for all of the individual parts of your restaurant.

Viral Landing Pages

Viral landing pages are usually fun flash games or funny videos with just a subtle reference to the company in the form of a logo or a reference in the video.

The goal of these pages is to have viewers spread them around to as many people as possible via social media, email, and word of mouth.

Viral landing pages utilize two key elements:

1. **Great Content:** Your content has to be cool or funny enough for your prospects to share them.

2. **Sharing Enablers:** Make sure you have a URL that is easily sharable vocally. You don't technically need social share buttons, but it helps.

Squeeze Pages

A squeeze page is specifically designed for visitors to submit their email address in order to proceed further into the site or your marketing funnel.

The copy of your squeeze page can either consist of a list of all the benefits that your service can provide to your prospect in order to grab instant attention or it can just be a teaser designed to quickly get the prospect's email address.

The image above is a squeeze page for a free download of a special report that will be downloaded on the next page after the prospect clicks through.

Unlike a lead capture page, if you put a lead-capture form on your squeeze page, it needs to be short. An email address field is sufficient for you to collect your visitors into your funnel.

What type of results can you expect from a landing page?

The Oyster Bar

Free Oysters Giveaway

Goals: Generate email leads for the restaurant while increasing awareness

Results:

- 9,294 visitors
- 6,137 emails collected
- 64 percent conversion rate

SUMMARY

You can now see just how essential landing pages are for just about any restaurant's marketing success. They are priceless tools for driving traffic, generating reservations and visits, producing leads, and creating buzz.

"Cooking is all about people. Food is maybe the only universal thing that really has the power to bring everyone together. No matter what culture, everywhere around the world, people eat together." — **Guy Fieri**

CHAPTER 8

Data Collection

"HOW BIG IS YOUR EMAIL LIST?"

That's the first question I always ask. Most restaurants either don't have an email list of customers and prospects, or don't think it's important.

If you don't have one, whatever world-beating restaurant concept you think you have is dead in the water until you do. The "better mouse trap" will fight its way to the top one out of every ten thousand times. The rest of the time a decent offer for an average product sent to a good list will win. "He with biggest database wins," has always been my rallying cry. That's why I have devoted twenty-five years of my life to lead generation, or in its basic form, list building.

In this chapter, you will discover:
- ✓ how to build a million-dollar email list,
- ✓ who to target to build your list,
- ✓ the importance of having a good customer-relationship management system, and
- ✓ 40+ proven ways to build your list.

Your Only Guarantee

The best way to guarantee your long-term income and success is to build an email database and, even though it may sound retro, a snail-mail database as well.

There Are Only Three Ways to Grow a Restaurant Business

1. Increase the number of customers.
2. Increase their incremental spend.
3. Increase their frequency of purchase.

That's it, folks. That is all there is, and number one and number three are directly related to the quality and quality of your list.

Increase Your List Size and You Dramatically Increase Your Business

I started my golf industry business from zero in the front room of my house and quickly built a mailing list of ten thousand (today it's seventy-six thousand). It took many long nights and lots of Heineken as I handcrafted it from scratch, but it turned out to be a multimillion-dollar list.

In addition to growing my own lists, I have helped over two thousand clients in a multitude of different businesses including restaurants, hotels and karate schools rapidly grow their email databases, often with amazing results.

- ✓ I have helped hundreds of businesses go from zero to over a thousand in less than a month. Some from zero to ten thousand in a month.
- ✓ One grew from a few thousand to over sixty thousand in a single year, with an increase in income over $1.4 million in the process.

The good news is that most restaurants need nothing near that quantity of names to do well. In fact, many can generate a million-dollars of business on just a few thousand names—but they have to be the right names. I will share with you every way I have used successfully to rapidly grow lists that you can mine for millions.

Why You Should Go to Ridiculous Lengths to Target Your Market and Handcraft Your Prospect List...If You Actually Want an Astonishing Response to Your Marketing

There is old saying that "close only counts in horseshoes and hand grenades." Nowhere is that truer than in picking the right people to whom you should target your marketing and **spend your hard-earned money in the hope of earning a profitable return.**

This is information that few people want.

Few people want it because it involves work—painstaking, mind numbing, boring work!

Everyone wants the quick and easy solution, so they buy giant directories or mailing lists of local magazine subscribers, new homeowners, or dubious "prospect" names from third party email vendors.

All these solutions are a start, but that's all they are. Most are suited only for starting to build a list of real prospects, not for actually making a direct sale. Those who think otherwise are always disappointed.

This year I bought two large email blasts from two different vendors. One batch of seventy-five thousand emails generated just 103 opt-ins. Another of fifty thousand emails generated just 90, and the guy emailed the list three times and said he added another twenty thousand names to help get the numbers up! While both lists were from creditable companies, they were barely above junk quality.

The success of all the campaigns I described in the introduction and, in fact, almost all "Legendary" campaigns, goes back first and foremost to spending a great deal of time and effort in defining your target market and building a great prospect list.

Multimillion-Dollar Marketing Advice Below

Here is a thought: Instead of spending $1,000 to do an e-blast to a list of twenty thousand people whom you think, because of a single criteria or two, are good prospects for your restaurant, spend $500 on building a great list of qualified prospects. These are **people who are willing to put their hands in the air and be counted**—then email those five hundred people multiple times.

The response will be a thousand percent greater and you won't spend a dime more that you have budgeted in the first place. In fact you'll spend a great deal less.

This is a hard concept for most people to grasp because almost everyone is seduced by the law of large numbers. But one hundred thousand people seeing your ad does not guarantee success. In fact, it does not even guarantee a phone call.

The First Secret to Massive Response to Your Marketing Is to Pay Attention to List Quality, Not Just List Quantity

The techniques I am about to share with you are simple and powerful techniques but most people won't follow them.

Why?

Because they take a good deal of time, effort and, in some cases, even talent.

Very often the skill, experience, and judgment of a senior player in your organization (most likely you) is needed to make a good decision about who exactly is an ideal prospect for inclusion on your list. Don't delegate this task to some frontline kid with the ink still wet on his AA degree or a temp service employee.

As Voltaire so eloquently said, *"There is nothing common, about common sense!"*

Target Your Prospects Precisely

The first key to any marketing success is focus.

Specifically, what are the characteristics of your best customers?

Plan your attack carefully. Focus only on those people who are most likely to do business with you and don't forget to focus on the people you want to do business with.

Many companies miss this critical piece of marketing advice. Do business with the right people, not just the people who want to do business. Use the 80/20 rule going in.

Set a Written Criteria for Prospect Qualification and Inclusion on Your Target List

First, decide on the criteria you are going to use to judge a prospect's worth. This is critical so you can weed out the suspects early on and *focus all of your time money and effort only on qualified prospects.*

For example:

If you are selling real estate and wanted to build a list, the prospect might have to answer these questions in order to make it onto the list:

- What price range are you looking at?
- What type of home, by size or type?
- When are you looking to move?
- Will the home be retirement, second home, or investment property?

If the prospect is looking for the price and property type you offer and wants to move in say, the next twelve months, you have a real prospect on your hands. If the person is looking for California beachfront for $125,000, you have a daydreamer.

For an up-market steak house, your criteria might look like this:

- Not vegan
- Not vegetarian
- 35–65 years of age
- Income over $100,000
- Drinks wine and spirits
- Dines out at least once a week, twice better
- Lives or works within 20–30 minutes

Now that's not to say a younger vegan, making $30,000 or less won't eat in your restaurant, it's just that they are not your prime customer even if you have vegan options. The more you can fill your restaurant with the "right" people, the higher your income will be. A family with one vegan and two small children will not spend the same as four guys from the local stock brokerage office.

Prime customers for a local pizza restaurant might look like this:

- Families with children
- Mom or dad under 45 years old
- Young adults 18–30 years old
- Live within 3–5 miles
- Local baseball, soccer or swim teams
- Not vegan
- Beer drinkers

Clarity Will Increase Sales

The clearer you are on specifically who your target market is, the more effective you can be in writing your sales copy, which of course results in higher sales.

For example:

I have just built an email list of people on Facebook who like an Italian restaurant.

Now I can start off my product solicitation knowing that they will respond well to this opening line.

"If you are like me, you probably think Italian food is awesome?"

Now that, my friends, is preaching to the choir!

One of my clients had a restaurant adjacent to a car mall. Not surprisingly, car salesmen where his number one customers. Car salesmen are, of course, a breed apart. But understanding they were his best customers, he was able to use jokes, memes and language designed to uniquely appeal to them.

Here are some key questions to consider when defining your list criteria:

- How old is your best prospect?
- Male or female?
- Family person, married, or single?
- Kids or no kids?
- Where do they live geographically—how far from your location?
- What language do they speak?
- How often do they eat out?
- What magazines, websites, and blogs do they read?
- What are their hobbies?
- What other restaurants might they be Facebook friends with?
- What other restaurants do they frequent?
- What is their income?
- What is their education level?
- What type of businesses are they in?

When you start making sales, narrow down your predicted criteria for real criteria. Keep narrowing your focus toward the highest performing segments of your lists.

Now let's go build us a million-dollar list. I am going to start with the simplest and most cost-effective ways to grow your list and work up from there.

1. Start Your Quest for a Million-Dollar List by Getting a Decent CRM System

Nothing is more important to your restaurant's long-term success than your database. (Okay, great food helps but plenty of places with great food still go under; places with great databases rarely do!) You should keep all that data in one place using a customer-relationship management system (CRM). There are hundreds of programs that will do the job; Your POS system may already have one. If not, there are plenty of other low-cost options to choose from like Salesforce or Zoho.

If you don't have a good CRM (an excel spreadsheet is *not* a good one), start with www.Zoho.com because it's free and it's easy to use. It will keep track of all your emails, snail mail, and phone numbers. If you have any type of phone follow-up, it will also provide a sales funnel so all your leads get tracked to their logical conclusion. Yes, it's a pain to type all this stuff up from the business card fish bowl, but the time and money this will save you in the long run is amazing.

Back up your list off your computer weekly.

Print out a hard copy monthly and file it just in case of a double disaster. Trust me, unless you make a real effort to keep all your data in one place, you may lose thousands in future sales if lists get lost or corrupted.

2. Start at Home—Look in Your Personal Email Address Book

Start in the simplest place: Hand pick family, friends, clients, ex-clients, coworkers, and prospects from your existing personal address list. Export all who may be interested in your restaurant into your list server and customer relationship manager.

Then ask family, friends, coworkers, and employees to suggest and invite people from their personal databases. Hopefully you already have your first handful of emails from the friends and family program. ☺

3. Make Your Business Card an Opt-in Promotion

Use the space on the back of your business card to make an opt-in offer; people who have met you in person are far more likely to respond. Few people do this, but it is a very simple, cheap, and high-converting way to generate high-quality leads. Be sure and mention it when you hand over your card.

"Joe, if you look on the back of the card, you can get a free appetizer with your next meal if you register on our website."

Equally good, you can use the back of your card for an opt-in discount—anything that gets them to go to your landing page and register.

Of course you can always place a bowl at the check-in desk with a promotion or contest where customers drop in their business cards. Talk about easy to obtain data—you just have to actually enter it for it to work! (Not everyone has a business card. Be sure to have some printed cards with blank spaces for customers to add their names, emails, business names, and phone numbers.)

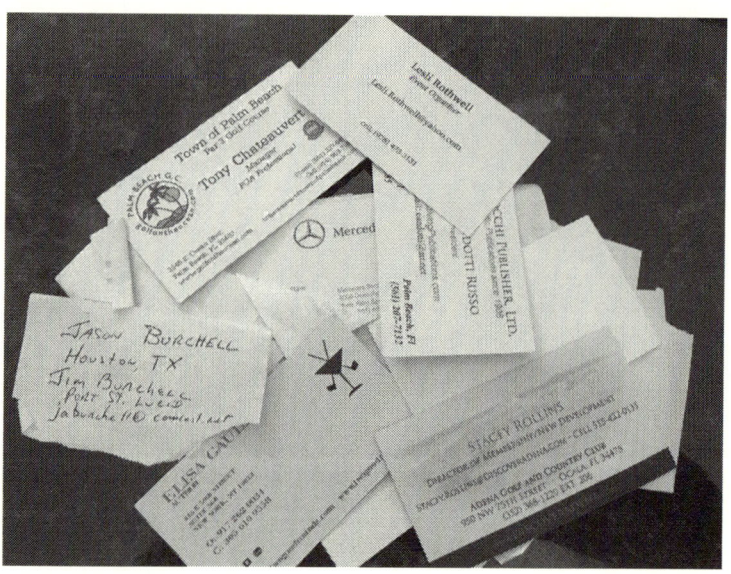

4. Use Old Business Cards to Handcraft Your Prospect List

Don't forget to go back and look for old paper copies of names and addresses you may also have in diaries or in filing cabinets. Remember, snail mail and phone numbers can still be a huge asset, so don't overlook typing them into your database, **even if you think you may never use them.**

Open your desk drawer, check your wallet, look in the top pocket of your blazer—do you see all those business cards from the people you met at local food fairs, chamber events, a party, or just the local bar? Some of these people are great prospects and need to be added to your list. But, let's face it, if you were ever going to type them up, you would have done it already, so give them to someone else; find a college kid, a virtual assistant, or call a temp but get them on your list.

People you have met in person are far more likely, perhaps a hundred times more likely, to pay attention to your sales message.

5. Harvest Prospects from the Internet by Hand

The web is by far the quickest and easiest way to build a handcrafted list, although gone are the easy days when you could you use a program like List Grabber, Address Grabber, Web Bandit, or a host of others and do it in a matter of hours rather than weeks.

Start with all the businesses around you and work your way out. Go to their websites and click on the "contact us" page or look for the info at the bottom of the page and copy down their contact emails. Here is a sample email you might send them:

Hi, my name is Jim:

I own the Legendary Café down the street, and I'd like keep you up to date on what we have going on here at the restaurant. Since we meet a lot of people every day, I'd love to know more about your business so I can refer some of our customers to you. We local merchants have to stick together—right?

Please introduce yourself to me when you come in and I'll offer you a free beverage. And don't forget to bring a business card for our local business wall.

Best
Jim Smith

No one is going to be offended by an email like that. Then I'd just keep emailing them. They can always opt out under the CAN-SPAM spam act, in which you are allowed to send one solicitation to ask someone to receive your emails. In a business-to-business situation, this still can still work to jumpstart your online efforts although you have to be very careful.

Warning: It takes very few complaints to your ISP provider to get your site shut down. You can't just send out mass email promos for your restaurant; you must engage, entertain, interact with, and connect with your reader. Your emails MUST contain a button or link to opt out of future emails.

You should also opt-in your list in very small doses, 50–250 or fewer names at a time. That way you can manage any complaints or tweak your content based on response.

I still harvest emails several times a year and it's still very effective as long as you follow my guidelines.

6. Sign Up for Other People's Newsletters and Reverse Engineer a List

Signing yourself up for multiple emails can be a great way to reverse engineer a list and a lot less hassle than online mining.

For example, if you want to target realtors, sign up for every realtor's e-list in your area and you will get back an email from them.

Thank you very much.

Best of all, technically you now have a legitimate business relationship since you signed up for their newsletter. In fact, I have had a few funny exchanges when people have asked to unsubscribe via email and I have emailed them back saying that I have taken them off my list but I will continue to look forward to their newsletter. This almost always prompts a re-subscribe action or an apology. ☺

7. Design Your Website for Optimum Data Collection

Set up your restaurant website with the number one purpose of data collection in mind. Most are not set up this way. Remember, each person has different hot buttons that will make them act to fill out your opt-in form; some will like information, others may prefer contests.

Most websites, because they are designed by web people, or design people, not marketers, miss the boat by employing only one way to collect email names, and that's usually buried at the bottom of the page where no one sees it.

Obviously, your number one goal is to get them to make a reservation so your booking button should be front and center, but you need to make your data collection prevalent on every page; lead generation is your website's number one job; everything else is secondary. Once you have their name, you will have multiple opportunities to sell them.

Use various different opt-in options on your home page; we usually have at least five or six ways to gather emails on most of the sites we design for our clients.

Opt-in options should always be in a very prominent position with a very prominent offer and benefit for registering now.

Some ideas for opt-ins on your website are: get a free dessert or appetizer for e-club signup, enter to win contests, banquet or event proposal request, wedding reception planner download.

It may even make sense to build your opt-in into the header or footer design so it shows up on every page automatically.

8. Use Your Blog Comments

To leave a comment on most blogs you have to register and that means you get their email. Encourage people to give you their thoughts and opinions on your blog. The more people you get to respond, the more emails you pick up.

Design some content for the sole purpose of getting people to opt-in and comment.

- ✓ Ask provocative questions.
- ✓ Ask people's opinions (for example, "What do you think of our new menu?").
- ✓ What's your favorite food?
- ✓ What would your last meal be?
- ✓ Post a top ten list and ask people what you missed.
- ✓ Do a Yes/No poll.

- ✓ Take a stand on a controversial issue.
- ✓ Ask for help.
- ✓ Respond to comments.

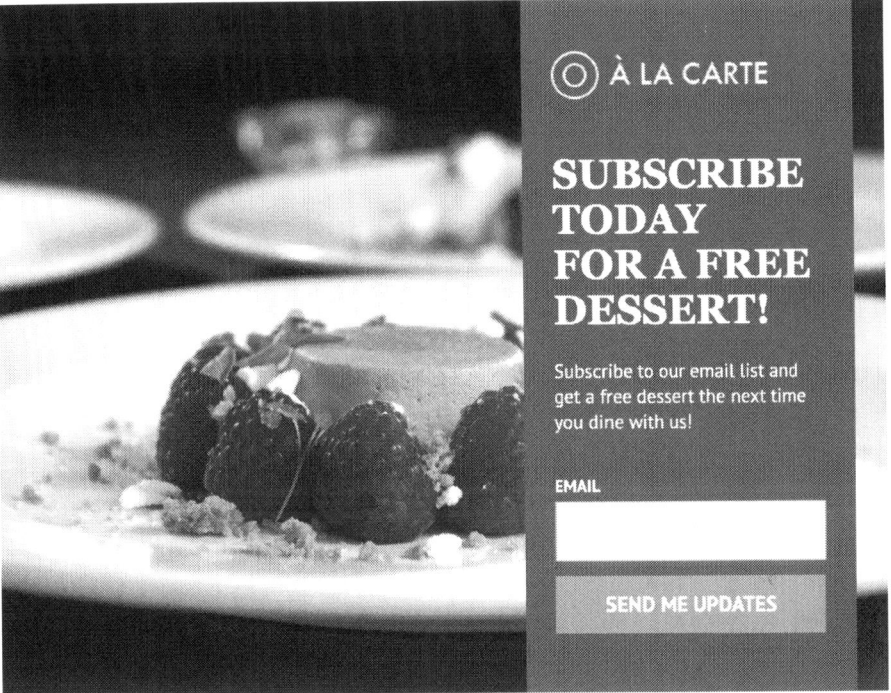

9. Use Your Pop-Up Ad To Collect Data

Hover ads are a special type of pop-up ads created using Dynamic HTML, Java-script and similar web browser technologies. Because they do not scroll with the web page, they appear to "hover" over the page, usually obscuring the content.

Hover ads have a 330 percent higher click-through rate than traditional banner or button ads so it only makes sense to use them to promote data collection.

As well as the primary page, you can also use hover ads to pop up on specific pages as people surf your site when the offer is relevant to content on the page they have chosen to be on. Matching specific offers to specific content and serving it up with a hover ad will greatly increase yours sign-ups.

Hover ads should be changed regularly to keep them fresh; I usually change mine every four to six weeks.

Many of my clients use hover ads to promote specific events or sales, which of course is fine, but in the long run you will always do better keeping an opt-in promotion there most of the time.

10. Make Your Banquet Brochures and Menus a PDF Download

Another simple way to increase data collection from your website is to offer your event flyer, brochures and menus as opt-in downloads. Even though all this information is readily available on the website through the main menu, we generated hundreds of extra leads a month for our clients by offering these materials as PDF downloads. Some people would rather print it out or share the PDF with others—whatever the reason, it's an easy way to collect extra data.

11. Use Your Facebook Cover Photo or Video as a Billboard to Promote Data Collection

Another simple yet little-used tool is your Facebook cover photo or video. This can be used to promote an opt-in action by focusing the visitors' entire attention on your free-download offer.

12. Use Photo Contests to Collect Data

Use photo contests to collect data in two different ways: first, from the people who are entering the contest; second, from friends they solicit to vote for their photos. We recently ran a contest for a client that netted them over eight hundred new emails.

The better the potential payout for voting for a friend's photo, a trip they might bring them on, event they can attend, and so on, the more data you'll be able to collect!

You can also do photo contests primarily to increase exposure on Instagram where you ask people to post a photo with a specific hashtag to enter to win your contest.

Another great part about photo contests is that you can then use the images that were submitted for marketing on your social media accounts or website, provided you put a disclaimer in the fine print stating that this will be the case.

13. Use Video Contests to Do the Same

Same as the photo contests, video contests can also be a massive data collector. With the technology available to use these days, you can easily splice together video from your contest submissions and use them as social media posts.

14. Use Facebook Pay-Per-Click Ads and Boosted Posts to Build Your Lists

The very best reason to use Facebook is not to generate a large number of fans, keep top of the mind awareness, or build your brand—it is to build your mailing list.

Facebook ads and boosted posts are the fastest, cheapest, most targeted way on the planet to boost your lists other than harvesting them yourself.

You can target geographical areas, interests, demographics, professions, and affiliations.

My Facebook ad strategy consists of the following:

- I spend little to no money getting likes – this used to be the way to go, but times have changed.

- I spend some money boosting posts I hope people will share and get me more likes.

- I spend some money on direct attempts to sell product.

- But 80 percent of my money is spent on getting people to opt-in to my mailing list.

Remember, Facebook fans are not yours; opt-in emails are. (More details on this later)

Skills & Endorsements

Top Skills

- 99+ Marketing Strategy
- 99+ Marketing
- 99+ Lead Generation
- 99+ Golf
- 99+ Advertising
- 99+ Event Management
- 99+ Online Advertising
- 99+ Social Media
- 99+ Online Marketing
- 99+ Sales

Andrew also knows about...

15. Use LinkedIn Connections to Grow Your Lists

LinkedIn obviously offers a quick way to build various professional lists but it's also a great way to add to your credibility.

- ✓ Invite your friends and colleagues to your restaurant.
- ✓ Upload any email lists you have into LinkedIn.
- ✓ Ask your LinkedIn contacts to recommend your restaurant to others.
- ✓ Contact a small number of people directly each day. If you do just a few they are unlikely to flag you. Technically you should only invite people you know, but very few people pay any attention to that rule. Just do it gradually and you won't get locked out.
- ✓ When people invite you, always send back a semi-customized response inviting them to get some of your high-value content for free.
- ✓ Do something similar every time a new contact accepts your invite.

16. Your Other Social Media

Obviously there are hundreds of options for social media beyond the obvious, but life is short and you can't do them all well. Depending on your audience, you might consider Instagram, Pinterest, Periscope, and many others. But don't just do them to say you have an account; you can only do so many well. Focus on the ones that give you the biggest bang for your time and effort.

17. Use Rented e-Lists

I own an ad agency, and so I buy lots of e-lists for my clients, usually at their insistence, after I try to talk them out of it.

Why?

Because 95 percent of them are garbage.

They are over-rented, overused, and send hundreds of campaigns a year that are of no relevance to the end user. Because they send so many campaigns, their emails are often blocked with many of the major IPs and never see the light of day.

Yes I know it sounds good that they have fifty-five thousand people just like the ones you are looking for...

I know it sounds like a quick fix...

I know is seems like a great shortcut...

All I can tell you is that unless you are okay with a very high acquisition cost, maybe fifty to a hundred sign-ups out of say fifty thousand names, then this is not for you. By all means try it, but test a small portion of the list first, say five thousand. If they are not willing to do a small paid-for test then there is a good chance they know the list won't work.

Email lists from a legitimate magazine that targets your audience have a far better chance of success, but I'd still be wary.

18. Buy Email Lists with Extreme Caution

The fastest way to get a large email list is to buy one. There are thousands of people with cheap email lists to sell and it's easy to get seduced by the large numbers they throw around at a very attractive prices.

Don't do it.

Realize that whatever list you buy, that same list is being sold to many other businesses.

Even more caution should be used when buying e-lists than when renting lists—in fact, it's even worse because when you buy a list those names are going to be sent from your server and you are the one who is going to get banned!

Unless you know the person personally or have a good history of where the list came from, don't do it.

It's a virtual guarantee to get banned by your email host and kicked off your ISP as well. I know of hundreds of sorry tales...

Here Is What You Can Buy

I have had great success buying lists of struggling companies or companies that had already gone under. I have also had success in soliciting lists from website owners who seem to have given up on their sites or blogs. You know the ones I mean—where the last post was three years ago.

Subject: I'd like to buy your list

Dear Blog Master Dave:

I have a new website I'd like to promote that I think would be of interest to your blog's readers. Do you have an email list I can rent or buy?

Lots of restaurants close each year. When a restaurant closes down for good, someone leaves with the list. If it's a restaurant with the same types of customers as your restaurant, find who has it and approach them with an offer. (Look in Google archives to find a contact person.) The thought of a quick couple of hundred dollars for nothing more than their email list can be very appealing to someone closing down a restaurant.

Obviously, what you pay depends how big their list is, how recently they mailed to someone on it, and how good it is. While there is no hard-and-fast rule, these days, a list that's a year old will have at least 30 percent deterioration. Any older and it may not be worth the hassle of cleaning it.

To do this ethically depends on the website/company's privacy policy, but while most *Fortune* 500 companies have pages detailing theirs, most small companies make no such guarantees. In fact, they usually have none.

19. Building the Perfect Squeeze Page

Your prospects are going to land on your main website, blog, Facebook page, or squeeze page. But wherever they land first they are going to ultimately end up on a squeeze page. (See also the earlier information on squeeze pages in Chapter 7.)

The squeeze page should have the same look and feel as your promotion for it. This includes colors, images, and headlines.

It should give several benefits to the prospect to build value into taking action.

It should tell the prospect to take action.

I am using three products right now to produce landing pages for myself and my clients:

http://unbounce.com

https://clickfunnels.com

http://www.kajabi.com

How Much Other Data Can You Get?

Standard wisdom is that the less you ask the prospect to give you, the more people you get to opt in. Various studies show a jump in response when you ask for first name and email only and forget the last name field.

Personally I have had good success in getting far more information—in fact in one campaign, much to the utter astonishment of my client who suggested I was crazy if I thought even one of his Irish countrymen would answer twenty-three questions to get a gift—16,884 people did in forty-eight hours! And that's a net number after we threw out the duplicates and errors.

How much data you should try and get depends on your:

- Type of restaurant
- Market
- Sales cycle
- Price
- Long-term strategy

Those questions provide me with more than enough information to make an initial qualification as to whether the person downloading the info is a prospect or a suspect. Based on which of the last options they choose, they also zone me in on their area of interest.

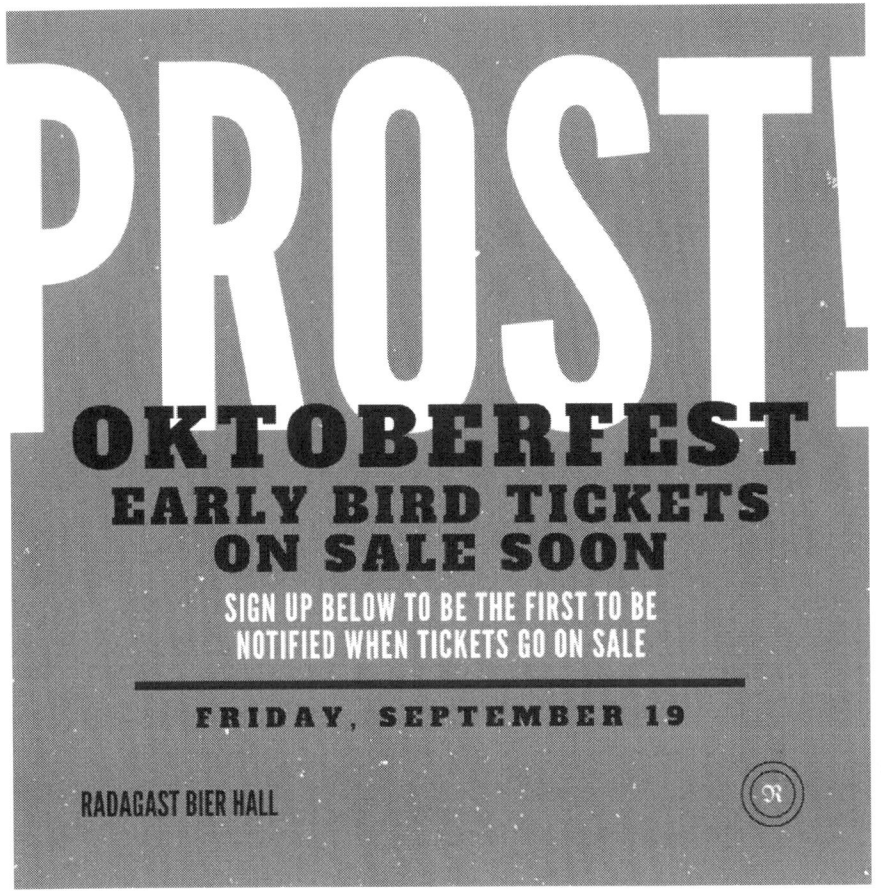

20. Let Them Be First

People will often sign up just to be the first to hear the details about a new restaurant, new promotion, or new event that you are going to offer—so emphasize that.

21. The All-Important Ethical Bribe

Without an ethical bribe to help things along, building lists is hard. Sure, some people will sign up to be first in line or for your newsletter, blog, or discount club, but to really turbo charge sign up, you need a bribe. The bigger and better the bribe, the faster you will build your list.

It's important to remember that different types of people respond to different types of bribes, so using only one type may severely limit your success. Some like to read, others prefer to listen or watch. Some like contests and sweepstakes; others might prefer discounts or VIP status. Some like free software, apps, and technology. The best list builders realize that people respond to different types of offers and incorporate all in their strategic plans.

21. Handcraft Your List Using Free Special Reports

Over the years, free special reports have been my absolute cheapest and best source of leads. It doesn't matter whether you call it a special report, , insider's secrets, an ebook, or a guide, free information is by far the quickest, most cost-effective and quality way of generating leads in any business that I can give you.

Who downloads a free wedding guide?

People who are thinking of having a wedding, right?

Who downloads a baby shower guide?

People who are going to host a baby shower.

Who downloads a guide on how to host a successful retirement party?

People who are going to host a retirement dinner.

Whatever the topic of your guide:
- ✓ Design an attractive cover.
- ✓ Add a benefit-laden headline.
- ✓ Add a bio page.
- ✓ Give five to seven bullet points on why the reader must download this guide now.
- ✓ Make sure the content is point specific and of high quality for your target market. Use it to showcase your expertise, not to sell. A lot of people run ads throughout the content for their actual products—while I am not against doing this, I usually try to keep mine clean.
- ✓ Make the last page an ad for your restaurant.
- ✓ Upload it to your website in a prominent spot on your home page (and the page that corresponds with the topic) and you are just minutes away from qualified leads.
- ✓ Set up some auto responder emails to upsell anyone who opts in.

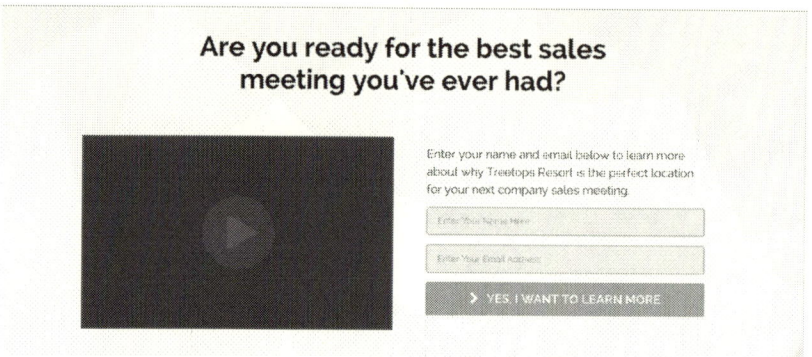

23. Build Your List with Informative Videos and Seminars

We live in a visual world and video is fast becoming every bit as important as copy. In my own research, people seem to be split fifty-fifty between preferring to watch a video or read copy so I often do both.

Obviously you can load your videos on YouTube but the chances of them signing up for your channel are minuscule compared with the absolute certainty of a squeeze page.

The Key Factor on Great Opt-in Video Is to Tell a Great Story

It could be a short five-minute cooking class on how to prepare one of your top dishes.

> **Here's the perfect video opt-in formula:**
>
> **Define the prospect's problem:**
> Your chocolate soufflés never turn out right.
>
> **Show empathy for the problem:**
> Don't feel bad, most people's soufflés don't.
>
> **Propose a solution:**
> I'm going to show you how to make all your friends jealous of your light, fluffy soufflés.

Report the results:

Take a look at this mouth-watering beauty.

Promise similar results:

Now I'm going to show you how…

Tell them what to do:

Just leave me your email right here (point to the box) and I'll share the secrets of spectacular soufflés video with you absolutely free. Leave your email now and I'll see you on the other side.

Two minutes is ideal for the opt-in but the actual video can be as long as you like, as long as the story is really engaging and entertaining.

24. Use YouTube to Build Your List

If you have not done so already, start your own channel on YouTube. It's not as good as a closed option like the above because you can't make people subscribe to your channel or your list. But YouTube will reach more people and so is a complementary strategy.

YouTube channels are also a very good way to present your restaurant in a visually appealing way that a photo just can't provide. A video allows you to portray an entire experience—the bar, your food, the kitchen and special events. It also lets you easily make people aware of other experiences you offer besides what you are most well known for.

Use informative segments to display your unique expertise. Always ask your viewer to opt in for more info at the end. Display a footer on the screen at various points as well in case they don't make it all the way to the end.

Remember to ask them not only to opt-in to your channel, which is good but you don't get their data, but also to opt in for your free info or gift where you do!

You can do this yourself with no technical skill by clicking on the enhancement button, which is the little wand icon next to the pencil. In addition to messages asking viewers to subscribe to your channel or opt-in to your list, you can also place hyperlinks directly into your videos.

This simple tip will significantly increase response to your videos as you drive people to your landing pages.

25. Use Free Webinars to Build Your Lists

Free webinars are another great way to get people to opt in—you can do video webinars, audio webinars, or slide show webinars. You can do live events for added excitement and interaction. With live webinars, depending on your preference, you can let people call in, email in, or post questions on Facebook to get real one-on-one interaction with your audience. You can also record the session so it can be played back at a later date. Webinars should follow the same rules as reports or video seminars in regard to headlines and content.

26. Use Contests, Vacations, and Sweepstakes

The quickest and easiest way to build a prospect list is to run a free contest, sweepstakes, or prize giveaway.

While you may think that people looking for *free* items are not ideal prospects, studies show that people rarely enter free contests for prizes in which they have no interest. *Therefore, if the prize revolves around your restaurant* you can assume with reasonable certainly that the person entering is in fact a prospect.

You can qualify the entries further by asking two or three additional questions that remove all doubt, such as their income, buying habits, or their timeframe.

At several locations, we have had no problem in getting people to answer twenty questions or more in return for the right incentive. You must of course be careful about the questions that you ask as people become more wary about giving away too much information. In most cases basic contact information, a postal code, and a couple of preferences should be enough.

27. Use Free Apps to Grow Your Lists

Free apps or software can often be developed at very little cost and can go viral fast, especially with the mobile market, which is fast becoming everybody.

What kind of app could you develop for your market? The key to apps is to make sure you have an upgrade that makes the consumer register to get more features; without that all you get is a download not an email address.

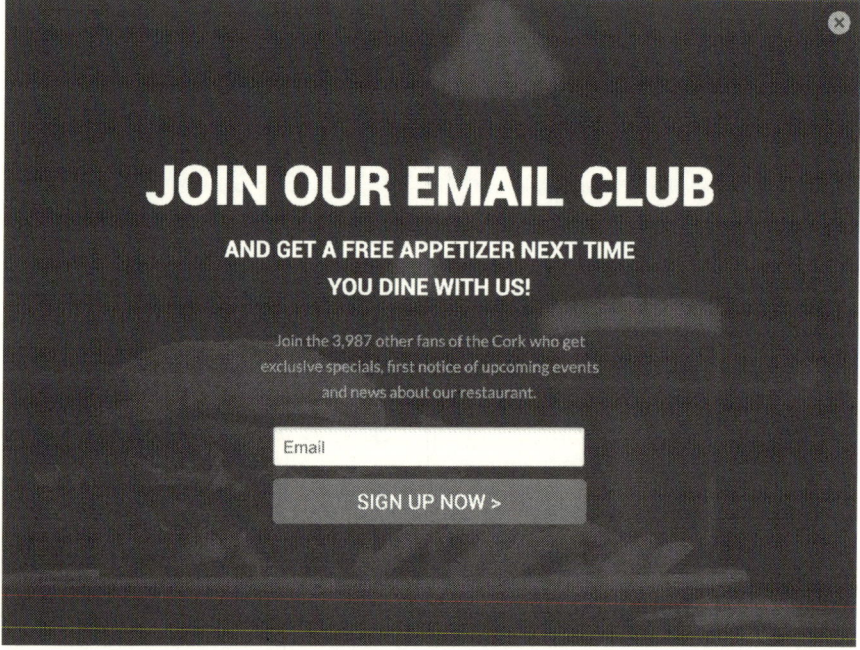

28. Use a Free e-Newsletter as a Way to Handcraft Your List

Opt-in newsletters are one of the very best ways to build your list. But don't just put a subscription form on your website; tell potential subscribers why signing up is a good idea.

✓ Tell them what's in your newsletter.

- ✓ Tell them how they will benefit directly from its content.
- ✓ Tell them how many subscribers you have already.

Do not make the fatal mistake of asking only for emails.

You should try to get their snail mail addresses as well. I know right now you may think you will never mail them…but you never know. Plus, even if you don't ever use the snail mail, it's another asset you have to trade, sell, or just add to the value of your business should you ever sell it.

To be effective, your free e-newsletter must be content-rich with the type of information that will be of prime interest to your customers.

28. Use Discounts, VIP Clubs, or Loyalty Clubs to Handcraft Your Lists

Other variations of this concept included asking prospects to sign up for special discount clubs, VIP clubs, e-special clubs, or whatever you want to call your subscriber list.

Invite visitors to sign up for your discount or e-club. Be sure to let them know that only e-club members get the best deals and VIP special events.

Provide special rates and other special offers only to those who register. Registering on the site and the benefits of doing so should be mentioned at various points throughout the copy on your site. Always be promoting the idea of registering for additional benefits. People are more and more cautious about giving out their emails and being bombarded by junk they don't care to read. Make sure you offer compelling reasons to register on your site because your competition for that email address is worldwide. (Also tell people how you will use their name. For instance, that you won't sell their name and will use it only for your email newsletter and special offers.)

Make your registration instructions clear. Ask the visitors to type their email *here*. Re-explain the benefits the visitors will get by registering.

After they register, make sure your site sends an automatic letter thanking them for signing up. Take this opportunity to mention once more the benefits they will receive from doing so. Suggest they might want to refer the site to a friend so that the friend too might benefit from the same information.

By making registration on your site rewarding and easy, you can quickly build your email list and slash your marketing costs.

29. Use Online Surveys to Handcraft Your Prospect List

Surveys are another simple and inexpensive way to generate a large number of qualified prospects in a short period of time. It really doesn't matter whether you do the survey on line, in an email blast, at the counter, at a trade show, or in a shopping mall.

Simply put your survey in front of people wherever and whenever you can find them and you will, with the right questions, quickly generate enough qualified leads to do a thunderbolt campaign.

30. Trade Old Lists with Others

Other than harvesting emails yourself, trading lists is the best strategy of all. I have left it until later in the program simply because until you have a decent list yourself you have nothing to trade. One company's old leads can be a gold mine for another. Beg, borrow, or trade with others to build your prospect list. Once you do have a decent list, people will line up at your door to get their hands on it.

31. Use Your Email Signature to Handcraft Your List

Create a signature file at the bottom of your outgoing emails with an ad or contest included. You should have your email software set to include a signature file on every email message you send out. This should go right after your name at the end of every email you send.

Your signature file should include an ad for your opt-in list along with your free bonus for subscribers. Once they are on your list, you build a relationship with them and sell them. Here is an example of a signature containing a bonus:

Andrew Wood
Legendary Restaurant

Download my *Free Special Report:*
The 12 Keys to a Killer Banquet

Automatic reply: video
Jim Callaghan
Sent: Friday, December 18, 2015 at 5:53 PM
To: Andrew Wood

I will be out of the office until Monday 28th December and will attend to all emails on my return. If your message is of an urgent nature, please contact

Tracey at clubhouse@haggscastlegolfclub.com for Clubhouse and dinner reservations

Linda at accounts@haggscastlegolfclub.com for accounts or general enquiries

For golf bookings, please call 0141 427 3355

Many thanks

Jim Callaghan CCM
General Manager

32. Use Email Inquiries to Handcraft Your List

Strangely enough, many great leads that come to companies in the form of questions, suggestions, and comments via email, never make it into the company's prospect file. *Make a habit of including such requests in future target lists.*

You should also look at your auto replies and bounced emails.

Very often these automatic messages contain a wealth of additional information that can be used to your advantage. This includes titles, phone numbers, and addresses. The names and titles of other people in the organization and the messages that tell you Joe is gone and the new owner is Frank.

33. Use Print Ads to Build Your Lists

Yes, print ads are costly and are dying, but they are not dead just yet. If the publication you are targeting is read by a specific enough market, a small ad for the specific purpose of opting people into your list can pay dividends by reaching people you might not have otherwise reached. This is especially true of trade journals, association publications, and business-to-business publications.

Most people run ads hoping they produce direct sales. Because they want their ad to end in a direct sale, they waste space and copy trying to make a sale. *The vast majority of print ads would be far better aimed at producing an initial contact rather than a sale.*

This two-step approach is remarkably more effective in generating long-term results.

Direct your copy, graphics, and CTA toward making an initial contact and you will produce far superior results. Use your print ads to advertise free reports, consulting, contests, freebies, and other incentives that get prospects to identify themselves, preferably by filling in their details at a contact point on your website. Once they are in your system, you can contact them multiple times and make a sale.

If you can accept this simple but potent paradigm shift, and use your marketing dollars to build a qualified prospect list instead of trying to make a sale, you are well on your way to astonishingly better results.

34. Go to Local Fairs, Malls and Events with the Express Purpose of Building Your List

Although time consuming and potentially expensive compared to other options, this is one of the surest and fastest ways to build a great prospect list of proven spenders.

Rent a Booth

Many of my clients go to local art and craft shows for the sole purpose of generating a mailing list. Rent a booth, grab some iPads, offer a contest, and perhaps even hire some talent. I have clients who grab three thousand emails in a single show.

35. Use Snail-Mail Postcards

Wait, you say, you want me to rent a mailing list of prospects and then print and mail postcards to them just so I can build an email list of the same people to mail to again?

Precisely, Dear Watson!

Using the same offers, reports, and freebies you offered on your website and through e-blasts, rent a snail-mail list of any group who might be in your target market and send out a postcard screaming for their response. Postcards are relatively cheap, easy to produce, and the most inexpensive thing you can mail.

This is an important strategy for two reasons:

One: The availability of highly targeted and storable mailing lists is still far greater than email lists. So if you need to reach golfing Corvette owners who love food and wine, you can actually do it.

Two: No worries about spam complaints, no worries about spam filters. In fact, very little worry at all that the great majority of your prospects will not even glance at your message. You will reach not only more people with a postcard than with email but you will also reach different people.

36. Use Snail Mail Letters to Build Your Lists

I have had some amazing success with snail mail, and I think that as fewer and fewer people send postal mail, the response rates will only go up.

The beauty of a sales letter over a postcard is simply that there is more space to tell your story and, with a high price or more sophisticated audience, that's important.

Yes, snail mail can be expensive if you do it wrong but you can test it very cost effectively and check your conversion rates before you ramp up. This is going to be cost effective only if you have a relatively high-ticket product, but you should not ignore it.

37. Use Scratch Cards to Handcraft Your List

Not everyone will want to take your free flyer, and a large percentage of those who do will ditch it long before they get in front of a computer to sign up. Enter the scratch card. People love scratch cards and will eagerly accept them. The key is to have a large grand prize, perhaps a free party for 12 people and a number of little prizes. Then have the cards set up so everyone wins something even if it's just a free appetizer. This is a very effective way to send people home with a little excitement in their hands and get plenty of opt ins.

38. Point of Sale—Make Email Acquisition Part of the Checkout Process

For retail stores, or seminar sales, asking customers for their email addresses at the point of sale (POS) is a proven technique that is quickly gaining momentum. In-person and in-store events were ranked second in acquisition quality and quantity, according to a recent research study.

- To put this practice into action, it's important that your associates:
- ask customers for their email addresses,
- explain the benefits of your email program,
- let customers know exactly what to expect in terms of email frequency and content,
- read back the email addresses to verify correct spelling and reduce errors.

39. Use Custom Memes to Build Your List

Use one of the stock royalty-free graphics services to find cool images to personalize with a slogan and an opt-in link, then post them on your social media. The right ones, ones that connect with your target market, can go viral quickly and can drive significant traffic and opt-ins. I post one on my Facebook page every single day.

40. High-Quality Emails Get Shared

No matter how small or large your current list is, quality content will always be one of your best email acquisition strategies.

- Quality content gets shared.
- Quality content gets commented on.
- Quality content sparks interest in your company and products.
- Make your content personal.
- Make your content topical.

Make content funny, controversial, opinionated, informative, thought provoking.

41. Add Share Buttons at the Bottom of All your Emails and Content

Encourage your current email subscribers to share and forward your emails by including social sharing buttons and an "email to a friend" button in your marketing emails. That way, you'll gain access to fresh networks, friends, and colleagues who might sign up for your list. At the bottom of your emails, include a "Subscribe" CTA as a simple text-based link so that those receiving the forwarded emails can easily opt-in, too.

Add a share suggestion on all your PDFs and videos.

42. Use Radio or TV to Handcraft Your List

Although very likely the last strategy you would use, due to lower cost it can be an option for the right restaurants. Radio is a better bet than TV because it's cheaper and radio stations are much more likely to allow you to use trade instead of cash or at least a combination. That said, there are often cheap slots available on local cable although it's not something I have used in a long time, so I'll stick to radio. Once again, the key strategy is just to drive them to a contest on your landing page that allows you to collect their data.

SUMMARY

Before you can expect to make any money from online marketing, **you must start by committing the time and resources to handcraft your prospect list.** Success in this endeavor is measured in quality, not quantity, but both are even better.

First decide what your specific written criteria will be for inclusion in your mailing list. The tougher the criteria, the better.

Once you have determined your exact criteria, you will use a variety of methods to qualify prospects into a high-quality list.

Start by combing your computer, desk, files, and pockets for all existing data, which, even though not current, can at least be re-qualified by mail or phone quickly.

Make your website the focus of all your prospecting efforts. Use ads, direct mail, radio, TV, and e-blasts to drive people to a contact point on your website or your landing pages. Entice prospects to register with contests, offers, emails, free stuff, VIP clubs, discounts etc.

Don't forget the obvious, existing customers, ex-customers, referrals, local fair leads, and existing vendors, they eat too! Look for alliances with non-competing restaurants to quickly enhance your prospect list by sharing data.

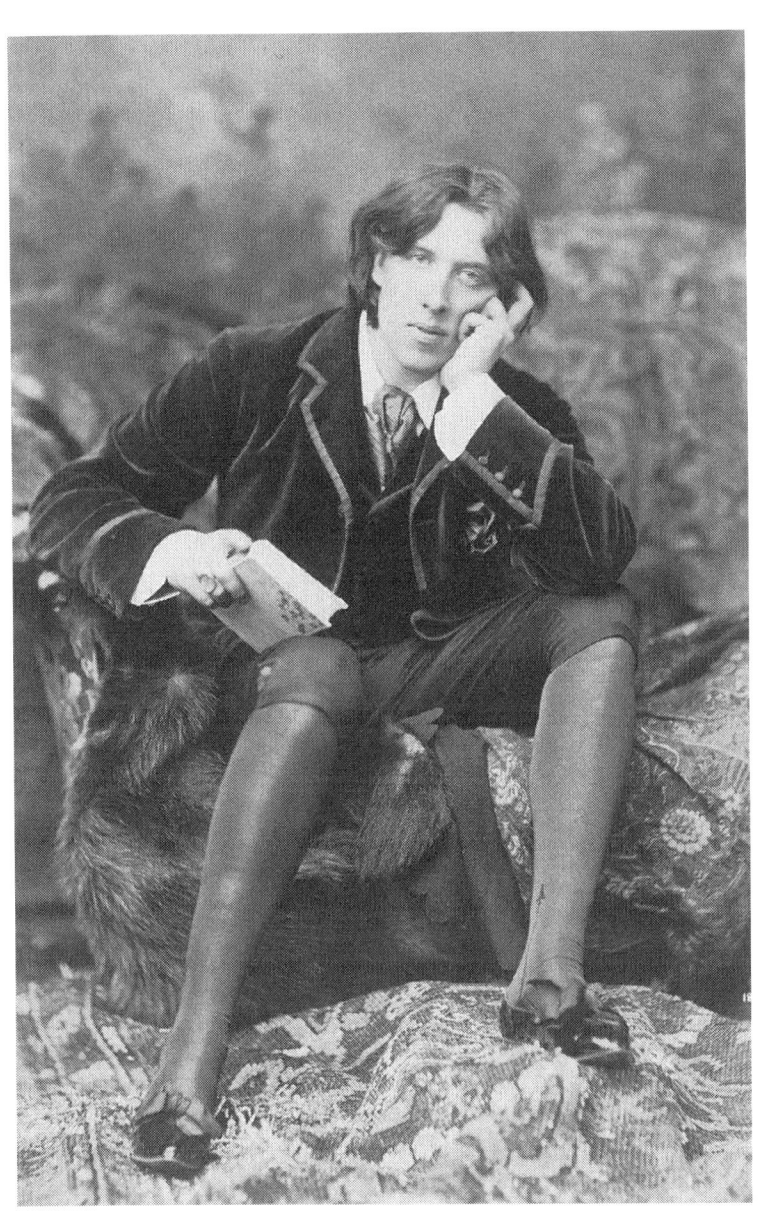

"After a good dinner one can forgive anybody, even one's own relations." — **Oscar Wilde**

CHAPTER 9

Legendary Email Marketing

Done right, email marketing is low cost, generates high returns, and provides instant gratification. Done wrong, you'll spend weeks trying to clean up the mess you leave behind, with irate customers who may never return. You have gone to great lengths to build a large email list. Now it's time to monetize it properly, which is not quite as simple as it seems.

Many restaurants get lackluster results from their campaigns, rarely seeing any significant spikes in business. Many more murder their lists with offer after offer, quickly destroying its marketing power in a storm of unsubscribes.

A good email marketing strategy is power at your fingertips, but you must take care in how you plan and execute your strategy. Random emails when the mood hit you is never the answer.

In this chapter, you will discover:

✓ 10 ways to connect with your customers using email,

✓ How to segment your lists for greater response,

✓ 10 ways to make your e-marketing more effective,

✓ How to personalize your messages for greater response,

✓ How often to mail your list, and twelve ways to avoid spam filters.

Connecting with your customers using email

It's a fact that the more often you connect in a meaningful way with your customers, the longer they will stay with you and the stronger your brand awareness will be. This in turn leads to more bookings, more referrals, and more profits. The key word here is *meaningful* ways.

Ten Ways You Should Be Using Email Marketing to Increase Your Business—but Aren't

1. **Sales**—This is obvious but is often the last of the ten things you should be doing, not the first and only thing, which is what most restaurants do. Even when you do sell, it's often better to wrap your message in a content sandwich rather than an all-out sales pitch.

2. **Data collection and enhancement**—This should be first on your list of email strategies. Email addresses change often and you must be constantly asking your people to update their data. You should also be using your emails to enhance your customer profiles. Request they forward your emails to their friends so the friends too can enter your contest or download your coupon and continue to expand your database.

3. **Entertainment and additional value**—Again this is something few really consider but your emails should be an extension of your restaurant's experience. In other words, your emails should provide additional entertainment and value to your guests. Think carefully about that last sentence for it's critically important to improving your response.

800-123-4567

WE HEARD YOU'RE CELEBRATING!

We heard there's a birthday in your party. Happy Birthday! Did you know that we can make a custom cake to celebrate the special occasion?

Let us know if you'd like us to get one ready for you, we just need 24 hours notice and the name of the person you're celebrating.

If you order a birthday cake we'll also throw in a FREE champagne toast.

Call us at 800-123-4567 to get the party started!

See you soon,
Twin Roosters Restaurant
hello@twinroosters.com

4. **Pre-dinner upsells and information**—The time between booking table and arrival at your location is one of the best times to reach out to your customers, catching them when they are excited about their visit and will be very receptive to opportunities for enhancing it.

The following is the strategy you should employ in your pre-arrival emails:

Remind. Remind your guests about their upcoming reservation by letting them know that you are looking forward to seeing them. Provide directions and parking instructions if applicable. Provide details to local taxis or limo services and let them know about any entertainment that may be offered.

Upsell. Including upsell options in your pre-arrival email is a great way to enhance your guest's visit and boost incremental revenue in the process. The more targeted the offer, the better.

Include a strong CTA that invites customers to contact you directly to make their request, or links to a portal on your website for adding extras to their visit. Perhaps putting a bottle of champagne on ice, pre ordering a soufflé or organizing a cake for a special occasion.

5. **Nurture** prospective customers with additional information to entice them in.

6. **Build brand awareness.** Constantly emailing consistently high-quality information will build a positive brand for your restaurant.

WE CAN'T WAIT TO WELCOME YOU!

We're looking forward to you dining with us. Is there anything we can have waiting for you? How about a bottle of our custom-made house white? It's a customer favorite and pairs really well with a lot of our dishes.

Just reply to this email or give us a call at 800-123-4567 and we'll have a bottle popped open and waiting at your table when you arrive.

If you have any questions before your scheduled reservation please don't hesitate to contact us.

See you soon,
Fish & Chips
hello@fishandchipsfl.com
800-123-4567

Upsells give you a chance to be creative

7. **Follow up** and thank your customers for their business.

Post-dinner emails are an effective tool for keeping your restaurant on top of your guest's mind. If you aren't sending out post-dinner emails, you're missing out on one of the greatest opportunities for turning customers into repeat guests.

Send out emails within 24 hours of your guests' dinner, thanking them for dining with you. In these emails you ask them for their feedback and request them to leave an online review on TripAdvisor or Facebook—include links to each so they don't have to find it themselves. If they didn't have a good experience, ask them to contact you directly and attempt to rectify the situation without it making its way online.

8. **Connect and engage with your guests**

After someone has dined with you, you may well have a wealth of additional information you can use to send out targeted marketing emails.

You can inform them of current or upcoming promotions or events that may be of interest—targeting corporate offers to businessmen, romantic packages to couples, and specials to families, results in more effective campaigns.

Remember, if someone is a big fan you can never connect with them too much!

9. **Keep them informed** on the happenings at your restaurant with a monthly, or even weekly, newsletter.

10. **Drive customers** to specific event landing pages. Like a wine tasting, beer night, couples night, street party, New Year's Eve or Valentines Day.

How to destroy your email list

If all you do is send emails offering nothing else of value to your readers, you will appeal to a very small percentage of those your list. You will rapidly increase your unsubscribes or people will simply ignore your emails altogether.

Most damaging of all in the long term is, you will brand yourself as being at the very bottom of the food chain. This is a place that's very difficult to come back from.

The information that you collect about guests in order to personalize their experience should be used to target your email campaigns.

Ten Keys to Effective Email Marketing

1. Clean lists

Before we get into the nuances of good email design let's start with something far more important...your email lists:

- ✓ How good are they targeted, opt-in segmented?
- ✓ How clean are they?
- ✓ Poor list maintenance results in poor delivery rates.

Manage Your Bounces

A bounce is when a sent email isn't delivered. If your provider isn't managing bounces correctly, he or she is flushing your email database down the drain.

There are two types of bounces that occur:

Hard Bounces—These are bounces that occur because the email address isn't active anymore. These should be immediately removed from your database, once they are confirmed as bad.

Soft Bounces—There are many reasons for a soft bounce to occur. The most common are "Mailbox full," "Email account unavailable," or "System not accepting message."

Hard bounces should not be immediately removed from your email database because the receiving server isn't telling you it's a bad email address. Your system should try resending to them and monitor the bounce that is received.

- If it continues to receive the same bounce message after a few tries, then it is acceptable for the email address to be removed. However, if it receives different messages, it shows that the receiving server is having issues. This is extremely common with a lot of the major mail providers such as AOL.com, Yahoo.com, and Hotmail.com.
- Resend to your soft bounces: soft bounces are usually errors that are occurring at the receiving end. Usually these issues are solved within a few hours and the email addresses start functioning again.

2. Target list demographics with your message.

The more ways you sort your lists by interest, gender, preference, and geography, the greater your open rates and the fewer unsubscribe requests. This is important data you can gain from the questions on your website, your landing pages, and from stays. Over time, you can build an insightful profile of your prospects.

Sort your lists into logical groups:

- Families
- Special events
- Businessmen
- Locals
- Dining events
- Drinking events—beer tastings, wine tastings
- Repeat guests

There are 101 other questions you can ask to create small responsive groups; after all, it makes no sense to invite a nondrinker for wine tasting or to pound your vegan list with steak dinner offers.

Targeted messages and offers can be designed for each group so that you can maximize your success. As with everything, the more targeted your groups and the more specific your offer is to meeting that group's needs, the more effective your marketing efforts will be. While it may sound like a lot of work, it's really just a couple of hours spent on programming. The computer will take care of the rest if you have the right software.

3. Great subject lines

The difference between an email blast that gets opened and therefore potentially acted upon and one that is not opened usually hangs in the balance of less than six words. Just like an ad, your emails will live and die on your subject lines. The difference in open rates between an A and a B subject line can easily be 500 percent or more.

The subject line is your ad for your email; make it count. The best email subject lines are short, descriptive, and provide the reader with a reason to explore your message further.

Trying to stand out in the inbox by using splashy or cheesy phrases will invariably result in your email being ignored. Promise the reader a benefit for opening your email.

Great headlines

- Kids Eat Free!
- Flown in Fresh – Florida Stone Crab!
- Free Wine with Your Meal Every Tuesday!
- 2 for 1 Specials
- 50% Off Happy Hour Drinks
- Free Appetizers

Subject lines are one of the most, if not the most important element in the emails you send. This is because it's one of the first things that customers will see in their inbox. If someone has twenty unread emails and little time to go through them, what do they do? They prioritize and make quick decisions. These decisions are based on who the email is from and what's in it for them.

4. Attractive design

Attractiveness is often in the eye of the beholder, judging by the deluge of pitiful emails in my1 inbox from "marketing people" at restaurants. Large pink type, purple block capitals, neon green and red do not actually make the email stand out, at least not for the right reasons.

The email should first and foremost be easy to read. That means no nine-point type, little to no reverse type, no overuse of block capitals, and sparing use of type over pictures. Designers love all these elements. But trust me, you will make more money if it's readable, not pretty.

Consider using a larger typestyle—55 percent of American over forty can't read this twelve-point type without glasses. Have one key the focal point and don't forget your social-media buttons in the footer.

800-123-4567

It's BACK! We're bringing back our most popular giveaway of the year for the 10th straight year.

Enter for a chance to win a dozen oysters on the half shell per week for the whole year. Use 'em or lose 'em, no oyster accumulations.

Winner will be announced at our annual Oyster Slurp Contest.

ENTER FOR A CHANCE TO WIN >

Good luck!
Codfish
shucks@codfish.com

5. Emails should add value to your readers' lives

Think of your emails as an extension of your service, or an additional way to entertain your prospective guests. With this key point in mind, you must add value to your emails; don't make them all about sales.

Make your reader pleased he opened your email even if he is not of the mind to book a stay today.

Make your emails a careful mixture of engagement, entertainment, and education. Build value into your emails, not just offers.

Include:

- Videos
- Contests
- Cool pictures
- Cartoons
- Stories
- Jokes
- Quotes
- News
- Events
- And, of course, offers!

Entertaining, engaging content will get passed around at astonishingly higher rates. More pass-around means more traffic and it comes with the healthy endorsement of a friend who thinks this is worth reading.

Example

Subject: Shuck Yeah!

6. Calls to Action

I see very few emails with specific CTA but the more time-sensitive, the more limited, the more explicit your demand for action is, the more response you will get. You must try and create some urgency to act in your emails.

- Limited to the first twenty callers
- Next 48 hours only
- Only four spots left in the wine event
- Only three Saturdays left this summer for wedding dates
- Deadline approaching for summer kids' cooking camp

7. Engaging graphics

Customized graphics add to the reader's engagement and entertainment so should be used frequently. The more creative you are, the better.

If it makes you smile, it will most likely make them too smile and that, my friends, is entertainment.

BEST DESSERT QUOTES EVER!

"All you need is love. But a little chocolate now and then doesn't hurt."
- **Charles M. Schulz**

"Seize the moment. Remember all those women on the 'Titanic' who waved off the dessert cart." - **Erma Bombeck**

"Cakes are healthy too, you just eat a small slice." - **Mary Berry**

"Anything is good if it's made of chocolate." - **Jo Brand**

In case you're wondering why we chose dessert quotes, it's because our Adult Smores are back on the dessert menu for a limited time. Come on out and treat yourself!

Space are limited call 800-123-4567 to make a reservation or click here to book online.

Hey Chris,

We know you love craft beer, so we wanted to let you know about a brand new event that's coming to Orlando in a few months, the Orlando Beer & Wine Festival.

Since you previously took part in one of our craft beer golf weekends, we wanted to give you first dibs on a special **VIP package** we put together for the event.

Here's what you get:

- Two VIP tickets to the event. A VIP ticket gets you in 30-minutes before regular admission
- Transportation to and from the event. It's only about a 15-minute walk from the hotel, but we'll take you there and pick you up.
- Two night's accommodations
- Two free beers and an appetizer of your choosing at our bar on the first day of your stay

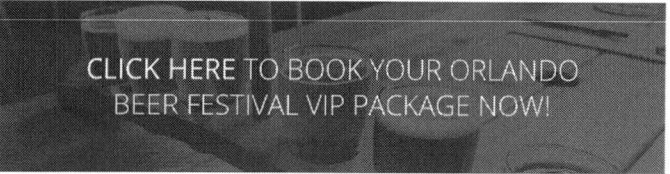

Best,

Patrick Clark

Patrick Clark
General Manager

Andrew Wood

Join us on March 17th for our annual
St. Patrick's Day celebration.

Dress in green and join us for:

Live music, Irish dancing, a bagpipe band
$2.50 Guinness Drafts, $2.50 Domestics,
Traditional Irish Food and more!

We open at 9am for a special Irish brunch.
Space are limited call 800-123-4567 to make a reservation.

8. Timeliness and Creativity

Getting Creative—How to Make Your Emails More Interesting, Engaging, and Effective

There are lots of simple ways you can make your emails stand out from the crowd of boring corporate-speak and mindless discount offers. Make your emails memorable, timely, and effective.

Memorable Dates

The more timely your email subject matter, the better it will be received by your audience.

The calendar is your friend: Holidays, tour events, birthdays, current events. The possibilities are endless.

What makes the St. Patrick's Day email good?

- Custom picture that matches the subject
- Offer tied into the actual day
- Fun fact included to spur them to action
- Easy to read
- Large call to action
- Facebook icon

People love contests and sweepstakes

Try to do at least one contest every couple of months:

- It creates excitement.
- It provides additional value.
- It refreshes your database with updated info.
- It often goes viral with people sharing emails.
- It mixes up your content and keeps it fresh.
- Vacations are great because of the high perceived value.

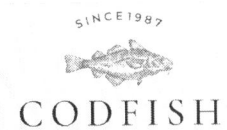

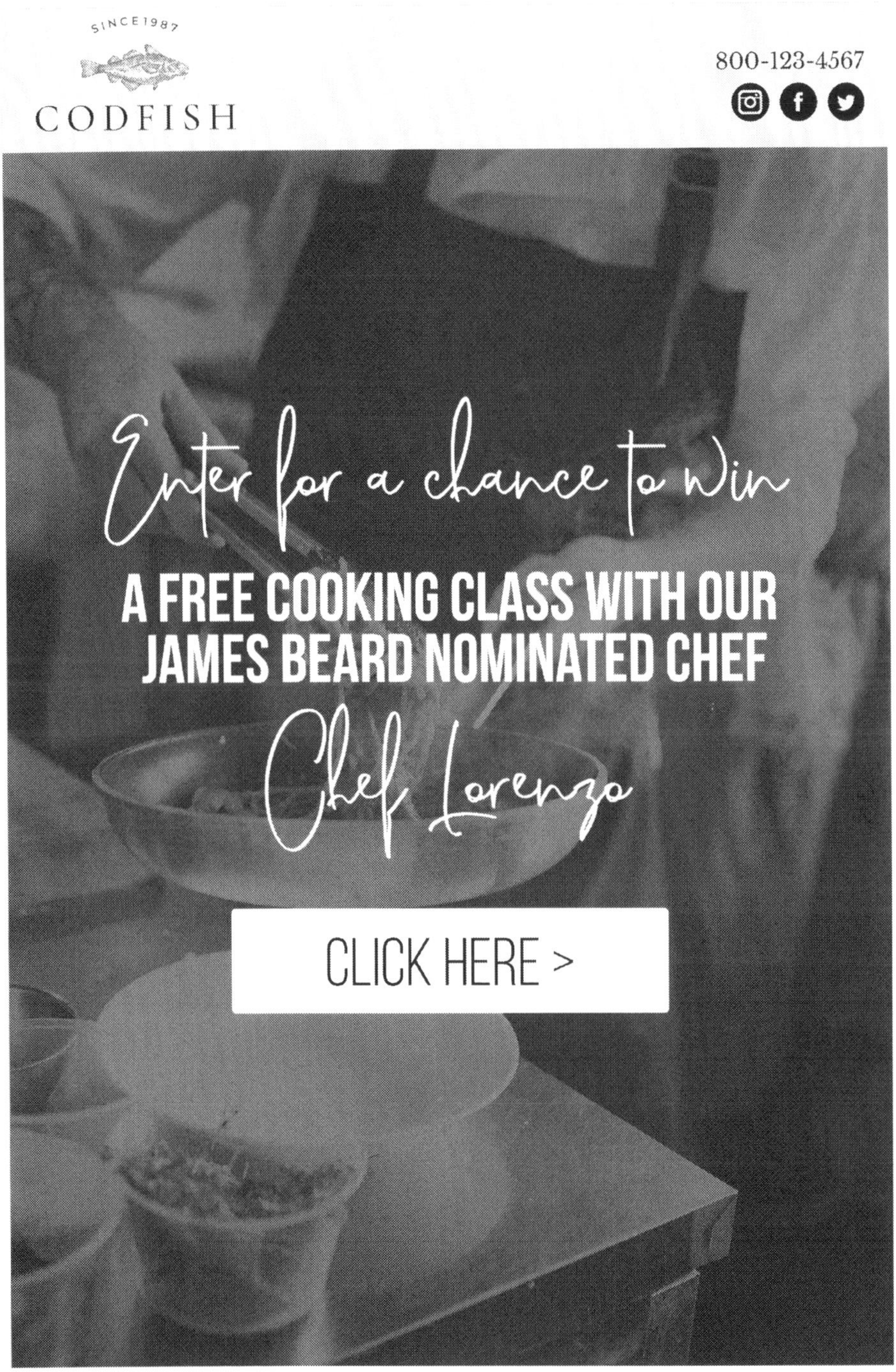
SINCE 1987
CODFISH
800-123-4567
Enter for a chance to win
A FREE COOKING CLASS WITH OUR
JAMES BEARD NOMINATED CHEF
Chef Lorenzo
CLICK HERE >

Like I mentioned, these contests are something we generally do every 60-90 days for our clients, and it gets great engagement:

- Provide value

- There will be some viral action

- Ensure that the call to action is clearly visible

- Tie offer into the email content

- Add a Facebook link

- Make it an easy-to-read layout

- And, of course, it would have a header and footer for positive association with your brand

9. Personalize your subject lines or the intro of your email

Most good email marketing providers allow the addition of fields such as a customer's name so the offers you send are more personalized.

One-to-one personalization is a proven key to building long-term customer value and higher response rates. We use our campaign manager to implement a true one-to-one marketing solution. Personalize your mailings to the people who have already indicated their interest in specific offers. It's all automatic and it makes them feel like you really know them.

10. Solid branding

Every email you send should have a solid header at the top with your branding—on longer emails you may choose to repeat this at the bottom.

Twelve ways legitimate emailers can avoid spam filters

Recently, several subscribers informed me that their spam filters were preventing their getting my newsletter. I checked and, sure enough, several factors were causing my own emails to get rejected. It's a sad fact that because of the massive amount of spam, perhaps as much as 20–30 percent of legitimate email does not get through to its intended recipient. Various spam filters such as Spam Assassin block some legitimate emails in addition to spam. That's bad news for restaurants looking to use their lists to attract guests. The good news is that by paying attention to some key factors you can still get most of your messages through.

Spam filters these days are much more sophisticated than the typical email filters of the past. The new ones can be made to delete an email message that contains a number of "bad" words. Filters such as Spam Assassin look for patterns and add or delete points for certain factors. If your total score reaches a predetermined level, the message is flagged as spam. By looking at what adds points (bad) and subtracts points (good), you can learn to construct emails that will do better with the filters, if not escape them entirely.

Make sure you get delivered to the inbox.

1. **You must authenticate your emails**—If you're not authenticating the emails you send from your mail platform, receiving servers automatically assume your email is more likely to be spam.

    Ways to Authenticate Your Email
    - **Sender Policy Framework (SPF)**—This record is a type of Domain Name System (DNS) record that can help to prevent email address forgery. This method adds IP Addresses of the servers that are allowed to send email from your domain name. SPF is the oldest authentication method that is still accepted by mail servers.

    - **Domain Keys Identified Mail (DKIM)**—This is another type of entry that is made to a Domain Name System (DNS) record. DKIM allows sending servers to associate a domain name with an email message, which will show it is authentic. This is done by "signing" the email with a digital signature, a field that is added to the message's header when it is sent from the server. The receiving server can then validate the digital signature using the DNS records and allow delivery. DKIM is currently the most popular authentication method.

- **Domain-based Message Authentication, Reporting and Conformance (DMARC)**—DMARC is the final type of authentication method, although it has not gained the popularity of SPF or DKIM. DMARC works with both DKIM and SPF, and builds off the success each technology has created. It uses both SPF and DKIM record to validate email, by testing the DNS records. If either record fails, the email immediately is flagged and will be handled by the receiving server to either be flagged as spam or rejected completely. DMARC is expected to grow in popularity over the next few years given the success it is having.

2. **Offer a Simple Unsubscribe Option**—Having an easy unsubscribe link is important to avoid being classified as spam. The link to the unsubscribe page must be functional, instantaneous, and easy to find in the email—meaning, put it at the top or bottom.

   Do not send users a follow-up email to confirm their unsubscribe. The majority of them will flag you as spam, blocking your sender address.

3. **IP Reputation**—Monitoring your IP reputation is very important. If your email provider uses the same IP addresses to send email for hundreds of different clients, all it would take is for one to import a bad list and cause spam complaints to hurt **your** deliverability.

   Legendary Marketing has many dedicated IP addresses, meaning that you don't have to share the reputation of your IP address with one hundred other users on your mailing platform. Systems are in place to monitor them regularly to avoid any problems that might occur. We also give partners and clients the option to upgrade to their own private IP address, virtually eliminating any deliverability problems.

4. **Use a Domain Name That is Linked to Your Website**—You always want to use an email address that is linked to your domain name.

   Example: Andrew@LegendaryMarketing.com

   If you use any other type of email address, even if you have all the proper SPF/DKIM/DMARC records created, your email delivery will fall dramatically.

5. **Make Sure Your Email Provider Can Use Throttled Delivery**—Throttling is the practice of adjusting your sending rate based on the rules ISPs (Internet service providers) and ESPs (Email service providers) have set. Yes, it is shocking to believe, but Gmail, Hotmail, Comcast, and many other providers do not want you sending ten thousand emails to them in under one minute.

   Your technology must be able to throttle based off:
   - The number of emails sent per minute or hour,
   - The number of connections per minute or hour,
   - The number emails sent per connection.

6. **You Must Monitor Spam Complaints and Use Feedback Loops**—Many ISPs and ESPs allow you to receive an alert when your email is flagged as spam, also known as a "feedback loop." When your email platform receives one of these alerts, it is best practice to immediately unsubscribe the email address that reported you as spam. If you do not, and you continue to deliver to the address that reported you as spam, your deliverability will be hurt.

7. **Manage Your Email Bounces Properly**—This is probably the most mismanaged process in any industry. If your provider isn't doing this correctly they are flushing your email database down the drain.

There are two types of bounces that occur:

Hard Bounces—These are bounces that occur because the email address just isn't active anymore. These should be immediately removed from your database.

Soft Bounces—There are many reasons a soft bounce can occur. The most common are reasons like "Mailbox full," "Email account unavailable," or "System not accepting message."

These should not be immediately removed from your email database because the receiving server isn't telling you it's a bad email address. Your system should try resending to them and monitor the bounce that is received. If it continues to receive the same bounce message after a few tries then it is acceptable for the email address to be removed, however, if it receives different messages, it shows that the receiving server is having issues. This is extremely common with a lot of the major mail providers such as AOL.com, Yahoo.com, and Hotmail.com.

You should instead be monitoring your bounces to see if any problems are occurring. Your providers should be showing you the reasons for the types of bounces that are occurring—if they aren't, they probably don't want you to see something.

8. **Send Emails Out Regularly**—If you do not send emails out on a regular basis, your subscribers will forget they subscribed. They then will most likely report you as spam, hurting your deliverability.

9. **Remove Inactive Email Addresses**—This one will be painful, but it's something everyone should do but no one does. If someone hasn't opened an email from you in the last twelve months, remove their email.

Yes, I know you've spent so many years building your email list to the size that it currently is, but the greater the number of inactive contacts, the more your IP reputation rate suffers, which will impact your deliverability.

10. **Avoid suspect spam phrases**—There are hundreds to avoid if you want your emails read, but here are a few key ones.
    - ✓ Free
    - ✓ You won
    - ✓ Amazing
    - ✓ Special offer
    - ✓ Promotion

11. Be careful with your subject lines. Spam Assassin is particularly interested in subject lines. Here are a few subject line no-no's to learn from:
    - ✓ Contains "FREE" in all caps
    - ✓ Starts with "Free"
    - ✓ GUARANTEED
    - ✓ Starts with dollar amount
    - ✓ Subject is all in capitals
    - ✓ Subject talks about savings

12. **Mobile Responsive Email Design**—Over 50 percent of all emails were opened on a mobile device in 2016. If your emails do not look correct on a mobile device, it hurts your deliverability and causes unsubscribes.

How often should you email?

This is one of the most asked questions at my live speaking events. Everyone has a personal opinion on this topic but, like most untested opinions about marketing, they are usually wrong. Most people email too little—yes, too little. It's a simple fact that the more you mail, the more you make. As long as the email is interesting, fun, entertaining, valuable to the reader.

General guidelines:

- Send your newsletter once a month.
- Segment your lists and target different groups.
- Make your emails add value to your guests' lives.
- Make your emails add entertainment to their lives.
- Make your email marketing a positive extension of your overall restaurant experience.
- The key to email marketing success is in consistency and creativity.
- Send emails at least once and preferably twice per week.
- Stay on a schedule find the best days and best times to send.
- Use a creative mix of offers and content.
- Varity is the spice of life. You have to keep readers on their toes by mixing it up so they open your email to see what you've come up with this time.

Give your emails a personality

One of the biggest mistakes I see being made by restaurants is not inserting their own personalities into their email. Part of the advantage of having a small business is that you are a real person. Readers can contact you, agree, disagree, and so forth. All of your articles could be from other people. The key is to add some of yourself to your content. What you need to do is add in a few paragraphs you wrote yourself at the top. Do an editorial section, just like in magazines to talk about what's going on at your restaurant. Tell your readers how you feel about your business, how it was built, what the design philosophy was, its history, and so on. Talk about what you love about the business. Be personal. You may be so afraid of making mistakes in this area that you don't do anything. So make some mistakes; we all do. It's part of being human.

What you say may offend some people and they may unsubscribe from your list. So what? They weren't planning on buying from you anyway. I'm not telling you to purposely offend anyone, just letting you know it's going to happen. Use spell-checkers and have someone edit your writing for you. But guess what? There are still going to be mistakes people will let you know about.

People always ask me how I have gotten my name published all over the web. Here's the secret...

Be a real person

It's not what you were expecting, is it? It's not exciting or highly technical. It's just the truth. People online are looking for people who are real, who have opinions, and who make mistakes. One of my most popular articles being published around the web mentions my dog Winston. Some people won't like you mentioning "daily life" items such as this. Let them unsubscribe. The ones who stay on your list will buy more once they know you. Personality is one of the most underused tools in the marketing arsenal.

Open 24 hours with email auto responder follow-ups

By installing auto responder software on your website, you can, in effect, be in business twenty-four hours a day. This option lets you preload a series of letters, answers to questions, tips, or any other printed material, and then email the specific information about your business back to the customer on demand.

Use marketing automation to take follow-ups to the next level

It's now possible to have custom emails triggered just by people spending time on specific pages, or watching thirty seconds of your video using marketing automation software.

Check your email often

Speed is king on the internet. Customers don't expect to wait until tomorrow for an answer. Check your email and respond throughout the day, not just at the end of the day.

Using these strategies will allow you to connect more often, provide better service, and acquire and keep more happy customers.

SUMMARY

Email is a powerful tool for online marketing. With its speed, low cost, and ease of customization, it should be your favorite tool. Always keep in mind, however, that your email is an extension of your restaurants experience. Engage, educate, and entertain before you try to sell anything.

"For me, I love food. It's my greatest pleasure and also the thing that could ruin you as well. It's one of those things where, if you're not thoughtful about it, it could be unhealthy. But if there's a mindfulness about it; it actually is a wonderful tool of emotional expression." — **Jon Favreau**

Andrew Wood

CHAPTER 10

Social Media—Facebook

Whoever controls the media—the images—controls the culture. —**Allen Ginsberg**

The power of social media has exploded across the world. Billions of dollars have been made on the backs of social media's astonishing reach, and there is an almost dizzying array of social media from which to choose: Twitter, Facebook, LinkedIn, Instagram, Pinterest, and YouTube to name just a few. It can be hard to know which are worth your time—and which are not—and harder still to figure out how you can profit from any investment of time or money in them.

In this chapter, you will discover:

- ✓ a powerful new way to look at your social media,
- ✓ which social media to use,
- ✓ the three secret words to social-media success,
- ✓ what to post, and
- ✓ how often to post.

Which Social Media Should You Focus on First?

With so many different social media available, it's very difficult for most people to figure out what they should do, what they shouldn't do, and how to do it. I'll give you a simple guide to the most effective forms of social media that, for most restaurants, begins and ends with Facebook. You may personally love Pinterest or Twitter but their ability to convert to sales is limited.

Facebook is so powerful and has such a major reach and the ability to allow you to target people with specific interests and demographics that no other social media really comes close.

The second social media you should look at is LinkedIn because LinkedIn is full of professionals, but this will be most use if you are in a metro location.

The third social media should look at is YouTube. Video is becoming more and more popular and more and more powerful as a means of getting your message out.

Fourth comes Instagram. It gets your delicious food pictures in front of a younger audience but has little impact on older age groups. I'd move this up to second if you are targeting the under-40s market.

Now we can fight over which social media should come next—should it be or Pinterest, Twitter or a hundred others? The truth of the matter is, you probably shouldn't even bother with any of these until you have a Facebook fully utilized, and very few restaurants ever achieve that. While all the social media have their own following, none of them are as effective in getting out real sales messages to your customers and potential customers.

Whatever social media you choose to use, the basic rules are the same. Engage, educate, and entertain. By engaging, educating, and entertaining your customers and guests, you essentially gain their trust and, by default, gain their permission to then approach them with a sales message. Too many restaurants bombard their fans and followers with sales messages without providing any real value.

Here's a paradigm shift that will help…

You Just Bought a Magazine

The best way to look at your Facebook page is to imagine that your Facebook page is in fact a lifestyle magazine. Your Facebook page should include all the types of content pictures, videos, articles, and links that would be interesting to your audience. Have back stories on wine and spirits. Where do they come from? What's their history. Where do you get your produce from—what farms and sources? Who are your staff? Tell us something about them. Share some recipes. Talk about your menu. What's your concept—your reason for being?

Think of your Facebook page as an extension of your restaurant's experience, something that continues to provide value and entertainment to your guests when they leave your restaurant.

The Three *E*'s of Social Media

Engage

Educate

Entertain

Educate Your Guests. Your content must be of value and should be timely to your customers. The more valuable your content, the more people will read it and pass it along to others, thus growing your list and your following.

Engage Your Guest. Be controversial; ask for opinions, tips, stories, pictures, feedback, and participation. Let your followers enter to win free prizes, discounts, and insider specials reserved only for them. Post photo-without-caption contests.

Entertain Your Guest. You must entertain your reader with funny pictures, cartoons, videos, anecdotes.

If your communications do each of these three E's, your readers will not mind that you have inserted a promotion or ad within the copy, just as they see in magazines. On the other hand, if all you do is bombard them with discount offers week after week without providing any of the above value, your lists and readership will shrink rapidly.

These three concepts are the mantras for all social media. The basic idea is that you should communicate with customers and form a relationship with prospects and customers *before* trying to sell anything.

Educate, engage, and entertain your readers with your social media. Then, and only then, try to sell them something.

PROFITING FROM FACEBOOK

The first question to ask is "What's your restaurant's goal for being on Facebook?" Ultimately the goal of most restaurants will be to increase retention of existing customers, build top-of-the-mind awareness, and find new customers. Like most marketing on the internet, this will happen over a period of time and will involve a number of phases.

STEP 1: BUILD AWARENESS FOR YOUR RESTAURANT AND ITS FACEBOOK PAGE

The first step of your Facebook marketing campaign is to build brand awareness for your restaurant and your page. People must know the general services your restaurant offers and the fact that they can find you on Facebook and learn more by visiting your Facebook page.

HOW DO YOU BUILD AWARENESS OF YOUR FACEBOOK PRESENCE?

Your existing website

Make sure you highlight your Facebook page on your existing website and let people know you are there, as well as promote all your other social-media links. It's best to do this at the top and bottom of every page.

Your existing email or snail-mail database

Use your existing email and snail-mail databases to let people know about your Facebook page. End every email with your social-media icon and make sure that all your ads and brochures carry your social-media logos and addresses. It's Marketing 101, but you'd be amazed how many restaurants forget to do this simple but powerful step.

Targeted ads

Take advantage of the Facebook advertising platform. The standard cost of acquiring a new fan on your Facebook page through Facebook advertising is always rising but still a good deal.

Organic growth

The very best way to grow your Facebook presence is organically. The golden rule of viral/organic growth online is: *Create great content that people will share.* It's honestly as simple as that, although this is much easier said than done these days.

STEP 2: EDUCATE YOUR VISITORS

For those visitors who already know your restaurant, you should go deeper. For the rest who are just learning about your restaurant or who are new to showing an interest in it, the education process entails answering the following questions:

Who are you?

When I say "Who are you" I'm not just referencing your restaurant as a faceless organization. As I tell people on a regular basis, you need to *humanize* your restaurant. Who are the manager, chef, bartender, waitstaff and frontline staff? By connecting with individuals on a personal level and letting them know that there are real people behind your computer, you'll build a strong connection that will help the individual associate positive feelings with your restaurant. Yes, you also need to let them know what your restaurant stands for, but the personal touch is much more important.

What does your restaurant sell?

This could be as simple as something within the information tab in your Facebook page that describes what your restaurant offers. Do you offer banquet, catering and take-out service? You could also create an entire tab dedicated to describing your USP.

Who's in your community?

When new visitors land on your Facebook page, one of the first things they'll look at is the number of fans you have. You'll notice that as Facebook pages grow in size, they also tend to increase in the volume of new fans per day. This is because having a large number of fans turns you into a trusted authority.

Users will also browse through the members on your Facebook page to see who else is part of the community. They'll also view the comments people are posting to see if your content is something they are interested in hearing about. Do you have brand advocates who speak up for you when you aren't around? Do you have people who have something valuable to add to the conversation?

They say that you are who your friends are, and on Facebook you are who your community is. Foster a valuable community and there's a greater chance you'll convert new visitors into fans.

Why do I want to join?

Finally, before becoming a fan, the user will try to figure what benefit he or she is going to get from becoming a fan of your Facebook page. The benefit could simply be an opportunity to express affiliation with your brand. Another benefit could be ongoing access to valuable content (for example, recipes and how to's). Discounts for Facebook fans only are also am popular way to connect with fans. If your Facebook page has nothing to offer the visitor, the only people who will become fans are those who are already your fans or those who are interested in existing community members. If your goal is to reach new customers, you'll need to present significant value through your Facebook page.

STEP 3: ENGAGEMENT WITH YOUR FANS

"Engagement" has become the cornerstone of social network marketing. While many marketers criticize engagement for their inability to quantify it, every online marketer knows that engaging your customers is the new form of marketing. Rather than speaking *at* your customers, marketing has now become a two-way dialogue, leaving many traditional advertisers feeling powerless and confused.

You aren't completely powerless, though, since you can control the environment in which much of the conversation takes place. While there are many other platforms for engaging your customer base, Facebook pages are a great environment for directly interacting with a large portion of your customers and fans.

The engagement process is also critical to building a relationship with your fans and strengthening their personal brand affiliation. One thing to keep in mind is the impact that various forms of engagement have on the relationship with your customer:

- ✓ *Low-impact activities.* There are a lot of low-impact activities that a consumer can engage in. One example would be "liking" a status update in Facebook. (For those who may not be familiar with Facebook, "liking" is the feature that lets you click "Like" under a feed story.)
- ✓ *Medium-impact activities.* Commenting on a status could be one example of a medium-impact activity.
- ✓ *High-impact activities:* An individual or brand could turn a medium-impact activity into a high-impact experience by providing one-on-

one dialogue to turn the experience from a single comment to an ongoing conversation.

For restaurants, the impact of the efforts will differ, which is why it's best to provide as many engagement opportunities as possible.

STEP 4: CONVERTING FANS TO ACTION

In contrast to search engine advertising, which involves clicking on an ad and then taking some sort of action (for example, filling out a form or purchasing a product), Facebook sales normally involve building a relationship and presenting multiple opportunities to take an action. At this point you've already converted new visitors and, in the engagement phase, you built the relationship. Now it's time to present opportunities to make a purchase, attend an event, book a room, join the club, or take some other form of measurable action.

Most Facebook users are not ready to buy when they initially become fans, which is why you need to present calls to action on a regular basis. One example would be instant discounts. For example, you may want to provide a twilight-special today only or for the next four hours only. Another example is entering their names and emails into a newsletter list.

STEP 5: CONTINUE ENGAGEMENT

Now that you've presented a call to action and some of your users have taken that action, you need to continue to engage them. If you use the relationship-marketing model on Facebook, you'll end up a winner.

Relationship marketing is not about a one-time sale or action. Instead, we are in the business of building relationships and Facebook provides a good environment for doing just that.

You've already subtly introduced calls to action and now that some users have taken action, you need to keep doing what you did in step 3: Engage them and keep on engaging them.

WHAT SHOULD YOU POST ON FACEBOOK?

First refer to the email chapter

Everything we discussed in the email chapter about using dates, news, celebrity birthdays, photos without captions, funny videos, tips, and in-depth articles to make your emails more timely and interesting, are fair game for your Facebook page.

Everyone on your team can contribute.

Everyone on your team has the opportunity to contribute to your Facebook page building additional esprit de corps for your team and making your people come alive for guests.

- Your chef can tell your readers how to cook great food, pair wines, or invest in the right vintages. He can talk about his herb garden or his favorite recipes.

- Your bartender can offer mixed drink ideas, discuss micro brews, or make wine recommendations.

Post special events

Create events to promote upcoming events, tournaments, dining events, live music, community events, and so on. When you create an event, it gets a fully featured page, much like a group, that includes a discussion, photos, videos, and links. Facebook Events makes it easy to get the word out to hundreds of people, manage your guest list, and build community around your upcoming event.

Highlight specific services or promotions

Most restaurants have a huge range of ongoing services and activities that should be constantly highlighted on their Facebook pages:

- Social events

- Seafood night
- Happy hour
- Meetings and weddings
- Fashion shows

Are all examples of things you should consider posting on your page.

Post pictures of people enjoying your restaurant

It is said that a picture is worth a thousand words and when it comes to pictures of people enjoying your restaurant and events, this could be right.

Make sure there are lots of pictures of every event and get them up fast so guests can share them with their friends while the event is still newsworthy.

If you find that you are having problems getting pictures of people enjoying your restaurant, refer back to the previous section on running Photo Contests. If you see people having fun and just ask if you can snap a photo for the *official* Instagram or Facebook page, you'll be hard-pressed to find people who actually say no!

To be on the safe side, it's a good idea to get permission (via email or on a written form) to use any photo that has people in them with faces visible. If you're on vacation and snap a photo in a public place that contains people, it's generally fine to post it on Facebook or other social media sites. But the rules are different for commercial enterprises —if it's for your business, permission is generally required. Most people are happy to give permission.

Also encourage guests to take photos. Servers are frequently asked to take a photo (using the customer's phone) of the table or group. Instruct servers to suggest that the customer post the photo on Facebook or Instagram.

Speaking of pictures, want to massively increase your following on Instagram? Run a contest! Here's what you do.

- Come up with a buzzworthy prize and post it on your Instagram account.
- Tell people they must follow you, like the post and tag a friend (1 tag = 1 entry; unlimited entries)
- Give bonus entries if they repost on their feed or story and be sure to tag you.
- **Sit back and watch your IG account grow**

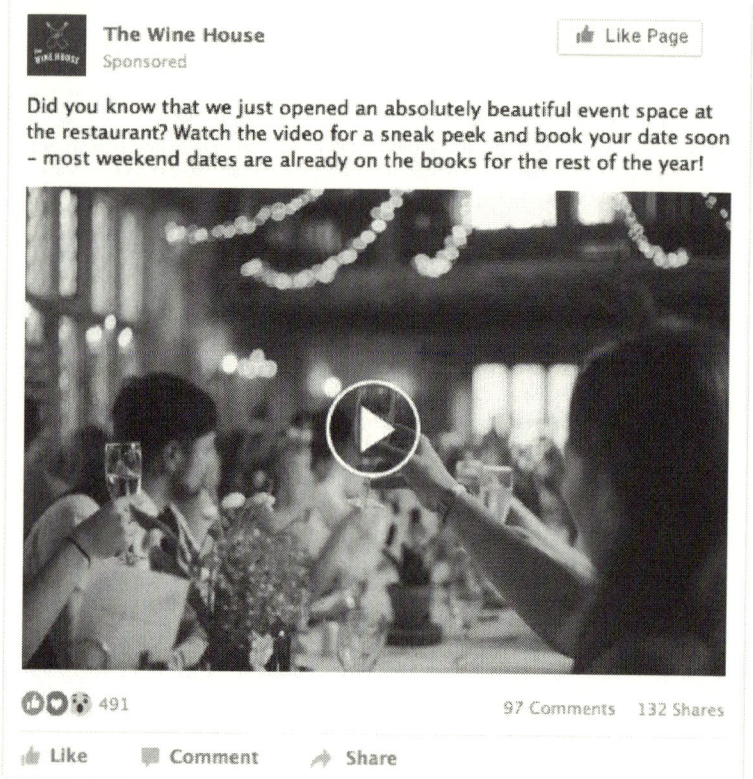

Post videos

The more multimedia you can add to your Facebook page, the more different people you are likely to attract. Post videos, audios, webinars, and slide shows. Some people like to read, others like to watch, so cater to both. Plus videos are more likely to go viral.

Post coupons and ads

Intersperse regular promotions and a special in between your news, event photos, and links.

You can do monthly, weekly, or even daily promotions, provided that's not the only thing you do and that it doesn't cheapen your image. Often it's best to offer extras rather than discount prices. Be sure to work real content in between your promotions and you will not risk offending your fans.

Everything you post will make it onto a percentage of your fans' news feeds, almost all if you boost the post. "Boosting" is paying Facebook to get your content (post, photo, video) on the newsfeeds of more people than your fans. You can specify characteristics of those who will receive your boosted posts, for example, people 35–55 years old in your town. Use this power wisely.

The 80/20 rule

Despite your best efforts, people do not log onto Facebook to seek out your new dinner package or deal, even if it's an amazing offer. We recommend following the 80/20 rule when it comes to posting content on your Facebook page.

The 80/20 rule is that only 20% of your content should be used for promoting your restaurant—your coupons or ads— while the other 80% should be content that engages, educates and entertains.

Remember to Focus on the "Three E's"

As I mentioned earlier in this chapter, focus first on the "Three E's" in order to build a relationship with your fans through great content. This is especially important if you have not begun to utilize Facebook as a marketing tool and are not posting often.

I see a troubling number of restaurants that post a deal once every few months and say that Facebook does not work! If the only posts your audience ever sees are you going for a sale, they will tune you out completely.

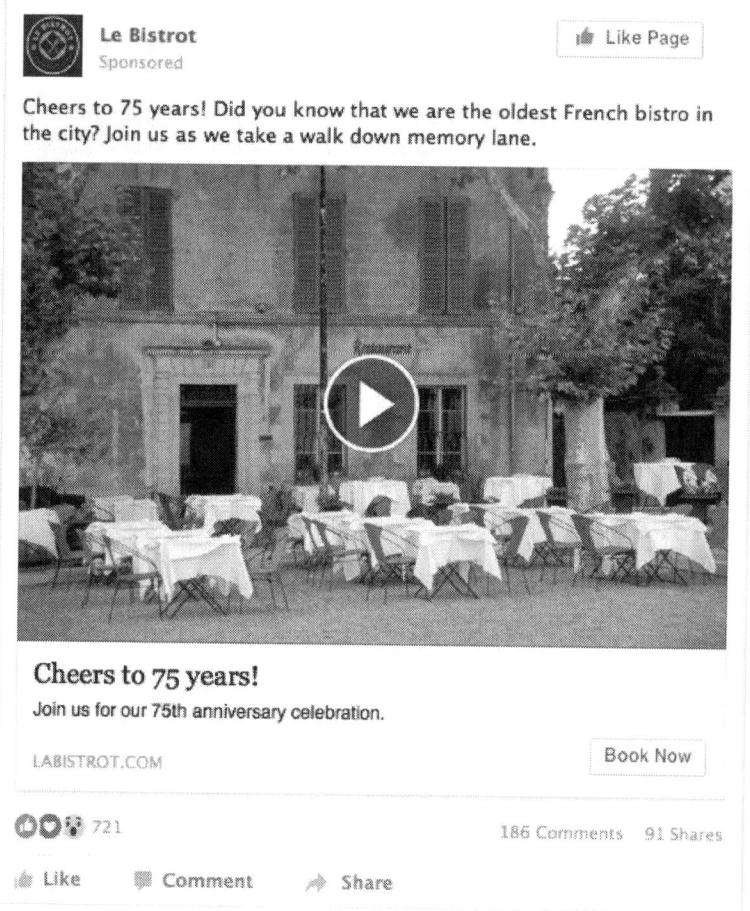

Share your restaurant's history

Facebook is the place you can share you restaurant's rich history. Pictures and stories from the past help to communicate the tradition and brand that your restaurant has. You can show past and present pictures, discuss remodeling through the years, or offer bios have the architect and prominent guests.

Promote gift certificates

Facebook is a great place to promote gift certificates, especially around major holidays.

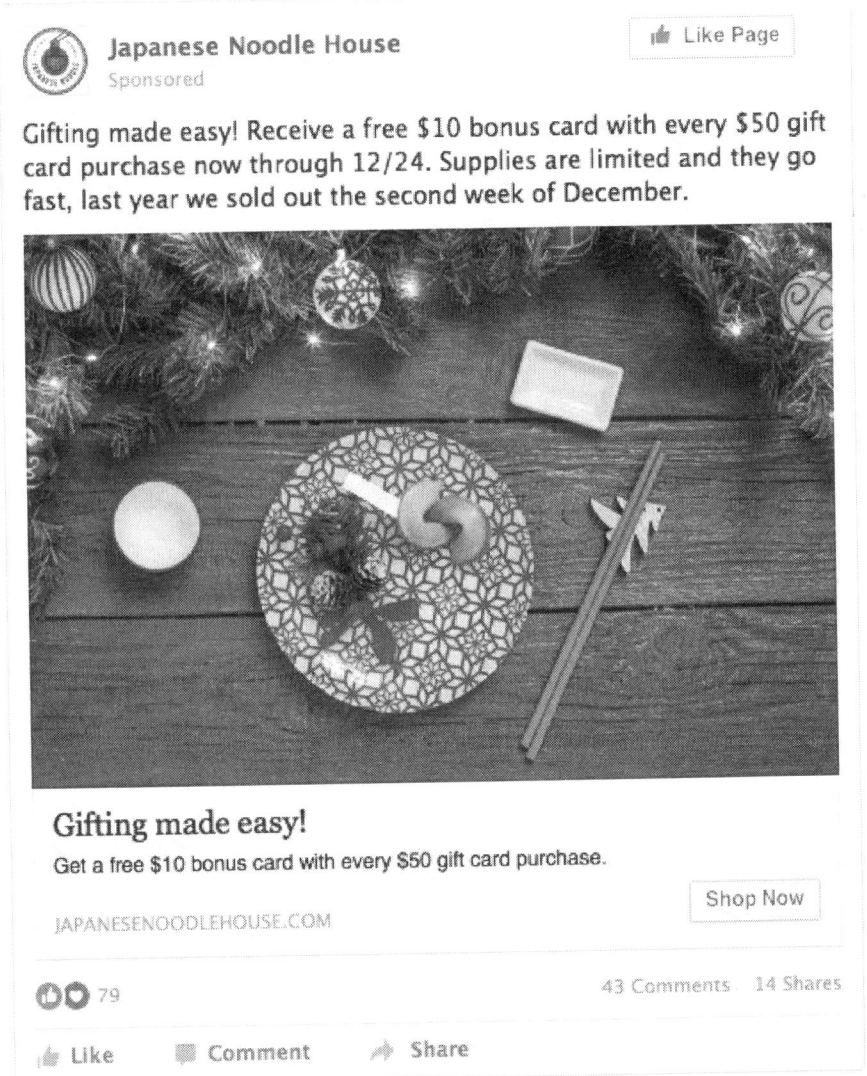

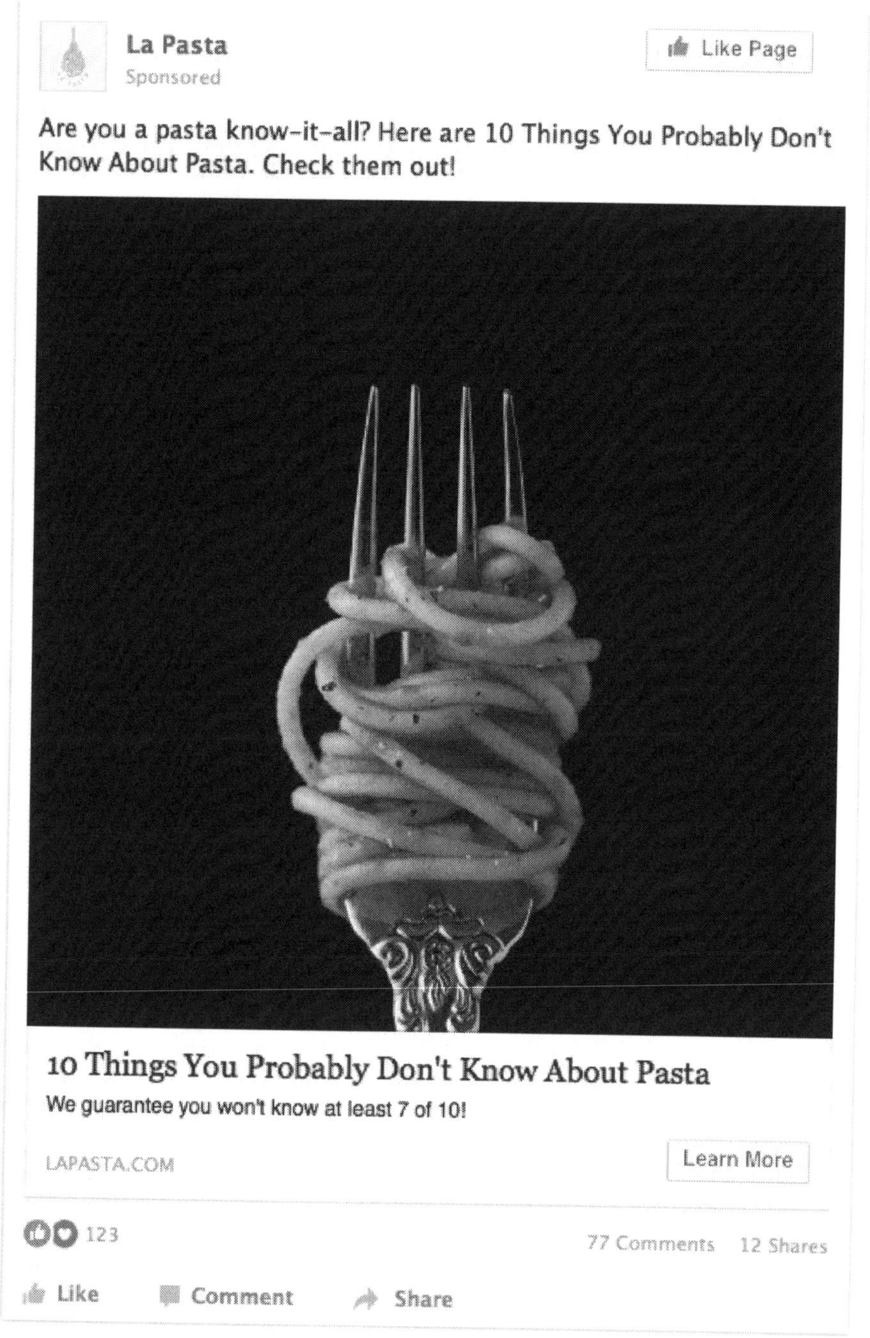
La Pasta
Sponsored
Like Page
Are you a pasta know-it-all? Here are 10 Things You Probably Don't Know About Pasta. Check them out!
10 Things You Probably Don't Know About Pasta
We guarantee you won't know at least 7 of 10!
LAPASTA.COM
Learn More
123
77 Comments
12 Shares
Like
Comment
Share

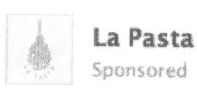

Post interesting facts and testimonials

Facebook is the ideal place to solicit testimonials or repost testimonials that have come in via email or snail mail. Repost your recommendations from LinkedIn, and stream video or audio testimonials. This gives your restaurant and its events great third-party endorsements that are proven to significantly increase response from prospective customers. Far too few restaurants do this!

Post links to interesting articles, sites, or videos

Use Facebook to bring attention to articles or reviews in other publications about your restaurant. Use it to bring attention to other news and blogs on the internet that you think your guests will find interesting or entertaining. Post links to new innovations in food, new drinks, etc. While you may think it defeats the purpose to send your fans to another site, the reverse is actually true.

Providing your fans with quality content makes you a trusted authority and a trusted source.

Run Facebook-only offers

Make your fan base feel special. Run an offer that only your Facebook fans can take advantage of.

Do a Facebook live video

Do a quick live video of happy hour, your chef plating a dish, a baby shower and so on.

These are just a few ideas for what you can post on Facebook. The possibilities for a post are nearly endless. Just remember to engage, educate, and entertain.

INCORPORATE THE TOOLS YOU'RE ALREADY USING ONTO YOUR PAGE

Do you blog? Do you tweet? Let's hope you do after reading this book. Do you read feeds? There are Facebook apps available for all these services. After you add the respective app, you simply do what you were already doing and let the app do the work. You can have your Tweets post to your Facebook page and vice versa. If your blog is on WordPress, you can add the WordPress app and your posts will automatically be pushed to your Facebook page.

Plan your Facebook ninety days in advance

We offer all our clients a ninety-day Facebook plan. That does not mean they can't or won't make spontaneous posts, but it does mean their core program is in place regardless of how many or how few posts they make in addition to the core plan. It also means we can get a good editorial balance of content and offers, humor and serious articles, videos and pictures. **By planning ahead, you'll be more organized and will be more likely to post items regularly.**

Remember, your Facebook page is a lifestyle magazine that emanates from the interests of your restaurant's guests.

ENCOURAGE HAPPY GUESTS TO LEAVE FEEDBACK ON YOUR FACEBOOK PAGE

As guests check out, invite happy guests to leave their feedback on Facebook and Trip Advisor.

"I am so glad you enjoyed yourself, Mr. Wood. Please consider posting your comments on Facebook and Trip Advisor."

JOIN GROUPS RELATED TO YOUR BUSINESS INTERESTS

Many groups on Facebook are nonsense, but there are quite a few that can provide useful information and professional connections. Rather than trying to search for groups, watch the groups that your friends are joining, as often you will find them of interest for yourself. After all, they're in your contact list because you have something in common, right?

How Often Should You Post on Facebook?

There is a lot of debate on what the right number of posts really is and I think it depends to a large degree how much you have going on and how interesting your content is. Remember, only a small percentage of your fans actually see any of your posts, so I would err on the high side. Based on my experience, four posts a day is the least you should do.

You might want to repeat important posts. Schedule them at different times during the coming days so they have a better chance of reaching fresh eyes.

How Long Can a Facebook Post Be?

While many people say everything today has to be in sound bites or no one will look at it, the fact is that's just not true. Some of my most successful Facebook posts ever were four pages long! It all depends on how interesting and how targeted the post is to your audience. Facebook also has a "notes" feature, which is more or less their version of a blog for longer articles but, while I like the feature and it typesets longer content far better, I have had more success with long posts on the regular page than with the notes feature.

LIMIT WASTED TIME ON FACEBOOK

Facebook can easily suck you in; it's very addictive once you get going. You, however, have important work to do. You won't help your restaurant or career if you fall behind on projects because you were too busy playing on Facebook. If you find that you're spending too much time reading Facebook message boards or reading about your friends' favorite book selections, then set limits for yourself. Check it only at set times of the day say—first thing, noon, and 5:00 p.m., and ignore all the game requests! Facebook can be a black hole. Use it wisely or you might get lost.

SUMMARY

Used correctly, Facebook can be one of the most powerful tools in your marketing arsenal. However, you have to remember that people are not going on Facebook buy into one of your dining events, so everything you post should not be sales-based. That's a sure recipe for failure. You must first build a relationship by engaging, educating, and entertaining, then you can go about collecting their emails for your database and offering them something. Think lifestyle magazine and you will do amazingly better than whatever you are doing now.

He who loves not women, wine, and song.
Remains a fool his whole life long."
— **Martin Luther**

CHAPTER 11

Building Buzz and Brand by Blogging

A blog is merely a tool that lets you do anything from change the world to share your shopping list. — ANONYMOUS

I have been blogging for a long time; it's easy for me because I love to write. Many people find blogging a hassle they can do without, judging by how few restaurant businesses are using their blogs effectively to engage customers, build brand, and produce sales. I often get people excited about starting a blog, only to find a few weeks later they have given up because they do "not have time" or because they did not get any instant feedback from their first few posts. Like most things in life, getting traction takes a little time.

A blog is important for several reasons.

1. A blog showcases your knowledge and positions you as an expert.

2. A blog gives your business a human face. Many customers may never have seen or heard from you or your key staff in person. A blog gives everyone the chance to connect with customers. A blog creates a feedback loop for customers and potential customers. They can comment, ask questions, and add to your posts. (NOTE: You get to review posts before they go up.)

3. A blog starts new relationships. A blog gives you a chance to attract new prospects and show them why a relationship with you would be valuable.

4. A blog strengthens existing relationships with customers. It gives existing customers a chance to bond with you. Featuring customers and how they have benefitted from your restaurant (for example, hosting a meeting or having the best anniversary dinner ever) on your blog or Facebook page will increase their level of engagement with your business.

5. A blog increases links back to your website from other websites; this increases traffic.

6. A blog dramatically helps your search engine positioning. The more relevant content you have on your site, the higher your rankings. Google loves relevant content and inbound links.

7. A blog builds into a large and searchable database of useful information, entertainment, and opinion that can be accessed over time. There is no doubt that blogging takes work but, if you commit to it, the upside is you'll have tons of content through which you can show your value to prospects and clients. You'll be able to use it on Facebook, Twitter, and other social media sites.

To blog or not to blog? Blog, I say, then blog some more. Blogging is real work, that many restaurants simply don't have the time to consider but it's a very valuable tool. Google loves fresh content for boosting search engine rankings and bogging twice a week will rocket you up the search engines.

One of the other benefits of blogging is that you can create tons of great content of one solid post.

Take this one for example:

Benefits of Drinking Red Wine

The quote at the beginning of the chapter may seem strange for Martin Luther, a priest, even though he was excommunicated. But I can only agree. Few things in life give as much simple pleasure in so small a space as a good glass of wine at the end of a long day. Nothing complements a good meal like it, and when we gather for a celebration it always finds its way to the table. Wine is happiness in a glass. It relaxes our minds, frees our tongues for conversation and brings smiles to faces.

We've all heard that a glass of wine here and there is good for you, but how exactly does it contribute to your health? New studies appear to be constantly backing up the health benefits of drinking wine for moderate drinkers. From decreased mortality rates to attacking cancer cells, a little wine can go much further then complementing your favorite meal. The next time you uncork a bottle, keep these impressive, science-backed benefits in mind (as if you need any extra reasons!).

1. Wine Is Full of Antioxidants that Support Longevity of Life

Red wine is packed with antioxidants. The substances that are found in the skin of grapes protect your cells against the harmful effects of free radicals, and that's great news for your health says the Mayo Clinic.

2. Wine Is Great for Your Heart

Resveratrol—one of the key ingredients in red wine—helps keep the heart healthy by preventing damage to blood vessels and preventing blood clots, says the Mayo Clinic. Drinking wine may also help in decreasing low-density lipoprotein (LDL) also known as bad cholesterol, which may cause artery damage. At the same time, wine increases the body's high-density lipoprotein (HDL—also known as good cholesterol) which may reduce the risk for heart disease. Moreover, wine prevents the formation of blood clots.

3. Wine Increases Bone Density

As we get older, our bones get more brittle. Red wine has high levels of silicon, which is great for your bone mineral density. It increases the density and reduces the chance of osteoporosis.

4. It Reduces the Risk of Cancer

Drinking a glass of wine can reduce the risk of colon cancer, prostate cancer, and breast cancer. Researchers at Harvard Medical School found that men who drink 4–7 glasses of red wine a week are only about half as likely to be diagnosed with prostate cancer as those who don't drink red wine, according to *Harvard Men's Health Watch*. Why red wine? They're not really sure, but doctors think it has something to do with the chemicals particular to red wine, like flavonoids and resveratrol. You can be sure they're taking one for the team and carrying out further research!

5. Drinking Wine Can Keep Depression at Bay

As most people know, alcohol consumption can worsen one's depression or anxiety. This may sound contradictory, but drinking a glass of wine per week can turn into a depression fighter. A seven-year study conducted by PREDIMED analyzed 5,500 individuals who were light to moderate drinkers and found that individuals who drank two to seven glasses of wine a week were less prone to depression than non-drinkers.

6. Drinking Wine Could Give You Healthier Skin

High levels of antioxidants in wine, when applied directly to the skin can inhibit the growth of acne-causing bacteria and are beneficial in maintaining a healthy skin. Antioxidants rejuvenate the skin, increase skin elasticity and keep the skin bright and glowing. Wine can stimulate blood circulation that can prevent wrinkle formation and skin aging. However, when one drinks in excess, it makes hormone flow lose its balance and may cause skin dehydration and aggravate chances of acne.

7. Drinking Wine Prevents Liver Disease

Drinking wine can reduce your risk of non-alcoholic fatty liver disease by half, flying in the face of conventional thinking. It has to be red wine though. A study by UC San Diego School of Medicine found that beer and hard liquor drinkers had more than four times the risk of non-alcoholic fatty liver disease than the wine drinkers.

8. Drinking Wine Protects from Sunburn

Scientists from the University of Barcelona found that drinking wine can help to lessen the effects of UV (ultraviolet) rays and protect you from severe sunburn. The flavonoids in wine inhibit the process that damage skin cells.

9. Drinking Wine Prevents Some Types of Blindness

Overgrown blood vessels in the eye can cause diabetic retinopathy and age-related macular degeneration, but the good news is that red wine can stop that blood vessel growth in its tracks, according to researchers at Washington University School of Medicine. The resveratrol found in red wine is the compound responsible for arresting the blood vessel growth.

10. Like you really need another reason—go uncork a nice bottle of Cabernet and let it breathe for later. ☺

Action Steps:

- This should be an easy one, drink more red wine!
- If you drink other forms of alcohol, try switching and experimenting with red wines until you find one you like. Another easy task!

Now let's break down how you can use that blog post:

- First, it's a rock-solid blog post.
- Second you can go back and turn each of the 10 reasons into Facebook or Instagram posts.
- Third, you could create a series of emails from them perhaps leading up to a wine tasting or wine dinner counting down from 10 to 1.
- You can create a nice slide show out of the 10 reasons
- If you wish, talk over the slide and create a video.
- Once the video is done, you can use each video as a social media post.
- You could even convert the post into a flyer for an event, handing it to your customer as they leave and suggest that your customers might pass it around at the office tomorrow.

That's a lot of great content out of one two-page blog post and I didn't even get to the best bit yet. Write two posts a week of a page each, 750 words and, if you add some pictures, you'll have written a book by the end of the year!

Write about:

- Wines
- Recipes
- Personalities in the kitchen
- Chefs' and servers' favorite dishes
- Funny incidents with customers
- Celebrity sightings

Don't Worry Too Much About Grammar, Spelling, Perfect English, or Emulating Mark Twain with Your Writing Skills

A man occupied with public or other important business cannot, and need not, attend to spelling. – NAPOLEON

I don't worry about spelling at all. I know this drives some people nuts, but at least it makes all those readers who are great at English feel good when they can point out my mistakes!

When readers point out my very common typos and other errors, I often send back this:

Typoglycemia

I cdnuolt blveiee taht I cluod aulaclty uesdnatnrd waht I was rdanieg The phaonmneal pweor of the hmuan mnid Aoccdrnig to a rscheearch at Cmabrigde Uinervtisy, it deosn't mttaer inwaht oredr the ltteers in a wrod are, the olny iprmoatnt tihng is taht the frist and lsat ltteer be in the rghit pclae. The rset can be a taotl mses and you can sitll raed it wouthit a porbelm. Tihs is bcuseae the huamn mnid deos not raed ervey lteter by istlef, but the wrod as a wlohe. Amzanig huh? yaeh and I awlyas thought slpeing was ipmorant.

All kidding aside, social media is informal; you don't need to be Ernest Hemingway or Mark Twain to get your message across. Sure, you can spell check it, but don't spend hours editing your blog. People are looking for content, ideas, entertainment, and education, not an English lesson. Twitter and Facebook practically have their own language that barely resembles English anyway.

Blog consistently, at least weekly, more often if possible. I like to get way ahead on my blogs in case something comes up. I usually have five or more drafts already preloaded so I never miss a deadline.

Don't Expect Tons of Feedback Right Away

You *will* get feedback, but it takes time. In the hundreds of useful marketing posts I make a year. It's the two or three controversial ones that always produce the biggest response, both positive and negative.

Sometimes to get the discussion going, you need to plant your own posts, feedback, or questions to stimulate activity.

The Fastest Way to Create a Buzz Is to Stir Something Up

Be a little controversial or provocative if you want to get a response. Offer bold statements and clear views that demand comment. You can even comment on local road conditions and other non-food topics. You're a local citizen, after all. (The old advice to stay away from politics and religion still holds.)

DO NOT expect all the comments to be positive. You have to be thick skinned when using social media. For some reason people say things on blogs and other social media they would never say to your face. Don't worry about it. Remember the idea of social media is to create dialog—to educate, engage, and entertain.

Also remember that this sort of discussion is going on by your clients and prospects whether you listen to it and address it or not. Many business owners are scared of what people might post, but burying your head in the sand is not a good idea. You always maintain moderator control over your blog and so can choose not to approve distasteful comments.

You don't have to be perfect to generate a ton of business from your blog. My spelling and grammar are appalling, and yet the response keeps coming.

"One of the very nicest things about life is the way we must regularly stop whatever it is we are doing and devote our attention to eating."
— **Luciano Pavarotti**

CHAPTER 12

Facebook Ads

With over 2 billion active monthly users, 65% of whom log in every day, Facebook is far too big a marketing platform for you to ignore if you expect to thrive in your market.

In the last chapter I showed you how to use Facebook as a tool in your marketing arsenal. In this chapter, I'll show you how to use the immense power of Facebook ads to reach a larger audience than you ever thought possible, at a fraction of the cost of many more traditional advertising channels, including Google.

In This Chapter You Will Learn:

- ✓ why Facebook ads are so important,
- ✓ what type of results you can expect,
- ✓ the various ad options (at this time),
- ✓ the anatomy of a Facebook ad,
- ✓ The Facebook Ads Checklist, and
- ✓ 15 ways you can get started with Facebook ads.

WHAT MAKES FACEBOOK SUCH AN EFFECTIVE ADVERTISING PLATFORM?

- The user base is continually growing and doesn't show any signs of slowing down. With over 2 billion people visiting daily, you can't afford to not be using the platform.

- Facebook has made it harder to reach even your own fans with organic posts.

- The wealth of user information that Facebook has makes it possible (and easy) to create incredibly targeted ads that your specific prospects can relate to and will take action on.

- Look-alike audiences make it easy to reach people similar to your ideal targets.

- It's easy to create brand awareness through Facebook—especially when the majority of your competitors are not taking advantage of it.

What type of results can you expect?

Leads

Driving conversions and leads is nearly everyone's top goal of online marketing. You can drive conversions straight from your ads using website conversion ads and boosted posts. One feature of Facebook ads is a call-to-action button that invokes people to take an action that is specific to your ad.

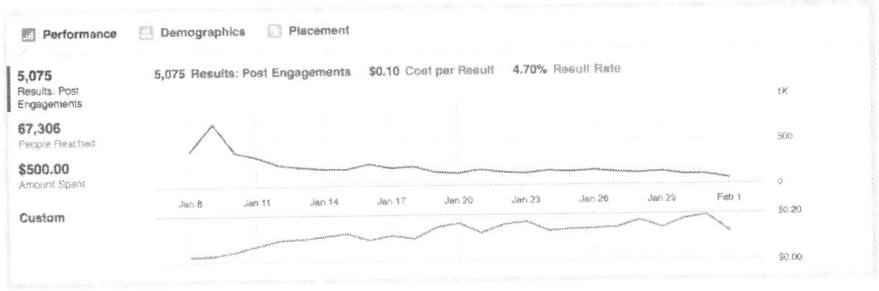

Visitors

Driving traffic to your website or landing page is another way to generate conversions from your Facebook ads. You can target relevant audiences and attract valuable visitors to your website by promoting offers, contests, downloads, and more. Use website click ads or boosted posts to drive your prospects to a landing page where they can enter a contest, sign up for a service, make an appointment, or download a coupon. (See Chapter 7 for more on landing pages.)

Engagement

You can also use Facebook ads to generate engagement on your page with your current fans and targeted audiences. Boosting posts increases likes, comments, and shares, which actually helps to increase your organic reach (that Facebook has made harder to obtain).

Ad Options

There are currently 13 different objectives you can choose from:

1. **Clicks to Website**—*Get more site visits.* "Clicks to Website" ads drive traffic to a particular page on your website. They are automatically optimized to reach people who are likely to click.

2. **Retargeting**—*Target people who have already been to your website or landing page.* If someone visits your site but doesn't take the next step, you can retarget them on Facebook.

3. **Website Conversions**—*Increase website conversions.* Website conversion ads encourage people to take a specific action on your website or landing page. These ads feature a selection of calls to action such as "Sign Up" that urges the user to take a specific action rather than just liking or commenting.

4. **Product Catalog Sales: Dynamic Product Ads**—*Promote your online products.* Dynamic Product ads are Facebook's version of Google's Dynamic Remarketing Display ads; these ads retarget users who have already visited your online or in-app store. While products won't be your main goal, offering your custom salad

dressing or BBQ sauce can help your branding online and in your restaurant and build your image.

5. **Page-Post Engagement**—*Promote your posts.* Promoting page posts increases interaction and engagement. You can promote any of your page posts—photos, video, or text post—via the Boost Post button on your timeline or by using the Ads Manager. You can target current fans and their friends, or people you choose through targeting if you're going after new blood.

6. **Page Likes**—*Increase likes on your page.* One strategy that we employ is using Page Likes ads to increase the number of likes on a page, then going after these new people with Page-Post Engagement ads targeted toward people who like the page.

7. **App Installs**—*Get more app installs.* Target people who are most likely to install and use your app.

8. **App Engagement**—*Increase engagement on your app.* Drive more traffic to a specific area of your app such as the store section of a freemium app.

9. **Offer Claims**—*Get people to take advantage of a special offer.* Promote exclusive offers that are available only to your Facebook fans. A great way to get more people engaging with your page.

10. **Local Awareness**—*Reach people near you.* Target people who are near you to increase awareness, to promote a special that you're running, or to take advantage of another special offer.

11. **Event Responses**—*Increase event attendance.* Have an event that you want to sell out? Use Event Response ads to promote it. People who click that they are interested will receive reminders and updates about your event as it approaches.

12. **Video Views**—*Get your videos watched*. Encourage people to watch a video about your restaurant, a new entree offering, positive testimonials, and so on.

13. **Lead Generation**—*Grow your database*. Obtain an email address without sending someone to a landing page. These ads fill out a form using the person's Facebook information so they don't have to do anything.

THE ANATOMY OF A FACEBOOK AD

Design

Every Facebook ad includes the following:

- a powerful main image or video,
- a small amount of headline text above the image,
- a heading below the image with teaser text,
- a "Like Page" button on the upper right, and
- a call-to-action button on the bottom right.

Andrew Wood

On Facebook, people *will* judge a book by its cover, so using attention-grabbing photos or illustrations will help your ad to stand out (and get clicked on) as people are scrolling through their news feed. Your prospects are going to look at the image before they read the text, so make it count.

Facebook removed the much-maligned 20%-text to image ratio requirement, meaning that your ad image could not include more than 20 percent text. However, although this rule is "gone," images with too much text will either be shown to very few people or not be shown at all. A general rule of thumb is to make sure your image doesn't rely too much on text and is more about illustrating various aspects of your restaurant.

The headline and teaser text must be compelling enough to force an action to be taken—whether it be a page like, website click, or app install. The message in your headline *must* match what is presented on your landing page and ideally be the first thing that they see when they click through, or they will feel like they were tricked into clicking your ad.

Ad placement

Ad placement is an important part of advertising on Facebook. Ads can be placed on desktop newsfeed, mobile newsfeed, right-hand column, and the Facebook audience network. Using Facebook, you can also place ads on Instagram, which caters to a different demographic than Facebook and should be a valuable part of your ad strategy.

Targeting

One of the reasons Facebook is so powerful is its targeting capabilities. It allows you to target users based on criteria like:

- Geographic area
- Local (radius or city up to fifty miles out)
- Designated market area
- National demographics
- Age
- Gender
- Level of education

- Income level

- Relationship status: married, single, engaged, and so on.

- Family demographics: have children (specific ages), expectant mothers, grandparents, and so forth.

- Interests and hobbies

- Behavioral traits

- Custom list uploads

- Employment and employer information

Other targeting options are:

- Lists you upload: People you already have in your database that you can target through Facebook

- Look-alike audiences: Users who are similar to those you're already targeting

- Engagement on Facebook: People who have engaged with your content on Facebook

- Website Traffic: A list of people who visit your website or landing page

Budgeting

There is no set amount of money you need to spend to achieve success in Facebook advertising. You can achieve good results with a small budget, but one thing to consider is that the more niche you go, the more expensive your cost per click will be. If your budget is limited, it's better to start broader before deciding to narrow down your targeting.

To test out how your ad will perform, start out with a small amount of money—it can be as little as five dollars—to see if it's worthwhile to devote more money toward it.

When I run ads, I run five to ten different ads targeting different areas, demographics, and interests at twenty dollars each and increase the budget only on the highest-performing ads. Nine times out of ten, the initial test is entirely indicative of how your ads will perform overall.

That's great, but how much do Facebook ads cost?

It's a fair question, because when you have a limited ad budget you want to know how much you're going to get for your money. The answer is, it depends on a lot of factors.

Facebook ads work like an auction; you're effectively bidding against other advertisers for that ad space. So, the more competitive the space, the more you will have to pay per click or impression.

Some of the biggest factors that affect how much Facebook ads cost are your audience, the quality of your ad, and the time of year.

You must remember that when someone has fine dining listed as an interest on his or her profile and you're a restaurant, you're also competing against the companies that are targeting that person's interests in travel, skiing, football, mountain biking, and whatever else they are interested in. You're not just competing against people in your industry; you're competing against everyone trying to market to these people, and Facebook limits the number of ads a person can see.

So how do you stand out from the competition? You create high-quality ads. With high-quality ads you could pay significantly less than your competition pays for their ad to the same exact user. The quality of an ad is determined by two factors: relevance score and click-through rate. Your relevance score measures how relevant your ad is to the audience you're targeting. The higher the score, the lower the cost of your ad. The second factor is click-through rate, which is the ratio of number of people who click on your ad to the number of people who viewed the ad. If you have a high click-through rate, your ad will cost less. Now isn't that motivation to create a great ad?

The final big factor is the time of the year. Holidays, the holiday season as a whole, and Black Friday will have higher ad costs because more businesses will be advertising during those times.

In the end, it's really all about return on investment (ROI). As long as you're getting a positive ROI on your Facebook ads, they're worth running.

Set yourself up for success.

Use the Facebook ads manager to track your ad performance. See how much you've spent, how many you have reached, your ad-relevancy score (very important in determining how often your ad will be shown), how many clicks, your cost per click, and many other important statistics. Checking this will enable you to tweak your ad so that you maximize performance to get the best possible results.

Facebook Ad Checklist

Getting Started

- ✓ Create a business page (if you don't already have one).
- ✓ Add or review business information.
- ✓ Add a profile picture and cover photo.
- ✓ Post frequently—engage, educate, entertain.
- ✓ Respond to comments and messages.

Creating Your Ad

- ✓ Determine your advertising goals.
- ✓ Determine your budget.
- ✓ Determine your target audience.
- ✓ Choose your ad formats.
- ✓ Create your landing page or dedicated page on your website.
- ✓ Craft your ads—image, headline, description, call to action.
- ✓ Create multiple ads with small budgets to test different target markets.

- ✓ Set your campaign live.

After Your Ad is Live

- ✓ Check Ad performance in Facebook Insights.
- ✓ Determine which of your test ads is high performing. Put more money toward them; deactivate the ads that are not performing well.
- ✓ Respond to comments on the ads.
- ✓ Track all relative key performance indicators.
- ✓ Tweak your ads to achieve maximum results.

What type of results can you expect from Facebook Ads?

Here are two case studies that prove the effectiveness of Facebook ads:

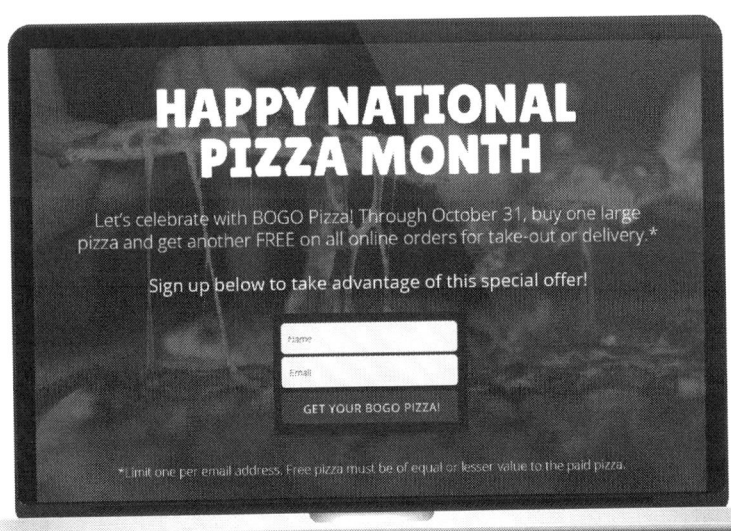

Pizza House

Jacksonville, Florida

BOGO Pizza

Goals: Build email list, increase awareness and generate revenue.

Approach: Facebook targeted ads were created and used to generate leads and sales for this campaign. We blanket targeted within 15 miles of our location in an attempt to reach the most people possible since everyone loves pizza!

Results:

- 162,426 reach
- 755 likes
- 519 shares
- $0.32 cost per click
- 9,294 unique visitors
- 2,993 leads
- 38 percent conversion rate
- $2,500 total spend

Looking for some ideas on how you can get started with Facebook ads? Here are 15 things you can do:

1. Gather email newsletter sign-ups.
2. Promote upcoming events.
3. Advertise services or sales and get clicks straight to your site.
4. Promote a new Facebook group you started.
5. Announce a giveaway and get more entries.
6. Promote the launch of a new program.
7. Increase your followers on other social networks.
8. Big on blogging? Send people directly to your latest blog post.
9. Teach an online course? Find some new students.
10. Have a daily special or sale? Promote it to your current fans or target a new audience.
11. Get presales on a new offering you're promoting.

12. Attending a trade show? Let prospects know where you'll be.
13. Promote a class, workshop, or group-coaching lesson coming up.
14. Have an awesome tip or trick? Use it to drive traffic to your site (or newsletter.
15. Promote an e-book download.

SUMMARY

Facebook ads are one of the cheapest ways to reach potential diners in your market.

Andrew Wood

"Food is everything we are. It's an extension of nationalist feeling, ethnic feeling, your personal history, your province, your region, your tribe, your grandma. It's inseparable from those from the get-go."
—Anthony Bourdain

CHAPTER 13

How to Write Legendary Headlines for All Your Marketing

In this chapter, we will tackle the first key task to creating a winning marketing campaign. Although the content of this chapter is specifically about the writing of great headlines for your landing pages, sales letters, or emails, the fact of the matter is, *this information holds 100 percent true for writing ads, brochures, websites, video scripts, and just about anything else* designed to be read and responded to.

In this chapter, you will discover:

- ✓ how to write legendary headlines,
- ✓ 12 formulas for writing headlines,
- ✓ examples of great headlines you can use for your own restaurant, and
- ✓ how to test your headlines.

In this chapter we will discuss the critical importance of crafting a headline that grabs your reader's attention and the perils of not doing so quickly.

We will detail twelve proven ways to create a winning headline. Each of the formulas given provides you with a systematic approach for creating excellent headlines on your own. While creativity is great, you'll find that sticking to a proven formula is far more likely to produce excellent results. You'll also get a whole slew of great examples to stimulate your own thinking.

How to Write Legendary Headlines

Few people outside the very top echelon of direct-marketing circles, including most ad agencies and copywriters, have any idea how to write compelling headlines. The difference between a total flop and a Legendary Marketing campaign can often be a single sentence, sometimes just a few words. The stunning difference your headline can make to the success of any landing pages, website, email, ad, letter, video script, or brochure cannot be overstated.

You need a headline that resonates with the thoughts and feelings a prospect has about your restaurant; a headline that speaks to their inner desires and aligns with their needs. A headline that connects at the very core of their self-interest and motivates the reader to action. That is a Legendary headline, one that's worth its weight in gold. Such headlines alone can easily increase your response by 500–1,000 percent or more.

Dead Before You Start

Instead of crafting compelling headlines, most people in the restaurant industry opt for headlines that are boringly descriptive, cute or very often just a corny play on words. In the process, they collectively throw millions of dollars down the drain, because if your headline does not hook the reader right in, the rest of your message will never get read.

How about these *impotent* headlines from my inbox from local restaurants;

April Specials
(Boring)

Good Food Good Wine
(Hmmm, I bet they have great service too?)

The Next Great Dining Destination!

(Three places are claiming that compelling distinction this week alone)

Worse than poor headlines are the stream of emails and occasional postcards that arrive from restaurants *that don't have a headline at all.*

The headline is like the ad for your sales copy and you only get a few seconds of a prospect's attention to make him bite. Studies show that prospects make their decision to read or not read your copy in just five to eight seconds.

What Gets Your Attention? A Simple and Practical Test

Get in your car right now and drive to a large bookstore or to your local newsagent. Stand in front of the magazine rack and look at the newspapers, magazines, and periodicals. Look at ones you might read and look at those you would never typically read; it's the ultimate headline battleground. All are seeking your attention. All are seeking your money. All are hoping that their headline will catch your eye and make you buy. Most magazines live and die on that fleeting moment.

Think about it, month after month:

- food magazines all promise delicious recipes,
- women's magazines promise beauty secrets,
- men's health magazines promise six-pack abs,
- travel magazines promise secret locations,
- martial arts magazines always have something on Bruce Lee (if they put his picture on the cover, it's always their bestselling issue of the year),
- money magazines promise wealth and early retirement,
- newspapers always sell death, disaster, sex, and scandal.

And, of course, the tabloids sell alien sightings and a fallen star's shocking weight gain. In fact, *The National Enquirer* (or any UK tabloid) is one of the best examples of headline writing in the world. *It's the only newspaper in the country that sells six million copies a week on the newsstand that nobody admits to reading!*

Each magazine carefully zones in on the small specter of interest that each target demographic has. *Then they play to those interests again and again because they have found that only a small number of their headlines actually work.* Only a small number of their headlines produce additional sales. They devise their short list and then play it over and over again like a TNT movie.

You must think the same way because of all the possible headlines you can use, only a few will really resonate with your target audience. Only a few of the headlines you test will actually increase response; the rest will fall short.

Why You Must Grab Your Reader's Attention with Your Headline or Kiss Your Money Goodbye

If you don't grab the reader by the throat with your headline, 95 percent of readers won't make it past the first paragraph or even your first sentence, which means no matter how long or short, good or bad your sales pitch is, it won't work!

Without good—no, great—headlines, everything that follows is a giant waste of time, money, and effort, for it will most likely never be read.

This is so important that I want to say it again: **Your headline is the ad for your sales copy. Therefore, a great headline has one job and one job alone—to get the reader to actually read what comes next.** You must excite him, intrigue him, titillate him, shock him, question him, project him into the future, and show him the better "life" that can be his.

But Wait, My Customers Are Rich, Smart,

and Sophisticated Diners

Perhaps the biggest mistake of all is to think that your clientele is above such tactics. But these are not mere marketing tactics we are talking about; **we are talking about something far more interesting—about deep, human nature.** People's natural inquisitiveness and self-interest changes little with social or economic status. Sure, what they buy may change, but the way you attract their interest changes very little. Delude yourself if you wish that your high-end restaurant is different and that your customers are so sophisticated that they will take your abstract copy and write their own sales pitch in their head…they won't.

Please think about it rationally:

- Everyone who dines out wants a great meal and a great experience.

- Every woman in her late thirties or forties wants to look younger, even the top movie stars.

- Every sports car owner wants a faster machine even if they never use its potential.

You must take these facts of life and use them to your greatest advantage in crafting your headlines.

For example, the headline below is a typical and at least an acceptable benefit-driven headline:

Ambience that Relaxes, Cocktails that Soothe and Food That Stimulates Your Senses

For That "Can't Miss" Dinner Date Choose Romeo's

Maxwell's—The Lunch Venue Where Deals Get Done!

Lunch in 15 Minutes or You Don't Pay!

Long Headlines

It is perfectly acceptable and often even desirable to have long headlines. Longer headlines give you a better chance to hook readers. And hook them you must, which is why cute, clever, or sophisticated headlines almost never work to drive readers to action.

But be warned, you must make every single word count, no matter how many or how few words you use.

Planning the perfect party is a tough job.

Few people realize what goes into pulling off a great event and seldom do <u>you</u> get the praise and recognition you deserve.

All that's about to change.

You are about to become a superhero!

This lengthy headline was part of a very successful campaign to book more events at a restaurant and uses a good deal of empathy, which takes a good many words to accomplish.

Let's go ahead and jump right into the formulas…

12 Formulas for Writing Headlines that Grab Your Prospects by the Throat and Make Them Want to Read What You Have to Say!

There are 12 proven formulas for writing captivating headlines. Formulas, you say—but isn't great marketing all about creativity?

No; let me repeat that: No!

Sure, creativity helps, but very often, in an effort to be creative, people ignore the basics of human nature, and the end result of their efforts is a campaign that is called cute, funny, or creative. It might even win an award but bombs where it counts—in actually increasing your response.

Great movies are the result of great scripts, very often formula scripts. So, too, are most bestselling books and great sales letters, letters that all start with great headlines.

You can very often borrow winning headlines from other industries and adapt them to your needs. Some of the world's best headlines still pull responses fifty years or more after their creation. They can do this because while the world changes quickly, people do not. People today have the same basic vanities, desires, motivations, fears, and hopes as their parents and their parents' parents, albeit with more money to satisfy them.

In writing headlines, never forget that people are emotional, irrational beings who respond to *their* wants and needs, not yours.

The Benefit Headline

By far the easiest way to write a great headline is simply to stick to the benefits approach. Lead with your number one benefit and squeeze in a couple more if you can, in the subheads or lead copy. If your benefit is strong enough, and targeted enough, you will be off to a great start.

Voted the #1 Seafood Restaurant in Orlando

The Best View on the Lake with Food That's Just as Spectacular!

Live Longer with Out New Health Guru Menu

The Perfect Location for a Meeting Free Valet Parking

Andrew Wood

The Only Ski-in Ski-out Restaurant on the Mountain

The Acropolis Restaurant—Any More Authentic and You'd Be in Greece

These headlines offer a clear benefit to the reader and are simple and effective.

The Old Jail Bar and Grill Just 150 Steps From the Court House

Note here that the benefit is specified as an exact number. Being specific and spelling out the benefits always increases response.

What Will You Do with the Kids While You Eat?

Leave Them with Upstairs with Us in Our Kids Camp! (for ages 5-12)

In the above headline a problem is stated, and a beneficial solution provided. This is one of the simplest methods to get your message across and one of the surest in helping you create a winning headline.

Decide what problem your restaurant is the solution for, state the problem, then solve it with your leading benefit.

For Example:

You need a nice location for your daughter's bridal shower
Our restaurant is the perfect location because…

You need a nice place for you son's Bar Mitzvah
Our restaurant is perfect because we offer kosher menu options, valet parking, a dance floor and the ability for you to entertain 120 guests.

The Offer Headline

The offer headline is another safe bet when it comes to making sure the reader gets the point quickly. Remember, the headline may be the only part of your message the prospect reads, so putting your offer in the headline makes a good deal of sense for most businesses.

Book Your Date Night Dinner Mon-Wed and Get Two Glasses of Champagne on Us!

Free Appetizers When You Reserve a Table Online Mid-Week ($20 value)

Two-for-One Desserts or Appetizers Sunday Night

Noting the value of your offer is always a good idea and helps the prospect put your offer in perspective.

So here is your basic offer headline formula. Tell the reader what you want him to do:

Book
Call
Join
Buy
Click
Go to

Then tell him what special key benefit he gets for his efforts.

Then if you can fit it in, tell him why he must act now or lose out on your offer.

Pretty simple.

The Discount Headline

In the discount headline, the lead benefit is not the restaurant itself but the amount of money that will be saved by acting. The discount headline also offers a good way to combine your key benefit, the discount, with a limitation designed to create instant action. Always make your discount limited by time or by the number of people you are going to allow to respond to your offer.

Discounts usually fall into two categories, percentage discounts or specific dollar amounts.

30% off All Meals between 5–6 pm

Two-for-One Tuesdays

50% off Every Bottle of Wine on Mondays

The News Style Headline

The news style headline is ideal when you have real news, like a new product service or offering.

New Chef the Talk of Birmingham with His Amazing New Take on Traditional Dishes

The other way to use the news style headline is to tie it into existing news. This can be very effective in aligning people with your offer. You can tie your headline into things like sporting events, the Olympics, Super Bowl, Ryder Cup, the holidays, or seasonally topical news.

The Bonus Headline

The bonus headline is interesting in that, instead of making the product the hero of the message, it makes the bonus the focus. The hero in this case, the reason for action now, before it's too late and is gone down the yellow brick road forever, is the almighty bonus.

Book Your Party of Six or More and Enjoy a Bottle of Champagne on Arrival ($45 value)

The Testimonial Headline

The testimonial headline is one of the most powerful and proven ways to get reader buy in. It tells your story, your offer, or your success through the eyes of an existing user. This perceived third-party endorsement is much stronger than having you say it yourself.

The key to having a good testimonial headline is to make sure the quote stresses the key benefits; it does not merely say you are a good restaurant.

"Any time I have a prospective buyer I bring them here for lunch or dinner. I love the ambience, menu and service. It has helped me close many sales and I hope to introduce a few new customers to your wonderful place. —**Sheila Layton, Local Realtor**

"Since my wife is vegan, she loves this place. Consider me a convert, the food is so tasty I don't even think about it being vegan!" — **Sam Hilton**

"Hands down the best ribs in town. Whatever you put in that secret sauce you've got me hooked" — **Jerry Norton**

While unsolicited testimonials like the ones above and below are great, it's okay to help happy customers express their thoughts by answering a few questions and you helping them put those thoughts on paper for their approval. It's also the only way you are likely to get all the key points you need covered in testimonial form.

A variation of the customer testimonial approach is to use a famous or empowering quote to capture a reader's attention and perhaps hope to get a little of the quote's power to rub off on your pitch.

Here are some, using quotes from famous people:

"There's no better feeling in the world than a warm pizza box on your lap." — **Kevin James, comedian**

Except one, when the pizza box says Rocco's on it!

"I can pick good food, but I can't pick a good man"
—**Debbie Reynolds**

Obviously she never tried Ladies Night at Charlie's—we have both!

"One cannot think well, love well, sleep well, if one has not dined well." **—Virginia Woolf**

Virginia, we couldn't agree more, but we've got you covered at Sam's American Grill!

Most people enjoy quotes and will indulge you for a few moments more to see how you have tied the words of Abe Lincoln or Albert Einstein into your copy. *You must make sure that the quotes can be tied directly into your headline or copy.* If the references are obtuse or the reader has to think too hard about what it all means, you will have lost him.

The How-to Headline

Like the benefit headline, the how-to headline is another safe bet for almost everyone. What do your customers want to know how to do?

- Plan the perfect party
- Reward your employees
- Get your date off to an impressive start
- Feed the whole family for under $50

Answer that question and you have the perfect how-to headline.

For example:

How to Pig Out & Lose Weight—Check out Our New, All-You-Can-Eat, Locally Sourced Salad Bar!

How Do You Feed the Whole Family Great Food for Under $50? Just Head on Down to Carter Buffet!

How Can You Guarantee a Great First Impression for Your Clients? Head to Mo's Steakhouse

Secret Headlines

Secret headlines are another variation on the how-to theme and once again should answer the question of what the reader wants to know.

Henderson's BBQ—We Invented Secret Sauce!

Three Secrets to a Perfect Date: Flowers, Champagne & Romeo's Italian Kitchen

The secrets variation has the added benefit of the seductive word "secret." After all, we all like secrets; they make us feel special. The answer to all these secrets is, of course, your restaurant.

The Guarantee Headline

A guarantee headline is a great way to remove the risk right up front and let your readers know how sure you are that your restaurant will meet their needs. We will talk a great more about the construction of guarantees. For now, I want to focus on the power a guarantee has as a great headline.

Removing the risk up front will always increase readership of your message.

Steaks Cooked to Perfection, Guaranteed

We Guarantee Lunch in 15 Minutes or You Don't Pay

Fresh Fish Guaranteed

While it helps that your guarantee is point specific, it does not always have to be to get the desired result. Rather than guarantee your actual restaurant, you could simply guarantee not to waste your prospect's time.

Question Headlines

Question headlines can work well but only on one condition—if you are absolutely sure that the person reading your headline will think of **the exact same answer you want them to think of** when they read it. *If they think of anything else, you just lost the battle before they even reached the copy.*

Don't think of a giant pink elephant.

What did you just think of?

Even though I told you not to, for a second he was there, wasn't he? That is what happens if you ask a question and the person answering it in his head does not make the connection you want him to make. He wanders off on a tangent and never returns. It is for this reason that I hate the often-used advertising phrase **"Why don't you?"**

Right now, I can think of about fifty reasons why I'm not going to do anything. Starting with, I'm going to an NFL game in a few minutes. The same holds true of other questions like **"What have you got to lose?"**

Well, since you asked, let me think about it. There is my money, my time, my prestige with my friends, and about 101 other things. The point is that if you use question headlines, I want you to think *very hard* about the readers' possible answers before you finalize your question.

You Have Been Working Hard— Isn't it Time You Treated Yourself to A Night Out?

Now there is a question most people can relate to; I mean who doesn't think they work hard and that it's time they had a reward?

Are You Tired of Eating the Same Old Things?

Come Experience the Exotic Tastes of India!

Yes, please!

Whatever it is, the mental images for the reader are good, his body language is positive and his interest is piqued. Question headlines are a great way to interest the reader and get the reader emotionally involved in what comes next.

Just remember to be sure you know the answer they will give to the question you ask.

Andrew Wood

Gang of Lobsters Attack Chef!

In organized attempt to stop the Maine Lobster Festival.

They failed. Come see us this weekend for Maine's best lobster roll.

The Shocking Headline

The shocking headline or provocative statement is by far the hardest of all these techniques to pull off successfully. It's very easy to cross the line and it's equally easy to simply miss the mark in making a statement so unrelated to the end result, or just so off base that nobody bothers to read the copy.

It takes a great deal of practice and insight to pull off the shocking headline with consistency and, even then, you will offend some people, but so be it.

Done right, the shocking headline can be a real winner because it instantly differentiates itself from "corporate speak" crap.

The key is to do something that will resonate with your target market.

Gang of Lobsters Attack Chef

Local Chef Abducted by Aliens
(Turns out they wanted his secret sauce recipe)

Divorce Lawyers Picket Restaurant
(for being too romantic and keeping couples together)

The Free Headline

While the shocking headline is by far the hardest concept to pull off successfully, I have saved the easiest for last. **Nothing works better than "free"!** Free removes cost; it removes risk; it removes disappointment. After all, how upset can you be if a free product or service fails to meet your expectations?

The most important reason to use free is that it opens up a dialogue with your prospect and allows you to engage in a two or perhaps even three-step sales cycle. In other words, the use of free anything, is primarily to start a relationship that will allow you to sell the prospect something down the line.

Many people wrongly shy away from free anything, as they feel it cheapens their product. However, even in the rarified air of very top people, with the world's most luxurious items, customers still expect a free something to be part of the sales process.

For example:

Almost everyone at my golf club is a millionaire and they all still talk about saving a few cents on gas or getting a golf club a few dollars cheaper on eBay. Never underestimate the power of free in attracting additional readership.

The ultimate puppy dog close—offer something for a no-strings-attached, free trial.

Free Beer

Free Wine

Free Desert

Free Appetizer

Free Wedding Planner

Free anything is always good in generating leads, no matter what end of the market you are selling to and no matter how high priced your product. The key to the successful use of free is in creating a good qualifying process.

Testing Your Headlines

You now have twelve solid methods for formulating winning headlines, but that my friends, is just the beginning. While you will already have surpassed the best efforts of your competition by using the information in this chapter, there is still more work to do. The final word on headlines is, test them.

A simple change of a word or two can make all the difference in the world. The addition of a guarantee, the use of a free bonus or a solid testimonial can all dramatically increase your response rate, which is why you should always be testing.

The first rule of testing is this—change only your headlines and nothing else. Leave your copy alone. Eventually you will find which headlines work best; those are the ones you can milk for year after profitable year to come.

SUMMARY

Great headlines are critical to your restaurant's success; without them, no one will ever read your sales copy.

There are 12 proven formulas for writing Legendary headlines. Whichever method you choose, you must work and rework your headlines until the promise or interest created by them motivates your reader to dig into the copy that follows.

Finally, you must put your headlines to the test.

Make sure the person writing your copy understands direct response marketing and is not a typical agency copywriter. Based on my search for copywriters, such a person can be found in about one in two hundred people who call themselves professional copywriters. Oh yeah, they can fill the page with words but most couldn't sell a nun a candle with their writing.

Brilliance without the capability to communicate it, is worth little, in enterprise.—
Thomas Leach

"Ask not what you can do for your country. Ask what's for lunch."— **Orson Welles**

Andrew Wood

CHAPTER 14

The Art of Selling Ice to Eskimos

Write in Tongues, How to Connect with Every Prospective Guest in Their Own Language

In this chapter you are going to learn a new language, the only language in the world that's basically universal. Without knowledge of this language—and few people even in the marketing business speak it fluently—your marketing copy will be dull and your response lukewarm.

I'm talking about Benefitize, the language that translates your restaurant's facts and features into sizzling reasons for the prospect to act now.

Benefitize answers the universal question of readers around the world—**what's in it for me?**

Why should I take the time to read your sales copy or watch your video?

Why should I believe what you say when I read it or hear it?

Why should I come in now?

And if I do decide to buy, why should I book at your restaurant and not that of your competitor?

All these questions are going around in your reader's head and must be tackled directly throughout your copy if you are to succeed in making a sale. As with almost all the information in this book, you'll find that the techniques outlined in these chapters are equally effective, no matter what type of copy you are writing. From letters to websites, brochures to print ads, emails to social media, benefitize is the language of profits! That's what this chapter is all about—turning facts and features into compelling benefits that make people want to act.

In this chapter, you will discover:

- ✓ how to speak and write in Benefitize,
- ✓ how to focus all your attention to gain the initial call, click or visit,
- ✓ how to organize your key benefits, and
- ✓ the importance of using testimonials to add credibility.

The Art of Selling Ice to the Eskimos—How to Make Your Sales Pitch Convincing

To have a successful marketing campaign, you must convince the readers or viewers of the value of your restaurant's offer. You must sell them on some kind of action, which often involves removing their doubts and fears. This is the point of the copy where you transition from your story to your sales pitch and it's the point where most marketing campaigns go wildly astray.

Are You Insane!

That was the headline of perhaps the greatest sales letter I have ever penned, my famous **"Insane"** letter. This one-page letter alone is responsible for over $7 million in income, but here's the real beauty of it. I have used the same letter for almost 15 years with the same staggering results in a number of different businesses—from selling franchises in the karate industry to software in the golf business.

The reason this letter has been so successful is simple—the concept and the copy resonates with the readers. The idea of doing the same thing again and again and yet expecting different results is, in fact, insane!

This type of connection and understanding of human nature, motivation, and buying psychology is what separates a $500 sales letter writer from a $5,000 or even $15,000 dollar sales letter writer, with a corresponding increase in response.

There is nothing, I repeat nothing, more powerful than a well-written sales letter! By well-written I don't mean spelling, grammar, punctuation, and all the things I seem to have missed by quitting school at fifteen. What I mean is, a letter that connects with a prospect at the soul. A letter that speaks the language of your prospect, not the corporate-speak language that some Madison Avenue type thinks your prospect speaks. And very possibly, not the language you speak.

It's that connection that makes your copy work and it's the lack of that connection that makes it fail, whether in a letter, brochure, postcard, website, landing page, email, video script or social-media post.

Learn to Speak and Write in Benefitize

It is critical that you learn and speak the world's most important language, Benefitize. Benefitize is the language that your readers will respond to and no other language will do. *All readers want to know what is in it for them and they will continue to ask this question from the very first time they glance at your copy until the very last word at the bottom of the page.*

Great marketing is all about salesmanship—getting the prospect to call, click, visit, or buy.

Perhaps the most common mistake in all of marketing is to waste time, money, and space telling the reader things that are of no importance to his or her actual buying decision.

Focus all of your attention on arousing enough interest for the reader to make the

initial call, visit, or click.

Converting Features to Stimulating Benefits

Charles Revlon, the great cosmetics magnate, once said, *"In the factories we make perfume, in the stores we sell hope!"* Of course, you'd come up with some pretty clever stuff too, if you were sniffing perfume all day. But the fact remains that, to sell anything, you must take basic facts and features and turn them into something wonderful, desirable, and magical.

The basic building blocks of all marketing copy are your restaurant's benefits. These are the foundation of your copy. The first lesson, in almost every study of advertising, starts and often ends with this point. You must list your business's benefits, not just its features. And you must know the difference.

Every copywriter worth anything has been plugging away for decades on this one principle. *Yet, I am honestly shocked that more than 90 percent of the courses I see on marketing still haven't figured this simple step out.*

Simply, a feature is your product's basic qualities. These are things such as how many seats you have, how big your space is, what type of restaurant you are and where you are located.

Benefits are prospect centered. Benefits are things such as telling them that

Our convenient location offers ski-in ski-out from the lifts for lunch so you spend more time on the slopes.

You have to make your marketing copy prospect-centered instead of product-centered. There are usually more benefits than you think and many of them are several levels deep. That is, the first benefit produces another, and it's the deeper ones that matter. For instance, a great meal gives enjoyment. The enjoyment helps you and your spouse relax. When you and your spouse arrive back home relaxed, you communicate better and are more patient with each other.

What's in This for Me?

Once you get in the habit of asking that question, you have half of the art of Legendary copywriting down pat. ("Me" being the prospect, of course.) Every time prospects look at your copy, they are asking that question. If all you tell them are the features, you'll never maximize your marketing dollars. You're better off asking those questions first. Then your copy will be ready to answer them when the prospect thinks the same questions.

Your prospects couldn't care less who you are or what you are selling unless there is something in it for them. Don't make people search through your copy to find out what's in it for them. Put it right up front in the headline, in the opening paragraph, in the offer, throughout the bullets, and all the way through the ad. Pack it full of benefits your prospects want and need.

Leave Nothing to Chance—Spell Out all Your Benefits in Detail

A picture is not always worth a thousand word, or even a few words. Stand in front of a large group of people and hold up a picture of large group of people standing up and you know what happens?

Nothing. I've tried it!

Ask those in the audience who feel like it to stand up. A few people shuffle in their seats but rarely does anyone actually get up.

Tell everyone in a room to stand up and to the last man, woman, and child, they all do.

What works with a real live audience works just the same in print. Show people a *picture without an explanation and they will all draw different conclusions.*

Provide wishy-washy instructions, and you'll get a wishy-washy response.

Expect people to finish off your sentences for you, and it won't happen.

Assume your readers will take your features and turn them into benefits in their head as they speed on their way to the next sentence—that's simply not going to happen.

Lazy and incompetent copywriters use features and bullet points that *do not* spell out benefits in clear, simple and direct language so there can be no misconception.

Let's take the feature: "Our restaurant is close to the freeway."

What did the writer want that sentence to mean or, to put it another way, what image did the writer *expect the reader to see in his head?*

> A. The restaurant is noisy and smoggy because it's close to the freeway?
> Or

> B. The restaurant is a quiet refuge but with convenient freeway access, cutting down your travel time so you can spend more time eating or relaxing, not driving.

That is exactly what happens when writers get lazy and fail to spell out exactly what they mean. Saying your restaurant is close to the freeway is open to all kinds of interpretations, not necessarily the one you want.

Spelling out what you mean, as in option B, leaves no margin for error.

This is the way in which you must approach each feature, each fact, and each benefit that you wish to impart to the minds of your prospect.

"Excellent wine list" **is not the same as:**

Excellent wine list, with fine wines to suit any budget.

The first assumes the reader knows what comes next; the other does not leave it to chance.

Feature

We have a bar.

Benefit

Try amazing local craft beers and make some new friends in our bar.

Can you really make every feature a compelling benefit?

Well, if you can't, then don't bother including it in your copy.

So what?

If you do this one thing and nothing else, your investment in this book will be worth a hundred times what you paid.

It's my age-old test for great copy and it's simply this—after each benefit in your copy ask the question, so what?

If the sentence you have just read does not answer that question, then rewrite the benefit because it is not compelling enough to be included in your Legendary copy.

Organizing Your Key Benefits

A great way to organize your thoughts in a logical manner to present to the reader is to write out all the key benefits your restaurant offers. Then simply arrange the benefits in order of importance and you will have competent, ready-made marketing copy. You will add details to each benefit as you enhance the copy with the following concepts.

Make it live, make it breathe, make it real!

- What will it feel like getting the whole family together to celebrate a special occasion at your restaurant?
- How are the views from your patio?
- Why is al fresco dining better?
- What dishes can they only get from you?

All you have to do is go down a list of features and ask yourself one simple question:

What does my customer gain from this feature?

Your Key Benefits

One of the most powerful exercises you can do for all your marketing is to sit down and list the ten most compelling reasons why people should do business with your restaurant.

The first five are usually easy and will be the ones you will use in your headlines, subhead, and leading bullet points; after that, it gets tougher.

Oh, and please don't tell me how great your service is or that you are committed to an excellent experience for your customers—that is neither compelling nor believable unless you are at the very pinnacle of your field.

10 Reasons to Do Business with My Restaurant

List each in the form of a complete sentence with a clear customer benefit.

1. _____
2. _____
3. _____
4. _____
5. _____
6. _____
7. _____
8. _____
9. _____
10. _____

To stimulate ideas, ask yourself questions from the customer's point of view such as:

- Does your location save me time? How much time?

- Can I get food I can't get at home, or is difficult to prepare at home?

- Am I going to get value? Who says so?

- Is the ambience conducive to meetings or is it better for families?

- Will it feel like home cooking? How?

- Will I feel comfortable and catered to?

- Will it impress my date? Is it romantic?

Remember, though, these ten reasons will be used for much more than just sales letters or landing pages. They should be woven into all your collateral material: brochures, information kits, flyers, and advertisements.

Whether you have seven key benefits or seventeen key benefits, these benefit statements are your "Basic Building Blocks" to better marketing. You will use these benefits as you create your headlines, offers, bullets, and all kinds of marketing collateral.

You Don't Always Have to Say It All at Once.

On a one-shot email campaign, you have to jam every possible feature and benefit into a single email because that's the only shot you are going to get. This is not the case if you drive them to an opt-in landing page and follow up with automation. In this case you are going to email your prospects multiple times so you don't need your entire sales message in a single email. In fact, you will very often use the first and last emails as overviews of the entire benefits package but use the letters in between to focus on individual benefits.

For example, an auto responder campaign might cover in different emails

- the history of your restaurant

- the food and drink options
- testimonials and stories from various "happy guests"

This will allow you to build on your story and its benefits with each letter you send and, over the course of your campaign, make a solid sales pitch that includes all your key points in detail.

Don't Be Afraid of Long Copy

Do not be afraid of explaining your offer in detail. People need reasons...they need benefits...they need proof...they need motivation—and it takes more than a few lines of fluff to connect on a meaningful level. Don't be afraid of writing copy that is long enough to prove your case. Even in today's world there is no such thing as copy that's too long, only copy that is too boring. If people are interested in any given subject, they want more information, not less.

The more wants you can satisfy, the more problems you can solve, the more needs you can meet, the more is in it for the reader.

Beware of the Opinions of Management, Your Spouse, Your Friends, Even Yourself; You Are Not the Customer!

I showed the an example of a long sales letter to several of my top resort clients and all but one said there was *no way they would ever send a letter like this to their clients.* It doesn't send the right message or portray the right image of who we are, they said. Perhaps not, at least not "who management thinks, they are" but it made my client, Garland Resort, $1.7 million from an investment of just $25,000!

What works in direct response marketing is almost always the exact opposite of what people think or wish would work and you have to realize this important fact when writing your copy.

Write Your Copy For One Person Only.

You must write your copy as if only a single person were reading it and it's that person and only that person's response to your letter that matters. That means is does not matter what anyone else thinks about your copy.

As one astute marketing manager said, "I have seen the customer and the customer is not me!"

Write your copy to appeal to your customer's unique demographic, psychographics, education, vernacular, ethnicity, profession, age, religion, and anything else you can think of that will bond you with him.

Ignore the pleas of managers, spouses, and marketing people (who couldn't sell a starving man a sandwich) to make your copy politically correct, corporate speak.

Remember, when developing any sales message, you are writing only for the tiny percentage of people who will read it, not for the people who will regard it as junk. Inspire them by providing more benefits and reasons to pick up the phone and take advantage of the unique offer you have made.

Back Up Your Claims with Proof

Testimonials from "happy guests," people who have experienced success and happiness with your restaurant, are the basic proof you can use to back up your claims.

Use any good press about your restaurant from newspapers, magazines, websites, and other media sources that can be used to back up your position.

Use social media like Trip Advisor, Yelp, Facebook, and others to showcase your restaurant.

Use Testimonials

Whether you personally believe it or not, testimonials are a very powerful selling tool. They're one of the most potent weapons that you can use to enhance your image, reduce buyer apprehension, build trust, and make sales. They should be used at every opportunity, throughout the course of your copy.

One thing that repeatedly amazes me is the number of solicitations I get that offer me no proof whatsoever of their veracity.

I want to scream out, "Why should I believe you?"

- Who uses your restaurant now and enjoys it?
- What authorities, publications, or experts back up your statements?
- What surveys, polls, or testing have been done that prove your claims?
- What do Trip Advisor, Facebook and Yelp have to say?

The power of testimonials cannot be overstated.

You are going to want testimonials for every different aspect of your business, not just for general satisfaction.

For each key benefit you promise in your copy, you are going to want two or three testimonials. Therefore, if your food variety is a benefit, you would be looking for the following:

"I love their lite bite small plates, great for a quick lunch. At dinner they give me the option of experiencing several different dishes without pouring on the calories! —**Frank Smith, Detroit**

"Great place for lunch. I go there several times a week and am never disappointed with the food or the service!" —**Elvis Patel, Senior Software Engineer**

You are going to need testimonials for different types of customers.

Testimonials should always be from real people with the same characteristics as your prospects. Women want testimonials from women, mothers want testimonials from others with children. Managers want to see that other managers are happy with your restaurant.

Use testimonials wherever you can to tell your story, highlight your benefits, and add credibility to your letter!

The more someone reading your copy can identify with the person making the testimonial, the better it is for you. Always personalize your testimonials, giving the name of the person making the testimonial, a title, company, area, or industry. The more real and identifiable the person making the statement is, the more credible it will be.

If you are looking to attract seniors, use other seniors and fathers and identify them as such. If you want to enhance your reputation in your state, use newspaper quotes and magazine quotes. The more you can slant your testimonials to your cause and the causes of those you service, the more effective they will be in enhancing your reputation.

Get Your Testimonials Together

Gather together your past testimonials, newspaper articles, PR, awards, and other positive feedback you have received. All these items can be woven into your copy to enhance your credibility.

If you do not have years of them sitting in a file as most businesses unfortunately do not, get on the phone right now and get some. Getting testimonials is easier than many of us think.

Simply call a few of your best guests and put a few words in their mouths while asking permission to attach their name and seal of satisfaction to your restaurant.

Make up a feedback form (with signature required) and hand it out to all your guests with their check. Let them know you care what they think about your restaurant. Make it easy for your clients to give you feedback and testimonials. (Of course, if any of the feedback is negative, reach out to the customer right away.)

Once you have testimonials, use them in all your marketing efforts.

Scan old newspapers, magazines, and web articles about your company for lines that can be pulled out and quotes that can be used as proof to your claims. Very often, previous management will have missed positive gems.

SUMMARY

Learn, understand, and write only in the universal language of Benefitize; it is the only language to which your prospects will respond. List your restaurant's key attributes in the form of benefits statements, then prioritize them in order of importance for inclusion in your copy. Spell out every fact and feature as a tangible benefit to your prospect; always answer the prospect's unasked question, what's in it for me?

Back up all your claims with testimonials, press quotes, surveys, testing results, and proof.

Andrew Wood

"Everything you see I owe to spaghetti" —
Sophia Loren

CHAPTER 15

Irresistible Offers and Iron-Clad Guarantees—Your Secret Weapon in the Battle for Massive Response

Thinking is the hardest work there is, which is probably why people do so little of it!
—**Henry Ford**

By this stage of the book, we have handcrafted our email lists, generated some legendary headlines, woven our restaurants compelling story with plenty of benefits, and backed up our claims with testimonials and proof. We have reviewed our sales message and improved it immensely by applying all the little tricks of the trade I taught you in an earlier chapter. Now comes the most important part of all, the offer, the guarantee, and call to action.

A full 95 percent of the hundreds of emails, sales letters, and social media I get a year from restaurants fail in the most basic of all marketing principles by simply failing to make me any kind of offer.

Instead they lose millions in the process, hoping to woo me and others with their pictures and vague promises of service, quality and prestige.

The offer is so important to the success of your campaign that in most cases it should be the very first thing that is written.

All the other headlines, text, and testimonials are just back up to getting the prospect in the right frame of mind to act and nothing will compel them to act faster than an irresistible offer. Nothing, that is, except an irresistible offer backed with an iron-clad satisfaction guarantee attached to it.

Coming up with the right offer takes a great deal of thought, backed up with a good deal of testing and tweaking to get it to the point where it will elicit maximum response. In this section, we will explore the various techniques that go into creating an offer so compelling that readers basically sell themselves.

In this chapter, you will discover:

- ✓ why irresistible offers are so important,
- ✓ how to maximize your marketing dollars,
- ✓ how to enhance your offers with guarantees, urgency and more, and
- ✓ a quick start action plan for crafting your irresistible offer.

Irresistible Offers and Ironclad Guarantees— Your Secret Weapon in the Battle for Massive Response

I want to expose the truth to you, one that no one else in the advertising and marketing industry dare to tell you.

Ninety-nine percent of all your direct marketing is doomed to fail because of one key missing ingredient: **The lack of an irresistible offer.**

You can't make a campaign succeed with a bad list.

Nor can you make campaign work with a bad copy…

But the truth of the matter is, *you can* take an average email or mailing list and average copywriting ability and still make a success of your campaign, *if you have an irresistible offer.* Most do not.

This is where it gets tricky, you see, because most people in the restaurant business have a totally distorted view of what it takes both physically and financially to get a new customer, or even a lead.

This makes them very reluctant to devise an irresistible offer, since they think that any offer is giving away or cheapening their product.

Very few of your competitors will ever answer the following questions or go through the simple but powerful exercise I suggest. This will give you a massive advantage because you will be working from facts, not vague guesses.

Do you know exactly how much it costs you to get a lead?

Don't feel bad, almost no one does.

The math is simple though, you just take your total marketing budget divided by your total number of leads generated per year. If you add in *all* of your marketing costs, newsletters, printing, parties, staffing, and so on, I can guess the number is almost certainly higher than you thought it was.

If you take out referrals, it may be staggeringly higher than you thought!

Do you know exactly how much it costs you to make a sale? (Cost per lead divided by actual sales.)

Do you know the lifetime value of your guests? (The number of new guests, times their yearly spend over the typical lifetime of a client, plus four percent a year inflation.)

Not a week goes by where someone does not call and ask us to do a massive e-blast on their behalf on a cost per lead basis.

No problem with that, we are all about response. The problem is that they typically want to pay something like a dollar per reservation. Which only goes to proves how out of touch they are with reality, since it actually costs $50–$100 for a typical restaurant to attract a new guest. (These are general figures that obviously vary with your area, product, and offer.)

Andrew Wood

What Is a New Guest Worth to Your Restaurant?

I visit my local sushi bar once a week with my wife and spend $80 on average. I'll visit about 30 times this year as I'm away a lot. Very often we have guests so the tab can be double that, but let's just settle for 30 times $80 plus another 10 times $80 for guests. My worth to that Sushi bar as a customer is $3,200 a year. Then you need to add in the intangible but almost as valuable fact that I promote this place constantly to my friends. I'm going to low ball that worth at $600. Making me worth $3,800 a year. Since I have been going there since it opened five years ago, my lifetime value so far is $19,000!

Now based on this information alone, what would you be willing to spend to acquire me as a NEW customer?

Would you be willing to give me a free meal to get me in the door?

Here's another example. About a year ago, a Mexican restaurant very close to my home opened in a tired strip mall. Despite driving past it a thousand times, I never even thought about going in there. The three previous restaurants there had all failed and I expected this one to fail as well. Finally, I went there on a Monday night when my go-to place is closed and—guess what?—it was awesome. They had spent real money to make the interior festive, the food was great and the service engaging. I love the place and have been back three times already.

Had they bought a mailing list of Pine Ridge residents—the upscale community I live in—and sent us all an invite for a FREE Meal to try it out, how much more would they have made in year one? I'd have been a customer a year ago. If they had made the letter personal, for example:

Dear Mr. Wood:

My name is Pedro. My family and I would like to invite you to try our authentic Mexican food at the Margarita Grill. We know that three other restaurants have failed in this location, and that the location is less than glamorous. Which is why I am sure you will be pleasantly surprised by our festive décor, wonderful food and friendly servers.

Please do me the favor of trying us. **Dinner for you and your wife is on us** in the hope that your first visit will not be the last and that you will share your excitement with your friends. This invitation is good for the entire month of June. Please introduce yourself to me when you come, I look forward to meeting you. Call now for reservation: 352-555-1234

Pedro Lopez & family

Margarita Grill

P.S. Due to Florida law, alcoholic drinks are not included.

Now if you had sent that letter to 500 Pine Ridge residents starving for close-by decent restaurants but skeptical of the location, what would the response rate be?

What would be the long-term value to the restaurant of getting these people to try it in month one of operation, or two, rather than month twenty-two?

What would the psychic debt be, having gotten a meal for free?

Would this have jump-started the restaurant?

In my experience: Yes! But few are willing to take the risk.

You minimize the risk up front by picking a perfect target audience. Risk is minimized even more by greeting those taking advantage of the offer in person and finding out a little about them. Then you seal the deal by having great food and decent service!

MAXIMIZE YOUR MARKETING DOLLARS

Now, let's say we spend $500 on an email campaign or a coupon campaign to twenty thousand potentials in your area—what will the response be?

I could tell you the typical response to a good list, with good copy is only half a percent, but even that would be a stretch. These days, typical mailings produce less than a one percent response rate.

The truth of the matter is that, all things being equal, the amount of your response will be based on the quality of your offer.

You can get 1 percent, even 2 percent or 3 percent response rates, but only to irresistible offers. In fact, we have had response rates of 10 percent, even 30 percent and more to well-executed campaigns.

Offer a ten- or twenty-dollar discount and astonishingly…the response will be lukewarm at best.

Offer 50 percent off and response will soar.

Offer a free lunch and response may or may not be good depending on the area. Offer free dinner and you should kill it!

Determine First What You Can Afford to Offer

In order to determine your optimum offer, you have to track your leads, conversions, and upsells. It may well be okay to give away $50 worth of meals to a couple to attract over one hundred new guests, as we did recently.

But Wait…My Product is Wonderful, and My Clients are Sophisticated; I Don't Want to Be Hokey!

What do you think is one of the key benefits for American Express platinum or black cardholders, the very elite of the spending scale?

Discounts, room nights, and champagne.

Discounts on cruises, free upgrades, free companion airline tickets in business class. Extra free room nights, $300 spa gifts, dinner with the captain. Free limo pick-up to and from the airport and a $3,000 certificate for my first private-jet rental. And these are just some of the offers I got this month!

The fact is, I almost never get an offer from a high-end American Express partner that does not offer a strong inducement to act now.

It's the same with the car-rental companies, the cruise lines, the catalogs I buy from, and the various high-end restaurants that want to sell me a quarter share. Even world-famous resorts like The Breakers, Pinehurst, or Pebble Beach send me offers that include large inducements, especially in their off seasons.

They all know that even at the higher end of the income scale, people are people. They want a deal. They want an offer. They want a special bonus, a justification for acting now, rather than next week, next month or never.

Make no mistake about it, the vast majority of the rich, the famous, and the world travelers are people just like you and me. They want to feel like they received a good value no matter what their income level. In fact, because they are successful professionals and entrepreneurs, they very often they take more pride in getting a good value than the average Joe on the street.

Inducements Do Not Have to Be Discounts

A good offer can include an attractive price point, but it does not have to be a discount. In fact, very often a value-added offer will work better than a discount since many people reading your letter won't know what the regular price is anyway.

The key is to offer the highest-value gift possible that you can get at the lowest possible cost.

That's why things like a bottle of champagne work well. There is a relatively high perceived value to the customer at little cost to you. (Not everywhere allows this, at least in the US.)

What Works?

Free Bottle of Champagne

15% Bonus on All Gift Certificates

Free Valet Parking

Like most effective marketing, the key to effective offers is test, test, test. Once you find ones that work, double up, heck, triple up, and milk it for all it's worth.

Reduce Risk and Build Trust to Make Your Offer Even More Irresistible

Add one final touch to your irresistible offer to increase response even further and reduce the perceived risk of your prospect. Offer a guarantee. Make prospects' act of choosing you a safe choice so that they can reap your benefits for themselves and their families. The more risk you take away from the prospect and place in your lap, the more response you will generate. The more you reverse the risk in prospects' favor, the greater your gains will be.

If there is even a hint of fear, loss or indecision in prospects' minds, they will choose to procrastinate.

How can you reduce risk for your diners?

- Money back if you're not satisfied with your meal.
- Free appetizer if we don't answer your reservation call in three rings or less
- Free dessert if your main course isn't delivered in 20 minutes or less.

Reducing risk increases business no matter what you are selling, no matter what your price point, or no matter what your offer happens to be!

Ask for Action

Ask for specific action from your reader in simple step-by-step language. *The more specific the instructions are, the greater your response will be.*

I use an interesting experiment at seminars where I ask everyone to stand up. They all do for one simple reason—because I asked them to. They take action because they are asked to take action. If they are not asked to take action, they will sit there for hours on end just listening, waiting to be asked to do something. Sure, one or two in a hundred will ask questions on their own volition; the rest will wait until you tell them you want questions from the audience or signal that you require their participation in some other way.

Create a Sense of Urgency

The very same dynamics are at work in your marketing offers—if you do not ask for specific action, very few people will take it on their own accord. It's imperative that your copy creates a sense of urgency to act.

Procrastination of any sort will destroy your response. You must get the reader to do your bidding as quickly as possible and give him valid reasons for doing so rather than keeping it in the "get around to it" later file. While some prospects will return, the vast majority will not.

Here are some examples of action-getting statements:

Go to your computer right now and click on the "Reservations" icon located on the top right of the home page.

Call and book your event now and we'll help you secure the best dates and choice of seating times.

Create a sense of urgency in one of the following ways…

Limit the amount you have to sell:

Only six prime wedding dates remain for this year!

Limit the date by which they can buy at this price, or talk of an impending increase in prices:

VIP cards are available only until January 31st

Talk of a limited amount of bonus items to accompany your offer:

We have limited supply of just three cases so don't wait to grab your free bottle of champagne. Book now.

Talk of lost opportunity:

Those who book early get the best dates and choice of private dining rooms.

Talk of social, financial, and prestigious gain:

You have worked hard to get where you are, now it's time to reward yourself with our VIP Dining Card

Use a Series of Different Offers to Reach Different Situations

While there is much to be said in any marketing for repetition, the words of W.C. Fields ring out loud and clear:

"If at first you don't succeed, quit! There is no use being a damn fool about it."

All kidding aside, because you are mailing multiple times you can vary the offer to suit different motivational factors in the reader.

This naturally brings us to the importance of testing.

Test, Tweak, and Test Again

Testing offers another area of marketing success that most people don't want to talk about. They don't want to talk about it because it costs money to test. Yet with the best efforts in the world, you cannot maximize your marketing success without it.

The plain truth of the matter is, some offers just work better than others, and it's not always the ones you think will work that prove to be the most successful.

You must commit to testing various offers in order to maximize your response.

SUMMARY

Most restaurant marketing, regardless of the media, fails for one simple reason—the lack of an irresistible offer to motivate the reader from procrastination to action.

All things being equal, campaigns with irresistible offers will always outperform those that do not have such an offer. Most people get so caught up in their own egos or image of what they think their restaurant offers that they fail to see it through the eyes of a prospect.

To create an irresistible offer, you should first determine what your Average Customer Worth (ACW) is. Based on that information, decide what you are willing to spend to acquire a customer.

Once you have that number in mind, it's time to see what valued-added features, benefits, or gifts can be added to your offer to change it from average to irresistible.

Guarantee your offer wherever possible to remove risk. Create a sense of urgency to get your reader to act now. Finally, when you have come up with your best possible offer, create a different one and test which produces the greatest response.

"You can't just eat good food. You've got to talk about it too. And you've got to talk about it to somebody who understands that kind of food."
— **Kurt Vonnegut**

Andrew Wood

CHAPTER 16

Designing Legendary Ads, Collateral, Sales Letters, and Direct Mail That Work!

Frankly, most restaurant print advertising, flyers, direct mail, sales letters, and collateral that are a giant waste of time, money, and trees. That is not to say that even today print ads, flyers and direct mail are not worthy of some of your ad dollars or that they're not an integral part of your overall marketing plan.

The problem lies largely in how poorly most ads, sales letters, flyers and brochures are constructed—they are simply designed to fail.

For starters, most ads fail by not grabbing readers' attention in the headline. Research shows that 95 percent of readers never get beyond the headline. (See the chapter on headlines.)

The text of the ad frequently fails by not expanding on the headline and by not turning features into real benefits. People buy for emotional reasons backed up by logic. The ad fails if it doesn't spell out benefits clearly. (See the chapter on benefits.)

Misuse of graphics is also common. Many ads feature pictures or graphics that is indistinguishable from their fifty closest competitors. Poor layout of the ad components often draws the reader's eye away from the sales message instead of toward it.

Failure to ask for specific action can turn an otherwise good ad into a waste of money. The whole purpose is to lead the reader to action, yet many ads do not spell out the action.

I have already devoted several chapters to the most important aspects of any ad, sales letter, or brochure—namely the headlines, copy, offers, and calls to action, so here I will focus on other topics, safe in the knowledge that you are already armed with this potent information.

WHAT MAKES A GOOD AD?

An advertisement, flyer, brochure, or direct-mail piece is not necessarily good just because it is funny, clever, or even easily remembered. A good marketing tool effectively motivates people to action—to sign up for your offer, visit your website, make a reservation, inquire about hosting a banquet, or buy a gift certificate. In other words, a good ad gets a response!

In this chapter, you will discover:

- ✓ why most restaurant ads fail,
- ✓ how to capture your readers' attention,
- ✓ how to write response-driven copy,
- ✓ which "gimmicks" can help you garner additional response,
- ✓ how to prove your value,
- ✓ how to create compelling offers,
- ✓ how to test your ads for effectiveness before they run.

And:

- why most direct-mail campaigns fail,
- what makes an effective direct-mail campaign,
- the most effective lists to generate response,

- the importance of the offer,
- the keys to copy and design success,
- how to test properly.

With these ideas in mind, let's look at the factors that will determine the success of your print and online advertising.

KEY FACTORS TO ADVERTISING SUCCESS

First, let's look at what an ad can and cannot do for your restaurant. Ads can educate, qualify, generate leads, and even handle some objections. In some cases, ads can propel readers to make a reservation or go into your restaurant. Ads cannot interest people who have no interest in your restaurant or food type. Ads can only attract and heighten the interest of someone who wants to buy something in your general category or market.

You do not design ads to be everything to everybody. You design them to attract either people who are already frequenting your restaurant or similar restaurants, or people who may be open to eating at your type of restaurant.

The key is to increase the number of people who actually read your ad.

Recent studies have shown that of the thousands of ads people are exposed to each day, only 4–5 percent gain more than two or three seconds of attention.

While each different ad vehicle obviously has its own nuances, these factors will hold up for all vehicles. Ignore one of these ten key factors and you will instantly decrease the power of your marketing message.

THE *BREAKFAST* COLLECTIVE

Your morning routine just got better.

Respect every inch of space.

The biggest reason that most printed material is a waste of trees (and their digital counterparts are just as bad) is that most ad agencies treat printed matter as a challenge to fill up space.

Problems

Problems include: logos are too big; pictures don't relate to headlines; and worthless copy without a real sales message, benefits, and calls to action.

To increase the effectiveness of each piece, you must treat each inch of each ad, flyer, letter, and brochure with the respect it deserves. That innocent piece of white paper is going to cost you lots of green paper, so make it work for you for all it's worth.

Never make a casual decision about even an inch of space. Make your ad into the best salesperson your restaurant has by committing to maximize its full potential. That means doing your ads well in advance of any deadlines.

The simplest way to maximize your ad is to remind yourself constantly that people buy for their reasons, not yours. This is Sales 101, but for some reason when people try to sell someone the idea of visiting their restaurant, logic goes out the window. They suddenly spew a host of mind-numbing statements like "committed to excellence," "in business for twenty years," and "we're the biggest restaurant in town." The reader doesn't care. Use space to sell, not to build your ego.

The Restaurant Marketing Bible

Andrew Wood

You must capture your reader's attention with the picture you use.

Pictures should capture your readers' attention and show your restaurant as an effortless, happy, exciting, and wonderful place to be! With a few exceptions such as fashion merchandising, pictures do not sell your product or service; rather, they attract readership and complement the copy. By all means use a photo of your best dish. But be warned: If it is not something spectacular, it's just another picture.

You will do far better in attracting readership, especially in a magazine that might feature multiple restaurants, if you add an element to stop the reader dead in his tracks.

For example, a man in a business suit dining with a woman in a swimsuit would get people to stop and look at the ad, read the headline, and then decide if they want to read the copy. We're not asking you to do something like this just for shock value; the picture must relate to the copy and the offer. In this case, perhaps the theme might be how you offer fine or casual dining. The point is that by adding an extra element you can greatly increase the extent to which your ad stands out.

Use graphics to point out features and benefits of your food or service. People believe what they see. Show how much fun your restaurant is; show how much enjoyment it brings; show how your readers' lives will be enhanced if only they come and try it for themselves.

For the most part, headlines work better if they are placed below a picture, not above it or next to it.

Very often, readers will scan captions to determine whether they want to go back and read the copy. Never waste caption space by describing what's in the picture—the readers can see that. Instead, use that space to remind them of key benefits, or restate your offer in different words.

Do not assault the reader's eye or make your ad hard to read.

Do not confuse the reader with off-the-wall typeface styles, fancy designs, and strange layouts. Some graphic designers understand the principles of effective advertising as do some advertising sales reps. About as many as understand the principles of nuclear physics!

Please remember that neither graphic design nor advertising sales have anything in common with designing printed material that increases your business.

People read from top to bottom and from left to right. If you make their eyes jump around too much, they will give up. If you make the type too small, they will pass. If you print your flyer on bright red paper, they will give it a miss. By all means be creative, but never at the cost of making your piece difficult to read.

Use all known gimmicks to increase customer response. There are a great many little tricks you can use in a printed piece to increase its effectiveness. On their own each may seem insignificant, but put them all together and you can increase the effectiveness of your ad tenfold or more.

- ✓ End the headline where you want the reader to start reading, not at the far side of the page.
- ✓ Always use a caption under a picture. It's the second place everyone looks.
- ✓ Make sure the caption sums up your key benefit or offer—you may not get another chance.
- ✓ Make sure all photographs with people have the people oriented looking toward the text so the reader's eye follows the picture and begins to read. Photographs of people who appear to be looking off the page take the reader's eye to the next ad.
- ✓ Use a graphic of a phone next to the phone number—it can

increase response by up to 25 percent.

- ✓ If you want readers to clip a coupon, show scissors—you'll get up to 35 percent more responses.

Always ask the reader to do something.

Not asking the reader to take action is the biggest sin of all. Surprisingly, this sin is often committed by people who up to this point have passed most of the key tests. They have grabbed their readers' attention, expanded on benefits, used the right pictures, and have their readers salivating like Pavlov's dogs. Then their copy ends. Readers are left lost, empty, and wondering what to do next. Should they file this information for future use? Should they throw it away, or should they call or click right now?

Use strong calls to action, such as:

- ✓ Go to our website right now and claim your offer.

- ✓ Pick up the phone right now and call for reservations

- ✓ Don't wait another minute to get the rewards you deserve. Clip out this coupon and present it on arrival.

Never end a printed piece without direct and specific instructions for what you want the reader to do next. Don't blow it by arousing their interest in what you have, and then letting them go to a competitor first.

Put all printed ads to the test before allowing them to leave your office.

All ads should be put to the test before they go to print. By all means, use family, friends, other business owners, graphic designers, and ad reps to gain feedback. But be warned. If you have followed any of our advice until now, they may tell you that you have too much copy (you don't). They may tell you to use fancier type styles or, worse yet, put your headline in reverse type (which makes it 33 percent harder to read). They may encourage you to use a picture of yourself or to make your logo bigger. Resist the temptation. Instead, do the Legendary Print-Ad test.

Use the following tests to evaluate the design-readiness of every ad:

Headline test

Does the headline promise a clear benefit to the prospective customer, such as:

Quite Simply the Best Food In Town

Alternatively, does the headline make a provocative statement or pose a very interesting question? If your headline does not pass the above criteria, it stands a 99.5 percent chance of failing.

Picture test

Look at each picture in your ad. Will it capture your prospect's attention?

Does it clearly differentiate itself and stand out from the host of other ads it is competing against?

Does it show people just like your target reader having fun?

Copy test

Is the copy written specifically for your most probable prospects? Does each line state what's in it for the client, with clear, compelling benefits?

The classic test we have developed is this: read two sentences of any printed piece, then ask, "So what?" If one of the previous two sentences did not answer that question, go back and rewrite it. Of course, the answer to "so what?" must relate to the customer's point of view, not yours.

Gimmick test

Have you used all the gimmicks you can to incrementally increase your response?

Have you used the captions underneath each picture to sum up your offer, rather than merely telling the reader what he can already see in the picture?

Are coupons flanked by a graphic of scissors?

Is there a picture of a phone next to the phone number?

Does your ad avoid hard-to-read type styles, colored paper, all capitals, and reverse type?

Is your ad designed so that the eye follows a natural path from the top left to bottom right?

Call-to-action and offer test

Have you asked for action? What do you want the customer to do? Be specific.

Tracking test

Have you used a unique web address and a unique phone number to track all responses to this ad?

Media test

Is this the right media to run your ad? Sure, they may have lots of readers, but how many of them fit into your "Perfect Customer" category?

MATCH THE MESSAGE TO THE MEDIUM AND DON'T BE SEDUCED BY NUMBERS

Even taking all of the above seven key ad-design factors into account, an ad can still fail. Many restaurant owners are unwittingly seduced by the lure of large numbers.

Ad reps love to seduce you with the power of large numbers, but a smaller number of the right target group will always beat a larger number of just anybody. Choose your media with care. Don't waste money on people who are not your prospects.

DEVELOPING EFFECTIVE COLLATERAL

To sell meetings, events, group business, and weddings you need some printed materials to use for prospecting such as a direct-mail piece or to physically put in the hands of prospects and aid in the selling process. Rarely should they look and feel anything like the puff-piece glossy brochures and info kits stuffed with everything but the kitchen sink, which passes for marketing materials at most restaurants.

This is not my personal opinion; it's real Marketing 101 as described by marketing gurus such as David Ogilvy, Claude Hopkins, Dan Kennedy, Jay Abraham, and others. The real problem is that most people who produce restaurant collateral are graphic designers or high-priced agencies looking to win awards on your dime.

Amazingly, rarely do they know the first thing about sales and marketing. You can instantly tell if you are dealing with this type of service provider when they start talking about image, look, feel, and brand rather than sales or results.

Let's run a quick test on your existing VIP brochure or kit to see if you are actually maximizing your opportunity or merely distracting your prospects from the selling process:

Take the Marketing Collateral 101 Test

1. Does it have headlines that offer clear benefits on *every page*?
2. Does it have picture captions that offer *benefits* beneath every picture that does not have a headline?
3. Does it have testimonials from happy members on *every page*?
4. Does the copy make a *complete sales presentation* about your restaurant?
5. Does your copy use stories to *connect with the reader* emotionally?
6. Do you focus the copy on your *ten key benefit* statements?
7. Does the copy *support your USP*?
8. Are the pictures diverse enough to *appeal to different segments of your patrons* (e.g., families, millennials, seniors)?
9. Is the brochure *easy to read*, with large enough text, no reverse type, indented paragraphs, and clear eye paths?
10. Do photos and graphics *support the main points* of the copy?
11. Is there a quick checklist of *benefits for review* at the end?
12. Do you ask the prospect to *take the next step* and actually join or make an appointment?

If your collateral is failing any of these quick tests, it can definitely be made more effective. If it's missing several of the items, then it should really be redone.

Most brochures are just graphic puff pieces that repeat the same things everyone else does like, how good your ambience is and how great your service is in the dining room. You must strive to do more with your brochure. Use real stories and emotions to draw prospective members into your brochure and get them excited about the prospect of becoming a member.

Great Collateral Sells

Great sales collateral makes the entire sales presentation for you.

The key to producing great sales collateral is simple: It must have a beginning, middle, and end. It must help qualify the prospect, sell the prospect, answer the prospect's questions, provide proof to the prospect, and close the prospect.

It is no longer or no shorter than that.

Great marketing collateral is in fact, quite simply, "Salesmanship in Print."

Few restaurant marketing materials do any of the above. Instead they have nice glossy pieces, with oversized photos, a few captions, and bullet points instead of a real sales presentation.

Simple and Effective Design Strategies for Producing Greater Response to Your Collateral

Nowhere do people have more opinions than on the design of collateral. That's exactly what they should be taken as: personal opinions that have no basis whatsoever in marketing science other than personal preference. Everyone has favorite colors, typestyles, and design elements, none of which mean they are the right choice when it comes to generating response or making sales.

The problem with graphic designers and most armchair designers is that they over design, thus making the collateral look nice at the cost of making it easy to read. Or they make it look nice at the cost of having nothing worth reading.

Graphics should be used to attract attention and aid in the selling process by creating emotion.

- Show pictures of people having fun, enjoying your restaurant.
- Put headlines *under* pictures; they are more effective there than at the top or on the picture itself.
- Use captions under any picture without a headline; the caption should reiterate a benefit, not merely describe what's in the picture. The picture they can see.
- Use an easy-to-read typestyle.
- Do not use reverse type, white on black background—it's 33 percent harder to read.
- Make sure the type is large enough to read; 55 percent of Americans can't read the twelve-point type in this book without glasses.
- Do not make a reader's eye path cross.

Your Mailer/Handout Brochure

This is the simplest way to design an effective brochure. List out all the key benefits in order of importance, and then spell out those benefits along with some pictures of your restaurant. It may seem like a lot of information to cram into a trifold brochure, but it's easy to scan should a prospect only be interested in one or two of your key benefits. Make sure you make the text easy to read. Notice the headline: *13.5 Reasons*. Why choose such a strange number? Simple—to be different, to stand out, and make people look twice.

This piece is versatile enough to serve as your main brochure on a budget, to use in conjunction with a sales letter as it will fold to fit into a number-ten envelope or as a handout at chamber meetings and local events. They are also cheap to print as ten thousand will run you about $2,000 on a decent gloss stock.

Your Meeting or Wedding Info Kit

Your information kit is a very important tool and must be designed to maximize your sales goals, not just look pretty.

Inside of your presentation folder you should include the following:

- A color four-to-eight-page 8.5 × 11 brochure or a series of cut sheets; cut sheets are step-down flyers you can place in a presentation folder for easy reference. (Step-down flyers means each sheet is cut a bit shorter than the one behind it so you all the headings are visible.)
- A sheet of options and fees.
- Copies of newspaper or magazine articles that support your sales pitch.
- A page or more of testimonials from previous brides or meeting planners.

How to Use Your Brochures Effectively During Your Sales Presentation

There is something magical about the written word that is so much more tangible than what is spoken. When it's right there in black and white in front of them, people are just a lot more apt, even in today's skeptical world, to believe what is written. This makes your brochure or info kit a very powerful tool in your sales presentation, but not if used the traditional way where the you simply hands the package to the prospect.

If you do that, you lose all chance to customize, personalize, and highlight the key areas of interest to your prospect. It is so much more powerful to be able to open up the brochure and circle a testimonial that talks about how easy parking was for banquet guests rather than to simply respond to the question verbally.

Use your brochures as proof of your sales presentation by highlighting, circling, underlining, and drawing your prospect's attention to their hot points addressed in print. The more you customize the brochure for the prospect, the more effective it will be as a sales tool or as a take-home tool if the sale is not closed on the first meeting.

To that end, do not give the prospect your literature other than perhaps a map of the restaurant until you have finished your sales presentation. Then, as you sit down and handle any objections or questions they may have, you can break out the collateral and customize it for them before you hand it over.

Giving out collateral at the start of the presentation takes away your ability to control the sales presentation, since they may jump ahead and start asking questions about something you will show them later, or they may simply read while you are talking, half listening to what you have to say.

DIRECT MAIL

Other than the internet, direct mail is still the best form of advertising for restaurants by far. Yet many restaurants have tried and failed with direct mail. There are usually two reasons for this: poor lists and the absence of a sales-oriented message. Instead, they hope pretty pictures and a few "impotent" features will sell. They will not.

Direct mail is the most scientific form of advertising. The majority of factors, such as lists, timing, offers, copy, and space, are all in your hands. Each variation can be precisely tested for effectiveness. There are proven techniques that boost response. Unfortunately, many people ignore proven techniques and try to be "creative." Instead, you should test each incremental improvement in the copy, layout, and design that can have a far-reaching effect on the success of your campaign.

No other type of advertising lets you target the market so specifically with income ranges, demographics, gender, and even occupation. Direct marketing is not cheap. But if systemized, the results can be quite astonishing.

Why most direct-mail campaigns fail

First, let me explain what I mean by a mail campaign. I frequently talk to restaurant operators who've just run a direct-mail campaign with terrible results. Upon questioning, we learn that their idea of a mail campaign is a two-by-three coupon included with fifty other coupons in a shotgun mailing to anybody with a mailbox. That is not what we mean by a direct-mail campaign.

We also talked to many who eagerly rent a mailing list of local magazine subscribers. They print a one-sided flyer with no letter, no offer, no headline, no sweetener, and then send it to twenty thousand people. They are shocked when the phone doesn't ring. That is not a direct-mail campaign either.

Creating your campaign

There are no hard rules about what a mail package should contain. It could be as simple as a one-sided sales letter or be as complex as a fourteen-page letter, complete with a color brochure.

However, if you take a look at the type of mail you receive, you'll find 70–80 percent will contain the following:

- An envelope with teaser copy that entices you to open it and find out what is inside.
- A three- or four-fold brochure.
- A two-to-four-page letter.
- A clear, compelling offer.
- A reply card or other response device.

Mailing lists—the first key to success

The best direct-mail package can fail miserably if you don't send it to the right people. If you're not careful, your letters will end up in the hands of dead people and people who aren't interested in your type of restaurant.

Lists can be ordered and sorted in almost unimaginable combinations. You can rent lists of people categorized by race, income, zip code, property value, business, or a thousand other identifying factors.

There is a huge difference between the performance of good lists and poor lists. For example, if your restaurant is high end, you will need a clear income qualifier.

First, figure out what your ideal prospects look like.

What characteristics do they have?

- Do most of your customers come from the same general area?
- Do they have a certain level of income?
- Do they have children, drive a Corvette, or root for the Redskins?

Once you've pinpointed the characteristics of your ideal prospects, check to see what lists are available with those exact criteria.

Lists are usually available in minimums of five thousand names and can be rented for one time or multiple uses. I suggest a one-time use and asking for a credit if you want to reuse it within sixty days. By then you'll know the response rate. Make sure you use a reputable list broker—there are plenty of sharks.

THE MOST EFFECTIVE LISTS TO GENERATE RESPONSE

While good lists can be found from third parties, the most effective lists you will ever use are the lists you build yourself. All the data you collect from your website and at the counter will pay off big time with direct mail.

These are people who already have had contact with your restaurant and that will translate into far greater response rates than any cold list you buy or rent.

Andrew Wood

The first trick is to get your mail opened

When a prospect gets a letter from you in the mail, the very first challenge is to get your letter in the interesting pile. Fail to do that and I don't care what you spent or what you sent; your campaign is doomed.

Have you ever watched someone open their mail? It's a very interesting study in human nature; take me, for example—I'm a sorter. First, I look through the stack for checks and bills. That's the accounting pile—pile A. Pile B is anything for my wife. Pile C is the "later pile"—catalogs that might be of potential interest (golf, car stuff, and, at Christmas at least, possible gifts for my wife) and periodicals. They get put on my magazine rack for later reading at night or for my next plane trip. Pile D is my favorite. That is the interesting personal stuff—a handwritten letter from a friend, books or tapes I ordered, brochures for interesting vacations, and direct-mail offers for things that interest me (books, tapes, cars, golf, and so forth). Catalogs and mailing pieces of no interest to me (credit card offers, insurance solicitations, stock pick newsletters, car dealerships of brands I don't care about) get instantly trashed.

Which brings me to pile E. Pile E is direct-mail offers that might be of interest to me—only pile E almost never exists because very few pieces make it through the sort-and-trash process.

For sure there are other methods of sorting your mail, but they all have one thing in common, some stuff gets thrown out without a glance, some gets saved for later reading, and some actually gets opened and read.

So how can you massively increase your chances of getting your letter opened and read?

How about an envelope with a handwritten address and a custom stamp from Stamps.com with a picture of your food affixed? How about some lumpy trinket inside the letter to create some interest? I have used everything from tea bags to seed packets!

They are not going to trash that letter like the rest of the "Junk Mail."

They are going to first put it on the interesting pile.

Grab readers' attention with your headline

When they open it to see what the lump is, a giant headline is going to grab their attention at once. If you don't grab them by the throat with your headline, 95 percent won't make it past the first paragraph. (Which means no matter how long or short your letter is it won't work.)

Just as in print advertising, writing good headlines is critical to the success of your direct-mail campaign. Without good headlines, everything that follows is a waste of time and money for it will most likely never be read.

With direct mail you have more space than a print ad and traditionally see much longer headlines. Longer headlines give you a better chance to hook the reader. (Re-read the headlines chapter.)

Whichever method you choose, you must work and rework your headlines until the promise created in them motivates your readers to dig into the copy that follows.

Make sure the person writing your copy is a direct response marketer, not a typical agency copywriter. Based on my search for copywriters, such a person is rare.

Long, relevant, interesting letters sell

Once you have your prospect's attention, the letter needs to tell an interesting story and make a complete sales pitch as to why the reader should act now.

This brings me to my favorite topic—long copy. Almost all successful direct response packages have a lot of copy. Most letters are two to four pages or more. Now, you might think that is too much to read. This is the biggest misconception people have about direct marketing.

For those who are truly interested in your restaurant, the more information the better.

Long copy always outsells short copy

Yet ask anyone and they won't believe it. In fact, they will flat out tell you that nobody reads anymore, but…

If people don't read anymore, why were there more books printed last year than in any year in the history of the world?

If people don't read anymore, why are there more magazine titles on the newsstand than at any time in history?

If people don't read anymore, why has the size of a local bookstore grown from fifteen hundred square feet to twenty thousand square feet (and that doesn't count the cappuccino bar)?

If people don't read anymore, why is the number one complaint of web surfers that they didn't find enough information when they got to a site?

I'll tell you why—because despite what the amateurs tell you, people do read but they only read things that are of strong interest to them.

At the very first marketing seminar I ever conducted, I asked forty small business owners whether they thought people would read letters that were four, eight, or even twelve pages long. They all said no. I then asked how they learned about the seminar they were attending, and they all said they received a mailing from me. This was an eleven-page letter with a four-page brochure and a personal note, a total of fifteen pages of text. I asked them how many had read the entire letter before committing $600 for the seminar (along with airfare, rental car, lodging, and meals). All but one said that they had read the entire letter before making the commitment. Some even admitted to reading it twice, including a husband and wife who had driven fifteen hundred miles from Houston to Los Angeles.

Has time changed anything? No, last year I repeated the experiment, this time attracting ninety-three people to my Golf Marketing Boot Camp at

$1,595 with an eleven-page letter. When the group was asked if anyone would read an eleven-page letter, every single one said no. But when I pointed out that it was the only way the seminar was marketed, most agreed to having read every page, with some admitting to reading the entire package three times before making their decision to buy. What people say they do and what they actually do is often different.

Don't be generic

Make your copy of great interest to your readers. Get them emotionally involved in what you have to offer. Do not settle for generic descriptions of what you offer.

- Make it live, make it breathe, make it real.
- Connect with the reader in a personal way.
- Paint a picture with your words, with them in it.
    - How will your wife feel after a bottle of bubbly and a fine meal?

People need reasons…they need benefits…they need proof…they need motivation—and it takes more than a few lines of puff to connect on a meaningful level. Don't be afraid of writing letters long enough to prove your case. There is no such thing as a letter that's too long, only one that is too boring. If people are interested in any given subject, they want more information, not less.

- Why is your restaurant better?

Remember, when developing a direct-mail campaign, design the letter, brochure, and everything else not for the people who will regard it as junk mail and just throw it away, but for the ones whose attention it will catch and whose interest it will pique. Inspire them by providing more benefits and reasons to pick up the phone or go to your website and take advantage of the unique offer you have made.

Have a conversation with your reader

The letter copy should be written as you would write a letter to a friend. It should be conversational and use simple, explicit language, free of technical jargon. It should excite the reader to want to learn more about your restaurant. It should be laced with benefits, testimonials, and true-life stories that will categorically back up your position. Tell your reader a story about someone who's really benefited from your restaurant. Someone who saved their sanity by choosing you for their wedding reception. Made a business deal, or saved a couple from divorce…thanks to you. Back up your story with lots of testimonials…fill them up with benefits, benefits, benefits. Add that real-world touch to your letter. Make it down home and folksy, like you've helped the person next door and can help them.

Make your great offer and spell out the action you want from the reader

Add in your irresistible offer using the principles in the last chapter.

The importance of your P.S.

Many people read the headline of the letter and then go straight to the end to see who signed it and read the P.S. For this reason, it is extremely important that you use both your headline and your P.S. to state your case as succinctly and powerfully as possible. Excite the reader and promise him specific and tangible rewards for taking his valuable time to read through the body of your text.

The brochure

Your brochure should be a graphical representation of your restaurant and should expand on the major points of your letter. The majority of direct-mail campaigns use either a four-page format (an 11 × 17 page folded in half) or a three- or fourfold format that is 8.5 × 11 or 11 × 17, printed on both sides.

Use the front cover for a good clean photograph or graphic that demonstrates the end result of your service. The better you can visually demonstrate the end result of your services in your lead photograph, the more effective your brochure will be. And don't forget to promise a clear benefit in the headline.

The inside of your brochure is where you repeat your story. Use a less personal approach that is full of facts and benefits. Make every line read from your prospect's perspective. If your benefits are unclear, remove that copy at once. To break up your text, use descriptive headlines, graphics, pictures, and charts. Always use captions under pictures or graphics to sell yourself or your service, never to describe what is in the picture. (Many brochures stupidly don't use captions or headlines with their photos.) Use facts, figures, statistics, surveys, comparisons, awards, and anything else to prove that you will do exactly what you say you will. Use the back panel or back page for summarizing all your benefits point by point, a brief biography dripping with benefits, or a new set of testimonials elevating your reputation. Also include a strong call to action.

The envelope

There are two different strategies when it comes to the envelope. One is to leave the impression that this is important and personal. That means using no copy, a first-class stamp, and at least a laser-printed address. (Handwritten is always better.)

The other strategy is to make it obvious that the envelope contains a solicitation, and make it so appealing that people open it anyway. Use a graphic and teaser that gets people excited and eager to open it up. Promise a clear benefit like unusual food, a better deal, or a VIP invitation.

Testing

Finally, test, test, and test. Mail some to one list, some to another list and see which letters and lists pull the best. You'll find that you can use your best lists and letters again and again with excellent results. Some say the typical response rate for a direct-mail campaign is 2 percent. Don't count on it. Figure closer to 0.5 percent until you've proven differently. Until you have a willing list of clients and followers, always figure on the low end. But follow-up telemarketing can boost your response rate much higher.

Work hard on the key factors that can make your mailings successful.

SUMMARY

The sole purpose of your print ads is to get people to take action—for example, to drive them to your website to register for an offer. Once you have their information, you do not need to run ads to reach those people again—they are yours. Let your competitors squander their money building their images. Design your ads to elicit response.

Overall, print advertising by most restaurants is poorly done. Use the rules and guidelines from this chapter to design effective ads. When you are preparing ads, run them through the Legendary Print-Ad Test and make sure they pass muster before proceeding with them.

Direct mail can pay the greatest rewards, but only if you do it right. A great offer with dramatic headlines sent to a good list is a start. Then test and refine until your mailings pull predictable, repeatable responses.

"Cheese is milk's leap toward immortality."
— **Clifton Fadiman**

CHAPTER 17

Meetings, Groups, and Special Events

Meetings, group business, catering and special events such as banquets, baby and bridal showers, wine tastings, quinceaneras, beer nights, and whiskey and cigar nights will use a variety of the tactics we have already discussed. They will also have some special strategies of their own.

Like any vertical market, the first key is to build a list of prospects, so adding specific questions to your landing page opt-ins will be key in building a list of specific interests. Having dedicated landing pages for weddings, meetings and special events will also be important.

Dedicated email blasts should remind prospects and guests of the meeting, banquet, and group services you offer. Caught up in the day-to-day or the promotion of the next event, it's amazing how few restaurants give adequate promotion to these important income generators through their normal email and social-media channels. Regular promotion of these services should be programmed into your media plan.

In this chapter, you will discover:

- ✓ how to give people a reason to come,
- ✓ how to effectively use LinkedIn,
- ✓ the power of the Guru Strategy, and
- ✓ the secret of Thunderbolt Marketing.

Dedicated Landing Pages

We provide all our clients with dedicated event landing pages. Every major event, be it a micro beer tasting or a ski picnic, gets its own dedicated page. Each can be targeted to specific customers by preference and vertical traffic will be sent from Facebook or other online sources.

Auto Responders

Each of our landing pages will often include an opt-in that in turn triggers a series of custom auto responders keeping the restaurant front and center in the prospect's mind and building the restaurant's story bit by bit along the way. At one restaurant we doubled wedding business in just a few months by adding nine auto responders to a landing page that offered a free wedding-planning guide.

Email Promotion

Meeting, weddings, and group event promotions should be included in your monthly newsletters and the occasional dedicated blast should be included in your marketing plan to remind all guests of the capabilities you have.

Social Media

Meetings, weddings, and group event promotions should be included regularly in your social-media posts. "Name drop" by welcoming groups to your restaurant, congratulating the happy couple and sharing pictures of everyone having fun. It's a kind of testimonial.

Program events into a ninety-day plan to insure they are neither forgotten nor promoted too regularly. I frequently see restaurants do none, then suddenly weddings are posted everyday using pictures, memes, and testimonials.

IN-LOBBY PROMOTIONS

Your lobby is a great place to set up a display of your private dining or banquets capabilities since every guest will come there sooner or later. In addition to a table-top or booth-like display, always provide a small brochure or flyer so guests can take the information to others who may have an interest.

Creating Unique Events Gives People a Reason to Book

Just about every restaurant in the world has New Year's Eve events and Valentine's Day events along with Christmas, Easter, Hanukkah, and whatever your local holidays may be. These events are usually sell-out dates and are highly profitable. But you don't have to wait for the calendar to provide the reason to book. Over time, you can create your own highly profitable events. Events that give people a reason to come on a specific week rather than whenever they get around to taking a break. Better still if that event is created to increase demand during traditionally weak dates.

Some of the events our clients have run include:

Garland Resorts Zhivago Night—this is the most fun, intimate, and exciting meal event held at Garland.

Imagine for a moment, Garland's thirty-five hundred acres of forests, lakes, and streams covered in a blanket of snow...The evening begins with a horse-drawn sleigh ride to the Bridge Inn, outlined with hundreds of tiny lights. It's there you'll recline by the fire, awaiting your five-course, wild-game dinner, accompanied by exquisite wine and other beverages.

This rustic log building is charming and homey, making you feel as though you've traveled back in time to a gentler, simpler era.

We set the mood, what happens back at the room... well that's up to you.

The Gourmet Glide: The Tastiest Ski Trail in the World
We've combined two of your favorite activities—cross-country skiing and eating.

The Gourmet Glide is a scintillating ski and feast trip covering ten kilometers of immaculately groomed cross-country ski trails. Five buffet stations are strategically placed along the route for your gastronomic enjoyment. The food is the very best we have to offer. In fact, it's so tasty that your biggest challenge is to leave each station and slide to the next. The entire family will love this event and it's guilt free since you'll burn off the calories as you glide.

Foodie Events—These are becoming more and more popular around the world with everything form cooking classes, to guest chefs (sometimes a celebrity chef), other times a guest who gets to help prepare the dish in the kitchen and, of course, invites all his or her friends. These are often combined with a cultural event as well.

Some examples of events you could run are:

- Winefest
- Chili cook off
- Farm to Fork dinners
- Events centered around a popular fruit or vegetable in your area such as a strawberry festival
- Beer tap takeovers with a local brewery
- Events for "national days" like taco day, pizza day, etc. There is something for every day of the year.

The list goes on and on, it's up to you to find something that will cater to your audience.

Beer and Wine Events—While Oktoberfest is always a winner, we are seeing a lot more events involving craft beers and locally produced wines.

Music Events—The Green Hotel in Kinross, Scotland, has its own music venue and books acts year-round that attract both local and out-of-town guests.

Comedy Night—A staple event at many restaurants. Who doesn't love a good laugh?

Take the Events From Other Cultures and Make Them Yours

In the United States, St. Patrick's Day is just as big as it is in Ireland as an excuse to drink, eat cabbage, and party but there are many more events around the world you can tie into to create a buzz at your restaurant.

Cinco de Mayo, or the fifth of May—This date commemorates the

Mexican army's 1862 victory over France at the Battle of Puebla during the Franco-Mexican War (1861–67). A relatively minor holiday in Mexico, in the United States Cinco de Mayo has evolved into a celebration of Mexican culture and heritage, particularly in areas with large Mexican-American populations. Cinco de Mayo traditions include parades, mariachi music performances, and street festivals in cities and towns across Mexico and the United States.

Guy Fawkes Day—Remember the fifth of November…

Guy Fawkes and twelve coconspirators spent months planning to blow up King James I of England during the opening of Parliament on November 5, 1605. But their assassination attempt was foiled the night before when Fawkes was discovered lurking in a cellar below the House of Lords next to thirty-six barrels of gunpowder. Londoners immediately began lighting bonfires in celebration that the plot had failed, and a few months later Parliament declared November 5 a public day of thanksgiving. Guy Fawkes Day, also known as Bonfire Night, has been around in one form or another ever since. In recent times it has served mainly as an excuse to watch fireworks, make bonfires, drink mulled wine, and burn Guy Fawkes effigies (along with the effigies of current politicians and celebrities).

So now you have a great excuse to hold a July fourth–type celebration in November.

Bastille Day—July Fourteenth

Parisian revolutionaries and mutinous troops storm and dismantle the Bastille, a royal fortress that had come to symbolize the tyranny of the Bourbon monarchs. This dramatic action signaled the beginning of the French Revolution.

Grab your wine and baguette—this is the best excuse we have ever heard for some great French wine and cheese.

British Night or Weekend

Bangers and mash, roast beef, and Yorkshire pudding, and some fine English ales.

Texas Week, Night or Weekend

Cowboy theme, with barbeque food and corn on the cob, country music, and line dancing.

The possibilities are endless and fun. All it takes is a little creativity and planning to turn a boring week into a fun-filled festival.

LINKEDIN STRATEGY

LinkedIn offers one of the very best sources of meeting and group business. Your manager should be very active on LinkedIn. That means expanding their connections daily, posting daily, writing articles weekly, and being active in groups. Yes, it's a lot of work but the payoff is equally large. You need to develop a daily routine to be effective. I do all this long before I go to the office:

Start each day by asking for new connections

I ask for at least ten a day. Choose your connections wisely based on their potential ability to do business with your restaurant. Use a custom introduction rather than the standard LinkedIn one. Focus local groups that make sense like "Orlando entrepreneurs" if you have a restaurant in Orlando.

Post something of interest each day

The LinkedIn post feature is really Facebook for professionals, albeit on a more professional level so the same rules apply—engage, educate, entertain, and then and only then sell.

Comment on posts

Like and comment on other people's posts; they want feedback and recognition of their efforts as much as you do. Try not to go with the generic one- or two-word comments that everyone else does; stand out with yours to ensure that the comments are memorable.

Contribute an article at least once a week

This may well be something you get your marketing company to do for you and might include a title like:

Ten Ways to Spice up Your Next Meeting

Each and every article you produce should offer a direct benefit to CEOs or meeting planner: Your restaurant can sometimes be one of the keys.

For example, to spice up your next meeting, point ten might be: choose the right surroundings. *The beautiful and pristine surroundings of our restaurant's mountain location are sure to stir the creative thinking of your audience.*

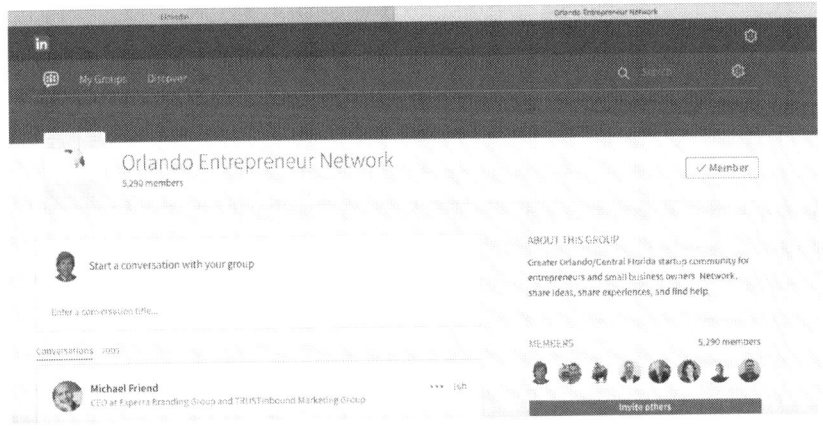

Share your articles with your groups

The power of joining groups is you can then share your articles with your groups. You can join up to fifty groups, which in my case gives me the potential to share my message with almost two million people!

Review your messages and respond daily

Like any social media, speed is a strategy and responding to something forty-eight hours later is most likely a day late and a dollar short!

THUNDERBOLT STRATEGY

Too many restaurants scatter their efforts to gain meeting or group business. I have had far greater response on a more strategic approach. Instead of blowing your budget on mass efforts, target five hundred handpicked people whom you know for a fact hold meetings or group events. In the chapter on building a list, I provided details on how to handcraft a list of prospects. That may involve the use of telemarketing to physically confirm that the person is alive and breathing and still in charge of a function.

Once you have a highly targeted list, you should focus all your efforts on converting that list to business. Since it's often impossible to tell when someone might make the decision to book a group or meeting, it's important that your restaurant be in front of those decision makers as often as possible in as many creative ways as possible. Which rules out sending the same boring corporate speak packages that everyone else does.

Most of our campaigns call for at least seven contacts, although the majority of business usually comes in after the forth. January through March, and September to early November are the most responsive months. I would avoid the summer months entirely.

While you can attempt to pull this off through email alone, mailing something by snail mail has more impact than ever. What you send will depend on your restaurant but here are a few of the creative ideas we have used to demand attention:

At springtime we included a packet of colorful flower seeds with our sales letter touting the beauty of our restaurant and the creative thinking it would inspire.

To a ladies group we sent a colorful, individual blueberry tea bag along with a sales letter that stressed our afternoon tea as a great event to get the group bonding.

When people get an envelope with something in it, they can't help but be curious, even excited, to open it. The more creative you are, the more impressed they will be, and the more likely they are to consider your restaurant. It's very important that the sales letter matches the gift in creativity and is not the same boring corporate speak they get from every other restaurant.

In today's market you have to be smarter and more focused. This strategy makes perfect sense, go ahead, and get started.

SUMMARY

Make your meetings, groups, and special events an integrated part of your marketing plan, not just an occasional add-on "when you have time." Use dedicated landing pages for each income source and indeed for each event. Create events that give people a reason to book now. Use the power of LinkedIn to grow your contact list and get your content in front of potential buyers. Hand pick a target list of prospects and focus a continual creative effort on them using my Thunderbolt Marketing strategy. Last but not least, build more personal contacts who can bring business to your door like the pied piper.

"The other night I ate at a real nice family restaurant. Every table had an argument going."
- George Carlin

CHAPTER 18

Legendary Sales—Get Ready to Maximize Sales

Recently I had a call from a well-known but struggling local restaurant asking what one idea I could give them to instantly improve revenue. The answer was easy and would have been the same had the caller wanted to sell more pizza, cocktails, sandwiches or steaks.

Train Your People How to Sell— Turn Severs into Sellers!

Nowhere in this entire book will you get faster results in terms of pure income than in this and the following chapter on how to sell.

Few people in the hospitality business genuinely love selling. Fewer still are good at it. In many ways, it's not surprising that most people don't like to sell. Selling not only has a bad image in many people's minds, *it often deserves it*. Telemarketing calls at dinner time, pushy salespeople who won't take no for an answer, and products and services that don't live up to the sales claims. These have all contributed to the bad image that sales has today.

In defense of sales, almost everyone sells in their everyday lives. Teachers need to sell students on the benefits of paying attention, spouses sell their ideas to each other, children sell their parents on staying up for that special TV show, and so on. Practice will bring comfort if you have the right attitude.

Increasing your sales skills by even a few increments can dramatically increase your restaurants income. Imagine if you closed two out of four banquet leads instead of one—you have just doubled sales at no cost! Even small improvements in how you answer the phone, handle objections, and close can have a massive impact on your restaurant's bottom line. Yet few, if any, restaurants engage in sales training. "Sales training" generally consists of a review of the day's specials and the wine of the week that needs pushing.

Before you can sell, there are several things you will need to understand in more detail. First, you must understand the fears that hold most people back from maximizing their sales potential. Next, you must learn about bonding with prospects and developing rapport. Finally, you will discover secrets for quickly qualifying your prospects so you focus more of your time on the people most likely to buy.

In this chapter, you will discover:

- ✓ how to overcome typical sales fear,
- ✓ how to develop instant rapport,
- ✓ how to separate suspects from prospects, and
- ✓ how to qualify prospects.

GETTING MENTALLY READY TO SELL

It is not the mountain we conquer, but ourselves. —**Sir Edmund Hillary, first man to stand atop Mt. Everest**

Sincerity sells

If you believe in what you are selling, your sincere attitude will communicate itself to your prospective customers. But you must have a positive attitude about the sales situation as well. If you feel uncomfortable selling, your guests will feel uncomfortable buying from you.

CONQUERING THE THREE GREAT FEARS

Before you can set off in pursuit of your quest for more business, you must overcome the three great fears that hold back mere ordinary mortals. These fears exist in some degree to almost everyone, even great salespeople. They are:

- ✓ Fear of money
- ✓ Fear of failure/rejection

Until you have confronted these fears and put them behind you forever, you will not achieve your true sales potential.

FEAR OF MONEY

Believe it or not, many salespeople are afraid to ask for money.

Why should a waiter or manager be afraid to ask for money?

They may be afraid to ask for large sums of money because they don't have enough money to buy the products they are selling. The fact that they are selling something like a $5,000 wedding rehearsal dinner that they themselves cannot afford may lead them to believe, at least subconsciously, that other people can't afford it either. The same thought often occurs with a $200 bottle of wine. People too often place a mental barrier on themselves and, in doing so, thwart their own efforts to obtain the success they deserve.

In my work with restaurants I still find that despite the fact that many of these people are working with some of the most affluent individuals in the country, most are desperately afraid of asking for money. In this case, it's not because they don't make decent money themselves but because they don't want to be thought of as salespeople. What they don't seem to appreciate is that 90 percent of the people they deal with are businesspeople who aren't offended by being asked for money. They expect it.

Overcoming your fear of money

It's okay to make money selling. The more people you help to enjoy the benefits that your restaurant offers, the more money you deserve to make.

Whether or not *you* can afford to spend a king's ransom on your daughter's wedding rehearsal or Bat Mitzvah does not mean that others can't. Whether or not you think it's expensive doesn't matter at all. Put your personal thoughts and prejudices away. Let your prospective guests decide whether or not they will spend their money. It's your job to give them the opportunity.

FEAR OF FAILURE OR REJECTION

One of the reasons mature people stop learning is they become less and less willing to risk failure.—**John Gardner**

Sometimes the problem that holds salespeople back is fear of failure or rejection. If managers had real faith in their restaurant, they wouldn't feel rejected when prospects say no, but would sympathize with the prospects for not having the wisdom or money to take advantage of the opportunity they are being offered.

What's the worst that can happen?

When you make a phone call, greet an appointment, or welcome an event planner for an on-site visit, what is the worst thing that can occur? I mean, after you have introduced yourself, made a presentation, and asked them to book an event, what's the absolute worst thing that can happen to you?

The prospect can hang up, walk out, call your mother names, or say no. That's it. Those are the worst things that can possibly happen. Compared to the millions of people who are dying every day, rejection is pretty minor. Great! Now let's move on.

There is one small problem we didn't mention—**ego!**

Our fragile human egos are such that when a person rejects our proposition, we take it as a personal affront. We feel humiliated, embarrassed, or even belittled. Rejection attacks our self-confidence and self-esteem.

Yet if we can let it go for what it is—a rejection of a sales proposition—we will have jumped a hurdle that many never cross.

Sales is a numbers game

You know that when people don't buy your restaurant for their group or event, they are *not* rejecting you. You know that when people can't afford what your restaurant offers, they're *not* rejecting you. You know that when people are looking for a freebie rather than a real booking, they're *not* rejecting you. How could it be personal when they don't even know *you*?

Yes, it can *feel* like rejection. But come on; it's not.

Sales are a numbers game. Depending on the quality of your leads, and the product you are selling only one in twenty or one in ten or one in five of the people you call may buy. So when most people say no, they're *not* rejecting you.

Yes, many people will say no to you if you're doing your job. But every no gets you closer to the person who wants to book. And even the people who say no can give you referrals to friends who are more serious about holding an event or whose needs are more in line with what your restaurant offers.

So even if you *feel* like you're being rejected, you're not. You can't get over your feelings immediately, but you can begin. Take control of your feelings and move on to successful sales.

Our greatest glory is in never falling, but in rising every time we fall. —**Confucius**

The power of persistence: the five reasons you must persist

Persistence is a virtue that many salespeople overlook. There are five key reasons why you must be persistent if you are to join the ranks of Legendary Salespeople. Knowing them will benefit both you and your prospects.

1. The customer doesn't always know what's in his best interest at first. You may have new information for him. You have to persist and educate him.

2. Prospects are almost always reluctant to change. You must persist and help them realize what the cost will be if they don't change.

3. Your prospects often have difficulty comparing different offer from different places and become confused. Confused people are afraid of making a mistake. Instead of buying, they procrastinate on making a decision. You must persist in your attempts to minimize the confusion and provide them with a clear path to enjoying the benefits of your restaurant.

4. Prospects have many different priorities. You must persist and help them arrange their priorities in such a way that your proposal moves up the list and helps them achieve their goals.

5. Some prospects are just not ready to buy right now. They might, however, buy next month or next year. You must persist to make sure you are still in the forefront of their minds when they eventually do.

BUILDING RAPPORT

Rapport is the ability to bond with another person as you would with a friend and, for a good salesperson, it is the most sought after of all conditions. Good rapport puts other people at their ease. They treat you as a *person* they are comfortable with, *not* a *sales*person.

You start most sales relationships with one strike against you. People assume that you have *your* interests at heart rather than theirs. Thus, they naturally don't trust you until you can demonstrate that you are interested in them and can be helpful to them. Because of this negative conditioning, it is essential that you go the extra mile to be courteous, friendly, and professional as you start building rapport.

Calming your prospects' fears

When people walk into your restaurant to explore their options, it is very probable that they do so with some degree of trepidation. They are unsure of what to expect. Maybe you'll put a lot of pressure on them, and it will be unpleasant. Maybe they won't be able to justify the booking to their boss, spouse, or partners.

One way to make most people more comfortable is to immediately tell them what will happen. For instance, you could say something like:

Here's what I was planning to do in our time together: Ask you a few questions about your events needs, tell you about our restaurant and our menus options, show you around, and answer your questions. Does that sound reasonable? Is there anything you want to know before we get started?

Your foremost task in the initial sales contact is to make your prospect feel comfortable with you. Until this happens, it will be impossible for the prospect to make a buying decision. Use the first few minutes to remove the prospect's fear and help him or her to relax.

If you don't sell yourself first, you won't sell anything

Men in general judge far more from appearances than from reality. All men have eyes, but few have the gift of penetration.—**Niccolo Machiavelli**

If prospects don't like you, they will not buy from you. That's pretty simple, isn't it? Consider for a moment. Do you buy products and services from people you don't like? No? Neither do most other people. Above all else, selling requires *selling yourself* to the prospect. If you don't do that, no sales technique in the world is going to save you.

The first few seconds of your contact with a prospect can determine your success in any sales interview. First impressions are lasting impressions and are usually the right impressions, at least as far as your prospect is concerned.

Your appearance

The way you dress is very important in selling. Always be careful to strike a happy medium between *over* dressing and *under* dressing. Smartly attired people have an air of success about them. Without overpowering the audience you will be selling to, make an effort to improve your image by improving the quality of your clothing and tailoring. In the words of Henry

Ward Beecher, "Clothes and manner do not make the man. But when he is made, they greatly improve his appearance."

Develop winning personal traits

When asked what great secret he had found to influence people to his way of thinking, Abraham Lincoln replied, "If you would win a man over to your cause, first convince him that you are his sincere friend." To a great extent, the way people react to you depends on the little things—like smiling. When you are introduced to someone, always respond with a warm and friendly smile. Shake hands firmly because there are few things that turn people off quicker than a limp handshake. Stand up straight with your shoulders back and chest forward. Make good eye contact and generally let the other person know by your body language that you are a successful, professional, friendly, and confident individual who is genuinely glad to meet them.

How do you sound?

Next to your appearance, the tone of your voice and the way you deliver your words are the most important parts of making a good impression on the prospect. Make your conversation enthusiastic, friendly, and professional. If the prospect talks in a loud voice, raise yours slightly above its normal level. If the prospect speaks quietly, lower your voice a couple of decibels. Mirror your prospect's speech patterns by speaking a little slower or a little faster as appropriate. Remember, people establish the highest levels of rapport with others who are just like them. Your voice can indicate to prospects that you are indeed like them.

Body language

The value of matching your prospect is equally true of basic body language. If the person you are dealing with has a military bearing and stands straight and tall rather than lounging or slumping, it will definitely pay you to do the same. In your office, if the prospect leans forward, so should you. In short, mirroring your prospect's largely unconscious physical demeanor is one of the most effective ways to rapidly establish rapport. Be sure to use this technique in conjunction with the others mentioned in this chapter.

Compliments

Giving genuine compliments about your prospect or his possessions will almost certainly bring a favorable response; however, use caution in this area. Prospects easily detect insincerity. If you are insincere, you will lose their confidence, never to regain it. There are ways to make sure this never happens to you. Never make a compliment you do not mean, and add a qualifying statement to all your compliments for added weight.

Qualifiers prove your sincerity. Your compliment is made more meaningful and personal if you add a brief remark to prove you mean what you say. For example, you might say to a woman who walks into your restaurant, "That's a beautiful sweater." Then immediately add a qualifier. "I gave one just like that to my wife last Christmas." You have demonstrated your sincerity. Why would you buy a sweater for your wife if you didn't find it attractive?

What's in a name?

One of the surest ways to develop rapport is to remember a person's name. In his classic book, *How to Win friends and Influence People*, Dale Carnegie stated, "The sound of a person's name said correctly is one of the nicest sounds in the world, at least to them." Using someone's name is indeed one of the sincerest compliments you can pay a person. It builds self-esteem and lets him know you think he is important.

How to open a rapport-building conversation

In order to build rapport beyond the superficial stages, you have to get the prospect to talk to you. The best way to accomplish this is to ask open-ended questions. Open-ended questions are questions that can't be answered with a simple yes or no. They demand a more detailed response.

Not only does this method build rapport, since you allow the customer to respond without interruption or contradiction, but it also provides you with valuable data for use in the sales presentation. After you exchange names, it's time to start casual questioning. You will be using the responses not just for data, but also to develop future questions.

- Where are you originally from, Jack?
- How long have you been with XYZ company?

Move smoothly from basic questions to more specific lines of inquiry.

- Where have you held your events in the past?
- What are you doing differently this time?

The more others talk about themselves, the more rapport you will be building, especially if you use active listening techniques.

Developing active listening techniques to increase rapport

Active listening means showing the prospect that you are not only listening to what he has to say, but you are also interested in what he is saying. Here are some of the ways you can do this:

- ✓ By holding eye contact and not looking around at anything else.
- ✓ By nodding your head at appropriate points.
- ✓ By raising an eyebrow to express surprise.
- ✓ By laughing, smiling, and making occasional comments like, "Yes," "Uh-huh," or "I see" to show you are an active participant in the conversation, even though you aren't doing the talking.

You will find that such active listening will draw people out and they will consider you an interesting person. In fact, the more they talk, the more they think you are a great conversationalist!

How people process information affects rapport

After all, when you come right down to it, how many people speak the same language, even when they speak the same language? —**Russell Hoban**

Essentially, people process information in one of three main ways—visually, aurally, and kinesthetically. Knowing which of these applies to a particular person can give you a much better chance of getting your point across.

If prospects comment on the view or the artwork, they are almost certainly visual (and the majority of people fall into this category.) If they comment first on the smell of food, they are probably kinesthetic. If they ask you to *tell* them about your banquet room or the menu options, then they are probably auditory. In cases where someone displays a combination of two, or even all three of these forms, you can use multiple approaches, but one of them will usually be dominant. Understanding this human characteristic can be invaluable to your presentation by helping you to communicate better and faster with your prospects.

Asking a kinesthetic prospect to look at something is not nearly as valuable as having him do it himself. If you prevent a kinesthetic person from "feeling" things, you risk losing the sale. In the same way, if you simply talk to a visually oriented person, you will soon lose his or her interest.

If you can't tell which method your prospect uses to process his information, try to use all three in your speech patterns. (It takes a little practice.) You will either find out what you need to know or at least will be sure that you have covered all the bases.

QUALIFYING YOUR PROSPECTS

Once rapport has been achieved, the next step in the sales process is to qualify your prospects. One of the biggest complaints by salespeople is that they have "unqualified leads." The corresponding complaint from managers is that their salespeople can't close sales from the "great leads" they are given. To have success in any sales, you need to set up a system and then measure the results to demonstrate its effectiveness. You need to produce qualified leads, train your salespeople well and measure performance.

Who is a qualified prospect?

Traditionally, a qualified prospect is someone who has a need for your product or service and the means to pay for it. So if you are a pizza and beer restaurant, almost everyone will be qualified. But if you are a high-end steak house selling group business events, banquets and corporate catering, you will want further qualifications such as high income or a hefty budget. And you will need further information about their "means." You need to help them justify the purchase. You need to find out how they would pay for it and you need to find out how they will measure the value they receive for their event.

Some prospects are more equal than others!

The success of group sales programs is based on generating the total number of leads needed to reach your goals. Successful programs recognize that leads come in various qualities even with qualifiers in place.

If you look at your prospects as a whole, you will get a very wide range of people—from those chomping at the bit to sign up to those with no intention of ever buying. Think of them as A, B, C, and D prospects:

- ✓ "A" leads include past guests, referrals, and event planers unhappy with their current location.
- ✓ "B" leads are considering several options and can afford what you offer if they are shown the service and value they expect.
- ✓ "C" leads might be prospects or might not. They could be a source of future business and should be kept on a tickler program.
- ✓ "D" leads are simply not real prospects, they can't afford you or their brother manages a competing restaurant.

The bottom line is that all leads should be counted and standards created for the conversion of each kind. Referrals might sell at the rate of one in two or three, while web leads might sell one in twenty or thirty. You should measure an average return from each source.

Questions to ask

You need to develop a series of questions that not only qualifies people but also goes further to expand their thinking about their needs and your offer. For instance, confirming that prospects have a need and fit your restaurant's income category isn't enough. You need to cover space requirements, dates, and number of attendees. Prospects need to see you as helping them satisfy their needs, not selling to them to meet yours. Your questions need to be interesting to them. They need to enjoy the conversation.

The key qualifying questions you ask will depend on the nature of your offer and on your location.

Here are some examples, depending on the situation:

- ✓ Where have you held your events in the past?
- ✓ What did you enjoy most about that location?
- ✓ Typically, how many people attend?
- ✓ What is your group's budget?
- ✓ What made you consider our restaurant?

Casually work the three or four most important questions you need into your initial conversation.

Qualified is not motivated

The key flaw in most sales systems is that they don't acknowledge that *most technically qualified prospects are not motivated to act now*. For meetings, weddings, anniversaries and banquets, motivation is usually not a problem. That is, those prospects need to contract with a facility in a specific time frame, so they are motivated.

For non-time specific events prospects may have an interest in making a purchase, but they have no urgency. The decision can be put off forever. Another reason people will delay acting is because they don't feel a connection to you. There is no relationship. They have no reason to trust you. They have no desire to please you. This is where long-term qualifying can come into play. If you approach prospects realizing that many will take a year to commit to action or make up their minds, you will design a sales system that allows you to keep in touch and build the relationship in addition to finding the short-term sales.

Why qualified prospects don't raise their hands

One complication in qualifying people is that sometimes your best prospects won't say that they want what you have to offer and can afford it. Why do people deny being good prospects? They do it for a many reason that vary from wanting to stay in control of the situation to wanting to make you jump through a few hoops. Another reason for sales resistance is the desire to see how good you are—how persistent and how skilled. These people are sophisticated in business. They are familiar with most sales approaches. If they have time, they may entertain themselves watching how you sell to them. They may also use resistance as a way to test your sincerity. They throw up obstacles but expect you to overcome them. They reason that if you're willing to put a lot of effort into signing them up, you may be more likely to put effort into making them happy once they buy.

False prospects

On the other hand, there are people who will lie about their interest. These people may be retired and miss the action of business. Or they may simply like whatever freebies you offer. Interestingly enough, there are also situations where people who have no intention of buying end up doing so. Timeshare vacation rentals are a prime example. Almost no one who goes to a presentation intends to buy, but enough do to keep the hard-sell sales practices going. You'll have to make your best guess on how hard to qualify prospects, and then test to develop a better profile of actual buyers.

SUMMARY

To maximize your sales potential, you must understand and overcome the common fears that hold back most people in sales—fear of money and fear of rejection. In sales, success is up to you. Manage your time well and realize that the more no's you get, the more sales you will make.

Learn how to quickly build rapport with your prospects by asking open-ended questions, demonstrating active listing techniques, and being aware of your body language. Once rapport is established, probe to qualify the prospect. There is no point in spending time selling to people who don't want to buy. By setting up a qualifying system, you will improve your results, make prospects happier, and have more fun selling. Design your system for both short- and long-term sales. While you harvest the "low hanging fruit," you will be building relationships for long-term sales. Even prospects who never buy may become sources of referrals and positive word of mouth when they are treated professionally and respectfully.

"What I say is that, if a man really likes potatoes, he must be a pretty decent sort of fellow."
— **A.A. Milne**

Andrew Wood

CHAPTER 19

Selling Private Events, Banquets and Catering

Selling private events, banquets and catering services in a competitive market takes real sales skills, skills that are often lacking in many restaurateurs. The higher price tickets involved in these transactions demand a higher level of skill and preparation on your part.

Once a prospect has been greeted, bonded with, and qualified, it's time to get to the meat of the presentation, handle objections, and close the sale. All presentations should be scripted and orchestrated for optimum results. If you do not approach presentations in a scripted systematic manner, your approach and results will differ from day to day and person to person—but you won't know what is causing the variation.

To get the most from your sales, you must follow a system and be prepared with perfect answers to any question. Since you can double your profits by doubling your sales results, it will pay you to keep track of what you're doing and what works.

Objections are a natural part of the sales process. While you might prefer that people come in with their checks in hand, already all made out to your restaurant, it's natural for people to have questions or concerns just as *you* would in any major purchasing decision. These concerns are generally expressed as objections. An objection is nothing more than a question in the mind of the buyer that has to be defined and answered. It gives you the chance to clarify or improve your presentation. A prospect who does not raise objections is not engaged in thinking about your presentation. Most sales are lost simply by not asking for the sale. Close early and close often. Find the closing techniques that best suit your style and audience and use them.

In this chapter, you will discover:

- ✓ how to build a perfect presentation,
- ✓ how to uncover and isolate objections,
- ✓ the five-step process to deal with objections,
- ✓ the *feel, felt, found* way to deal with objections,
- ✓ exactly what to say to specific objections,
- ✓ how to spot closing signals, and
- ✓ how to close.

I never learn anything just by talking. I only learn things when I ask questions.
—**Lou Holtz**

MAKING AN EFFECTIVE PRESENTATION

Because each presentation is different, this book can only give you pieces to use and an approach to put "standard" pieces together with your own custom material. As you design your presentation, start by assuming that everyone who has qualified as a prospect wants to buy and buy *now*. This may eventually prove to be incorrect but assume it anyway. Many people who are on the "edge" will make the decision to buy without your having to make a great deal of effort simply because you are so confident, they want what you have to offer and today is the day they should buy. Use phrases like *"when* you hold your meeting here" rather than "*if* you hold your meeting here."

Getting the audience involved in the action

The more senses you can bring into play during the presentation, the better your chances of making a sale.

Using questions for involvement

Questions can be an important part of your presentation by getting the prospects *involved* with your points. Prospects can't just sit back and pretend to listen when you ask them questions. And often, even if they wanted to remain detached, good questions will "hook" them into considering you more seriously. As mentioned earlier, open-ended questions—questions that can't be answered yes or no—are best. Ask questions that get them talking about things that relate to features or benefits of your restaurant.

The points you need to cover

Many people think that giving a great presentation requires the gift of the gab or a certain type of personality. Not so. There are many ways to give a winning presentation, the best of which is to write a script and practice it until you can deliver a legendary performance.

A good presentation script will read a lot like a good direct-mail letter. It will be full of features and benefits. While features are more objective, your emphasis should be on the benefits. There are usually more benefits than you think, and many of them are several levels deep.

List the features of your restaurant that you want to cover in your presentation. They should include features such as:

- ✓ History
- ✓ Meeting and banquet space
- ✓ Food and beverage options
- ✓ Outside gathering areas

Now list the benefits that come from your features. (You may skip many features and go straight to benefits in your presentation.)

- ✓ Family recreation and togetherness
- ✓ Great location, easy to get to
- ✓ Relaxation
- ✓ Fabulous wedding pictures
- ✓ Status location
- ✓ Amazing food with great craft beers and local wines
- ✓ Team of professionals to do the work for you

When you simply spell out each benefit you want to convey, you have your basic presentation. Add a few testimonials and you're well on your way.

Quitting while you're ahead

One thing that epitomizes Legendary Selling is knowing exactly when to stop presenting and start closing. The key to selling anything is getting the prospect excited about your offer. Once that has been accomplished, you must provide him with logical reasons why he must buy *today*. Then you must close. Continuing to talk after the prospect is ready to buy is overkill and often leads to lost sales rather than successful closing.

Anticipating objections

When Abraham Lincoln was a lawyer, he always summed up his opponent's arguments before he gave his side. That way the jury saw him as a fair man and he got to "frame" his opponent's points the way he wanted to. If you *know* that certain concerns will be in the prospect's mind during your presentation, you are usually better off dealing with them as part of your presentation. Otherwise, prospects will tend to not listen to *your* points as they think about the problems on their own. For instance, price is often a concern, so acknowledge it and show how the value that your restaurant delivers outweighs the cost. Another example is competitive restaurants. You need to know how they compare to your restaurant on all important dimensions. When people are looking at other restaurants you need to deal with them briefly in your presentation. Never "bad-mouth" other restaurants. Say something like you hear they are very nice, and then cover your relative advantages.

Too many choices

Complexity is your enemy. It only confuses prospects. Design your presentation to offer no more than three options. If you have to present more than three options, do it in stages. For example, if you have nine menu options, offer three groups of three. Help your prospect to reach a decision on which group of options appears to be most suitable, then concentrate on those three options in detail. When you give people too many choices, they become confused. When they are confused, they become scared, and when they are scared, they rarely make a buying decision.

Reduce risk, build trust

Another thing you can do is to use guarantees to reduce people's perceived risk. Make their choosing you a safe choice so that they can reap your benefits for themselves and their families. Written testimonials can produce some trust effect, especially if the testimonials are from people similar to them.

The to-the-point sales presentation

The entire banquet sale process should, in most cases, take no longer than fifteen minutes from contact to close. If you take too much time, your prospect will probably become bored or confused as the presentation drags on, and you will be frustrated as a result. Tighten up your presentation. Be fast, fluid, and professional. Act as if completing a sale is second nature to you, and you do it every hour of the day, week in and week out. After all, selling *should* become second nature to you.

Use emotion backed up by logic

You want to use emotion: the excitement the prospect experiences as a result of his perception of the benefits your restaurant will bring him or her. Your prospect should feel that this pleasurable sensation is real and waiting for him or her alone.

Once prospects have decided to buy, they use logic to come up with good reasons to justify their decisions. Back up their reasons with your own supporting evidence. Indicate features and benefits that they may not have considered and you will make the sale. Help them to see that their emotional reasons are also logical ones. Reinforce the buying decision by complimenting them on their choice and assuring them, sincerely, that you know they will get satisfaction and pleasure from their event.

What's in it for me?

A basic motivating force that drives nearly everybody is "What's in it for me?" Some salespeople are so busy selling that they can't see the forest for the trees. Few, if any, prospects will be initially interested in the *quality* of the service you offer them. That may come later. Initially, they will be much more concerned about what the restaurant and *you* will do to make them and their event shine. You must understand that their decisions are often exercises in positive selfishness.

Write it down

You should address all the above points and actually type up a script for selling groups, banquets, and anything else you sell. This should include diagrams of the very best places to stand as you deliver your lines and point at something of interest. It takes time, but once you have done it you will reap big dividends, and the script will always be there for training as staff come and go.

OVERCOMING OBJECTIONS

Objections are a necessary part of the sales process. Learn to deal with them and you will close a much higher percentage of the prospects you meet. Unfortunately, many salespeople take objections personally and their ability to complete the sale is adversely influenced by this negativity.

It's not personal. They are turning down buying, not turning down *you*.

Think of objections not as rejections but as steps toward your final goal. Rather than fearing objections, you need to ask good questions to bring them out. An objection is not the *end* of the sales process; it is the beginning. Many objections mask a real or perceived problem. Hidden objections are often associated with money. They will not want to admit that they are not qualified or don't have decision authority.

Overcoming objections is usually taught in a one-step sales approach, and it *is* one step for smaller items such as booking a table for twelve. But for group and wedding sales, you can't expect everyone to make a fast decision. As long as you have permission to keep in touch with the prospect, you are in the game. Keep in touch for the short term when they're in the decision-making mode. And if necessary, keep in touch for the long term as there will always be other meetings. Some objections will dissipate over time. "I'm happy with restaurant we use now" may change—either their current restaurant will make a "mistake," or you will use the repeated sales contacts to better build value. When you keep in touch with them, you build your credibility and sincerity. Put them on an email nurturing list and they will see all the activities they are missing. That gives you something to build on to resell them at a later date.

Sometimes you have to break out of the cycle of sales resistance that can be created between you and a prospect. You have to step back and say "George, I've talked to you several times about bringing your group here and we don't seem to be making any progress. I don't want to keep bothering you—should I just leave you alone?" This will often turn the situation around—they'll start to sell you on why you should keep in touch. And they'll often tell you their true objection. The key is for them to talk to you person to person, *not* prospect to salesperson.

Some objections arise as the result of nothing more serious than a lack of understanding. Your presentation doesn't come across. In these cases, it is necessary to further define and explain the benefits of your restaurant in clear and simple language. Use your banquet info kit as the excellent business tool it should be. Put it in front of the prospect and check off the listed benefits, giving a short explanation of each benefit as you go. When features and benefits are there in black and white, any misunderstandings should soon vanish.

Anticipate the objection

As mentioned earlier, many objections can be dealt with in the sales presentation by bringing them up before the prospect does and taking away the objection before it is even voiced. Those that can't be dealt with during the presentation should have already been anticipated and a perfect answer scripted out as the response.

> **In a system, there can only be one perfect answer to any objection.**

The answer to each objection should be carefully crafted to be the best answer possible, then should be learned and used by everyone on staff exactly as scripted. This is the type of approach used by Disney, Ritz Carlton, and other world-renowned companies for a simple reason—it works.

This may sound very rigid, but, if you really think about it, it's true at least 95 percent of the time that a scripted answer works best. Sure, intuition and experience can come into play 5 percent of the time, but 95 percent of the time a well-orchestrated response will produce better results. That's why movies have scripts. That's why comedians have scripts and practice them so they don't sound like scripts. Remember, 95 percent of the jokes you ever heard from Jim Carrey were scripted, rehearsed, practiced, and timed to be delivered as if they were natural and spontaneous.

Five Steps to Successfully Dealing with Objections

There are five important steps to remember when dealing with objections.

1. Listen carefully to the objection. Resist the temptation to jump in before you have heard the full objection. Use active listening techniques like nodding in understanding to show you are fully engaged in what your prospect is saying. Sometimes the prospects will talk themselves out of an objection before you even say a word.

2. The first thing you should do after an objection has been voiced is to thank the prospect. This changes the tone of your interaction from adversarial to cooperative. It shows that you're not defensive or trying to avoid the objection.

For instance, you could say:

- "I'm glad you brought that up."

- "Thanks for asking that question. It gives me the chance to explain…"

3. Never argue with a prospect. Remain calm and pleasant. They may just want to be listened to.

4. Isolate the objection. If the objection is unclear, as in, "Well, I have to think about it," then ask more questions to isolate the real objection. You must attempt to get the prospect to voice his objection in tangible terms like, "I think the price is too high," "I must get approval from someone else," or "Your competitor made a lower bid." When there are several objections on the table, many times most of them are minor. Don't be distracted with secondary objections. Focus on finding the major wants and the major objection.

5. Counter the objection with an inescapable solution.

When you have all the information you need, you can deal with the root of the objection using carefully thought-out and scripted answers that clearly demonstrate a benefit to the prospect. Remember there can only be one perfect answer to any question.

OTHER WAYS TO DEAL WITH OBJECTIONS

"Fast forward" your prospects to help them understand the benefits

In order to overcome an objection, it's very helpful to involve your prospect emotionally in how his future will improve from the moment he agrees to your proposal. This is particularly true when dealing with money issues. By "fast forwarding" your prospect into the future, you can help him see how his life will be different.

I understand your hesitation about the investment, Mr. Miller. Lots of our first-time groups felt the same way. Even when they could easily afford it, they didn't want to make a mistake. For instance, Cheryl Smith from ACME had her doubts but found that the peace of mind she got from having a professional events team and state-of-the-art AV at her beck and call were more than worth it. She's already rebooked for next year.

The biggest problem in the world could have been solved when it was small.
—**Witter Bynner**

The One Sales Objection Technique Everyone Should Learn First: Feel, Felt, Found!

This is one of the most powerful objection busters there is. It's called the feel-felt-found solution. It can be adapted to handle many types of objections.

When the prospect raises an objection, you listen attentively then follow up using these three agreeable steps:

1. "I understand how you *feel*." This statement avoids being argumentative and takes prospects' objections seriously. It tells them you were listening and shows that you do indeed have their best interests at heart.

**2. Many of our clients *felt* that way before they invested in an event

with us. "For instance, Mr. Miller is in your line of work [church, age group, or other category]." This shows prospects that their concerns are valid, and the fact that you name other customers they can relate to who had the same concern builds trust in you.

"He worried about that but…"

3. What he *found* was that… [your answer]

The feel-felt-found solution is one of the strongest techniques for dealing with objections. Add it to your repertoire.

Killing the Competition with Cunningly Clever Innuendo

I don't always agree that you should never say something bad about your competition—sometimes they deserve it. You'd be doing yourself and your prospect a disservice by not bringing to light key information that might be considered negative. For example, you may know for a fact that a competitor is in financial trouble and on their way out of business and thus won't be able to stand behind any of their claims. But even when justified, it's a dangerous game.

Obviously, as a general rule, bad-mouthing the competition is something you want to avoid. It often comes off the wrong way, making you look bad instead of them, even if what you say is true. A far better way to deal with competition is to praise their strengths but raise subtle doubts about their weaknesses.

If you raise doubts about the competition through subtle questions and innuendo and allow the prospect to come to his or her own conclusion, it's far more powerful than anything you will ever say. For example:

Objection: *Your competitor charges far less that you do!*

Answer: *Why do you think that is?* [Then just wait for an answer.]

Wait…

Keep waiting...

Frequently, when this type of objection arises, and you invite the prospect to guess why the restaurant down the street charges 30 percent less, he will. Even if he doesn't respond at once, he is almost always sitting there thinking, "Because their product is inferior," or "Maybe that's all they are worth," or "The private rooms are not that great," or "The whole place needs a refresh." But if you wait, they will think of something.

Here is example of how you can easily change the thought process by planting some doubts in the prospect's head about his objection:

Prospect: The restaurant down the street is offering a better deal.

You: *XYZ is a fine restaurant although you probably won't be dealing with the same person for very long. They have had seven mangers in the five years I've been working here.*

Now you haven't really said anything negative. In fact, you praised the restauarnt. But in a single sentence you told the prospect that if he likes dealing with the same person, which of course most people do, then he'd be far better off dealing with you. Plus, that many managers in that short a time obviously implies that there may be something very wrong at the other restaurant. Although you did not actually say that, I guarantee you that's what the prospect is thinking.

Sometimes I like to use humor here:

Prospect: The restaurant down the street is cheaper.

ME: Yes the restaurant down the street is cheaper and a decent restaurant as long as it never rains.

Wait...

Keep waiting because the prospect cannot resist asking the next question.

Prospect: Why do you say as long as it never rains?

ME: Just that none of their outdoor areas have an awning so they can't cover the guests if it rains and the whole party has to move inside.

Once again, I haven't really bad-mouthed anyone, but I have planted a seed of doubt about the value of booking somewhere that does not offer cover for their outside areas.

With a bit of practice this can be a very fun way to dismiss a competitor and, in my experience, to get a chuckle from the prospect as well.

Casting doubt on your competitors is best done by making a casual comment or phrasing a question in such a way that prospects draw their own—negative—conclusions!

Testimonials

Just as examples about another event planner are important in dealing with objections, written testimonials can be invaluable. Gather a portfolio of letters from your satisfied groups, wedding, meeting, Birthday, Bar Mitzvah, and banquet guests. Together they should address all the objections that your prospects will have.

The easiest way to obtain a range of testimonials covering different issues is to ask satisfied guests to address particular issues. Your portfolio of testimonials will be impressive by itself. It can even be given to prospects while they wait. By organizing it according to the type of objection, you can also use it when specific objections are raised. For instance, after you answer a couple of objections, as a change of pace, you might say "Instead of me answering that question, why don't I let one of our groups do it for you," and bring out the relevant testimonial.

Isolating objections

There are two times when you need to isolate objections. When people make vague objections like "I need to think it over," "I'm not sure," or "I need to talk it over with___," you don't have much to work with. In the specific objections dealt with later, we show you how to ask for the real objection. These approaches acknowledge prospects' needs to think it over and then ask them what they need to think over.

The second time you need to isolate an objection is to find out if this is the key objection. When there are several objections on the table, many times most of them are minor. Don't be distracted with secondary objections. Focus on finding the major wants and the major objection. For instance, if there is an objection that you know you can answer, don't just say yes. Say something like "If I can arrange flexible payments for you, are you ready to commit today?"

By isolating the objections that really matter to the prospect, you can answer them and move to close the sale.

What will others think?

A key decision blocker that is often overlooked is how others' feelings and views may affect the buying decision of your prospect. Where most banquet bookings are concerned, the question is, "What will my boss,/spouse/partner think about the buying decision?" Sometimes, but by no means always, this question is verbalized as an objection. However, a person's ego may not allow him to tell you that he must consult with someone before making a buying decision.

Any time a third person is brought into the sales decision, your presentation must take them into account. You need to give your prospect the ammunition they need to "sell" the other person.

Answering objections is not solving every concern

While I can give you a *lot* of ammunition here to answer objections, some can't be eliminated. For instance, your restaurant does not have outdoor dining. You can't change that. You can only suggest that it is not crucial.

You'll add to your rapport and credibility by being frank about things you can't change. At the end of answering objections, you or the prospect might agree that there are a couple of points that are not perfect. But that can still compare very favorably to other restaurants. Nothing is perfect. Help your prospects make a decision anyway.

COMMON CONCERNS, OBJECTIONS, AND STALLS

Location—too far from where prospective guest lives/works.

Our guests believe it is worth the drive. Our restaurant is located in the heart of the Pine Barrens, which is why the property is as magnificent as it is. Our front entrance is almost one mile from our location. One of the best things about Pine Barrens Restaurant is what it is missing—no cars whizzing past, no housing developments, and no distractions! And believe it or not, remote as it seems, we are actually very close to both the Garden State Parkway and Interstate 95. We promise, once you're immersed in the tranquility you won't even remember the commute.

The price is too high!

Too high compared to what, Mr. Miller? Wait…prospects will often answer for you…

If not, help them differentiate your value…

After all, our views, ambience, outdoor patio and menu are unique. What other restaurant in the area would you say was comparable to the Legendary Restaurant?

Or

We have a great downtown location, valet parking, free wi-fi, the city's best wine list and four private dining areas. What other restaurant is actually comparable?

I see on Trip Advisor or Yelp not all your guests are happy.

Every now and then you will get prospects who have heard something from a disgruntled guest, the social media rumor mill, an ex-employee or, possibly even, a competing restaurant. They will raise a question about how happy your existing customers are. As with all objections, you don't want a protracted discussion about this. You simply want to quickly and concisely answer the concern and go back to your presentation.

Objection: *I hear not all your guests are happy.*

Solution: *Really, Bob, I'm surprised to hear you say that. But as Lincoln so aptly said, "You can never please all of the people all of the time." Wouldn't you agree?*

Think about it—who is going to argue with Honest Abe? By using this well-known quote, you simply help the prospect align with a concept that most people agree is a universal truth.

Abe Option Two:

Objection: *I hear not all your guests are happy.*

Solution: *Really, Bob, I'm surprised to hear you say that. But as Lincoln, so aptly said, "Most people are about as happy as they make up their minds to be." Wouldn't you agree?*

Most of the time either approach will work. If the prospect persists, casually ask for an example of what the prospect means, for example:

Is there something specific you've heard that I might address?

Make Abe your ally in dealing with unhappy people.

I want to think it over.

It isn't that they can't see the solution. It's that they can't see the problem. **—G. K. Chesterton**

Time objections are often masked by the sale-killing words "I want to think it over." This is your classic objection but one that you, as a battle tested salesperson, should have removed earlier in the sales process by handling most common objections in your presentation. Nonetheless, for most salespeople, it's a stall you should expect to hear often.

To deal with this stall, you must pin the prospect down to a more specific objection in order to deal with the true objection.

Objection: *I need to think it over.*

Solution: *I agree that any decision such as this should be thought about carefully. May I ask—is it the location (facilities, rooms, menu etc.) or the price that you are thinking about the most?*

Probe and close on the issue that is causing the procrastination.

Objection: *I need to think this over.*

Solution: *What exactly is it that you need to think over? You told me you liked the facilities. Is there a money issue?*

Objection: *I want to think it over for a while.*

Solution: *When people say that, it usually tells me that I've left something out of my presentation or that there are questions I haven't answered thoroughly. What other questions do you have?*

Objection: *I want to look at some other venues.*

Solution: *I understand. That's exactly what I would do myself. That's why I always carry a comparison sheet of our closest competitors and us. (Show them.) As you can clearly see, we offer not only the best facilities, but the best price too.*

Objection: *I'm going to wait until September to make a decision.*

Solution: *I understand you wanting to wait until September to book, but if you do that, I won't be able to guarantee the dates. Most groups book at least six month in advance.*

Or

Let's go ahead and take care of all the paperwork now. Then you'll be all set as soon as September rolls around.

Objection: That's more than we have in our budget for food.

Answer: We can lower the cost easily if we choose a different menu.

Or

Answer: Saturdays in summer is our prime time. If we can move your event back a little or choose a different day, I can certainly save you some money. Would that help?

Or

Answer: I understand, Mr. Smith. Perhaps if we were to narrow the guest list a little—most people tend to overestimate the number of people who will attend.

Objection: I am just so afraid something will go wrong.

Answer: I understand, Sally. That's a perfectly natural feeling for a bride-to-be, but let me put your mind at rest. We have a dedicated team of professionals here that have been running perfect wedding rehearsal dinners for over twenty years.

Objection: I think the location might be a bit too upscale for us.

Answer: This is your daughter's special day. Surely you want her to remember how special the location and event were?

Andrew Wood

Objection: I am not sure the restaurant has the right ambience?

Answer: I certainly understand what you mean but that's because you are not seeing how we transform this room for a rehearsal dinner. Here, let me show you some photographs with all the tablecloths and flowers in place.

The Restaurant Marketing Bible

"People who love to eat are always the best people." — **Julia Child**

CHAPTER 20

Legendary Closing

Well done is better than well said.—**Benjamin Franklin**

Closing a sale is the key step in the sales process and the first step to starting a serious new relationship. You've spent time and money to generate leads, given tours, and answered questions. Now you need to communicate your enthusiasm to the prospect and close the deal.

All the money, time, sweat, and skill you've put into your sales effort mean nothing if you can't get the prospect to buy. Many people get so caught up in their sales pitches that they fail to observe that the prospect is radiating all kinds of buying signals. The prospect is ready to book, but the salesperson doesn't know when to be quiet and go for the close. In fact, studies show that an astonishing 63 percent of all sales presentations are given without the salesperson actually asking the prospect to buy.

Close early and often

"Closing" a sale means that your prospect has agreed to book the event. To be even more specific, he or she needs to have signed the contract and given you a credit card.

Closing is *the purpose* of the sales process. Many people are uncomfortable actually asking for the sale. As mentioned in the last chapter, most of us have a bad image of sales and don't want to seem "pushy." That's one reason people don't try to close often enough. Another is that they think closing should come only *after* all the other steps in the sales process. In fact, sometimes the prospect is ready to be closed early. You won't know this unless you try.

The prospect may be ready to buy when he walks in the door. You will make more sales if you ask for the sale early and often. Another benefit of trying to close early in the presentation is that it will get you over your discomfort about asking for the sale in general.

Early attempts to close the sale are called "trial closes." You don't necessarily expect them to work, but they sometimes do.

SPOTTING CLOSING SIGNALS

Let's look at some common closing signals that will alert you to when your prospect is ready to buy.

Verbal closing signals

Often you can tell that a prospect's level of interest has risen by the type of questions he starts to ask. These questions suggest that the prospect is now thinking like a customer.

Prospect: Is the first Saturday of August (or any specific date) available?

Prospect: Can you accommodate 150 guests for dinner?

Prospect: Can we get a better rate if we sign a two- or three-year contract?

Stay focused on closing

When the prospect asks questions like the ones just mentioned, try another trial close. Answer each question quickly and professionally in accordance with the answers in your presentation and objections scripts and then go directly for the close. Ask for the sale.

Note: Do not allow yourself to become distracted from selling by answering a series of questions that do not lead to the close. Always draw your prospect's attention back to closing (or your presentation if necessary). If the prospect persists in a series of distracting questions, excuse yourself and leave the room for a moment. This will help you regain control of the conversation. When you return, sit down and get right back into your closing sequence or structured presentation. Lead and remain in charge, but never be "pushy."

Just because someone asks a question doesn't mean you have to answer it immediately, or even at all. For instance, you could say, "I'll be getting to that point a bit later." You are in charge of the situation. It's up to you to dictate the pace and control the interaction.

When a prospect asks if he can pay for his event in three parts, don't say yes. Instead, say, "Are you ready to book if I can arrange a three-part payment?" The answer will tell you if it was an idle question (or one trying to distract you), or if the prospect is ready to go.

Nonverbal closing signals

You must not only listen to what your prospect says but watch his body language as well. The majority of communication is not based on what your prospect says.

Signals that will help you pick the right moment to close:

- ✓ Nodding in agreement.
- ✓ Making more frequent eye contact.
- ✓ Eyes dilating slightly and brow relaxed.
- ✓ Raising one eyebrow, smiling, and appearing to be imagining himself in the scenario that you have described.
- ✓ Body language relaxed, as opposed to stiff and formal.
- ✓ Leaning toward you.
- ✓ Picking up your sales literature and intently studying it.
- ✓ Taking unusual care in reading the agreement.
- ✓ Starting to reach for his credit card.

Be alert for such signals. When you observe any of them, bring your presentation to a pause point and try a trial close. You will find your sales volume increases significantly when you raise your level of alertness to nonverbal signals.

GETTING TO THE CLOSE

In order to ask for the sale smoothly, you need to set it up in advance. The way to do this is with your trial closes. As just mentioned, usually you'll attempt a trial close after the prospect has shown buying signals. If the close works, great! If not, follow the procedures in the objections section to isolate and answer any concerns and then float another trial close.

SAMPLE CLOSES

The professional salesperson knows that every prospect has a close that fits him or her—one that appeals to him on a most personal level. The secret is to find out which one will resonate most deeply with your prospect, so you can obtain a favorable response and make the sale.

There are several closes below that have been successful for decades in selling group business and events. Although you might know them by other names, anyone who has been in sales for even a short period of time will recognize many of them. Others may be new to you. Some of them you might like; others you might hate. It's important to be completely comfortable with the closes that work best for your style and personality. As you go through the following closes, adapt them to match your style and selling situation. Whichever closes you choose to adopt, practice them, role-play them, and perfect them. The more you practice, the more they will flow naturally. The one thing that is certain is that if you don't ask prospects to buy, they won't.

The straightforward close

"Ms. Garcia, based on what you have seen, do you think that Romeo's Restaurant is the type of facility in which you would like to have your event?"

or

"Ms. Garcia, shall I go head and lock in your event date today?"

The assumptive close

Always assume that the prospect is going to buy. The assumptive close handles the sales interaction as if you were certain that the prospect would buy.

"Mr. Miller, based on our conversation it seems like Joe's Steak House meets most of your criteria."

"Mr. Miller, you probably want to go ahead and fill in our banquet reservation form today to lock in your dates and rates."

or

"Mr. Miller, based on our conversation, it seems like our facility meets most of your criteria. I assume you would you like to go ahead and get the paperwork out of the way right now while you are here?"

The alternative close

The alternative close is perhaps the best known of all closing techniques and has many variations, depending on the exact circumstances. Another common name for it is the "either-or" close. This close gives the prospect the choice between buying and buying, between yes and yes.

Do you want to book room A or room B for your event?

or

Would you prefer the $100 bar credit or twenty free appetizers as your bonus gift?

When your prospect is on the verge of making a buying decision, the most direct way of closing the sale is to ask how he intends to pay for it. This approach can best be used when a prospect has made the decision to buy but is asking unrelated questions—the kinds that prevent him from giving you the order. At this point, "Will you be using a credit card or check?" is the best way to take control of the sale and complete it. Each one of the previous alternative close offers the prospect a choice. No matter which one they choose, they will feel committed to buy once they have made the choice.

The action close

In the action close you ask the prospect to *do* something to accelerate the process and help them make a positive decision.

> *"Ms. Garcia, I've gone ahead and filled out most of the booking agreement for you. If you would like to go ahead and approve it, I can get your event on the calendar at once."*

Hand the prospect a pen and casually slide the agreement across the desk.

Once the prospect accepts whatever action you have asked her to take, she has already mentally booked the event or agreed to hold the event with you.

The Ben Franklin close

The Ben Franklin close is ideal for prospects who are considering other options or who are very detail-oriented. It is so named because it was the method employed by the legendary statesman to help him and others make a decision. It is an excellent way to summarize your benefits and the positive response you have received from the prospect during the sale presentation about various features you have to offer. When written down in black and white, the total impact of the words is greater than the spoken word.

Start with a blank sheet of paper and draw a large "T" on the page. At the top, write on either side of the line Pro/Con. Look at the prospect and say:

> *Mr. Miller, when Ben Franklin had an important decision to make, he'd make a list of the pros and cons and make a decision based on them. I always think it helps in any important decision to write things down on paper. Would you like to give it a try?*

Now give them the paper and pencil and ask them to start with the "pros."

Why don't you start with the things you liked that we offer here at The Cove Restaurant?

One of the keys to this close is that your prospect states the pros and cons, and that you give him lots of help with the pros.

You agreed that our restaurant is in a great location?

You like the banquet space?

Prompt the prospect to contribute additional positive benefits to his list.

Then tell your prospect to write down the negatives. Because he's done the positives first, his mind will have a harder time changing gears to come up with negatives. And you don't help! This is one reason it's important to have the prospect do the writing (unlike some ways this close is taught). You might even say, "Now that you've got the hang of it, list all the negatives you can think of and I'll be right back."

When the prospect is done, he will typically have ten or more items in the positive column and no more than three items in the negative column. This alone gives you a psychological advantage in closing. You may be able to say, "It looks like the positives far outweigh the negatives. I guess that's it," and go into final closing mode. For instance:

Mr. Miller, it certainly looks like the benefits of holding your event at The Cove are in favor of you holding your event here. What do you say we go ahead and complete the paperwork?

If there are any important negatives, you now have the chance to deal with the objection and close. It's the hidden objections that create problems. (See the Objections section for more details.)

The minutes or cents close

If you have a prospect who is stuck on price, the way to handle it is to break it down to ridiculous proportions. This is how life insurance has been sold for decades, but this type of close works just as well selling anything, especially to value-oriented prospects. When you show people how little your restaurant will cost them on a per head basis, it makes it much easier for them to justify, or rationalize, the purchase.

> Ms. Garcia, when you think about it, an event at Charlie's works out to less than $100 per attendee, per day. Wouldn't you agree that's an amazing value for a world-class restaurant?

When all else fails, there are three more closes you can try to get a positive outcome.

The thermometer test

This simple technique helps you measure the degree to which your prospect has been sold—up to this point in your presentation.

Here's how it works:

> Mr. Miller, we've covered a lot of ground so far, and there's still more to show you. But on a zero-to-ten scale, zero meaning you have no interest in our property and ten meaning you have already decided to book, where would you say are?

If he says ten, game over. Sign the paperwork and get out of there!

If he's less than a six, you've got a problem. He's agreed with all your qualifying and review thus far, and he's less than a six?

> Mr. Miller, based on what you've told me so far, I don't understand that.

Whatever he says will reveal something that your earlier answers have not alleviated. Be patient. Listen. And begin the process again.

Most of the time, at this stage of the presentation, the prospect will be higher than six. In that event, you say:

> Mr. Miller, what do you need to see [hear, understand] to get to ten?

And then, whatever he has to see or hear is what you show him or tell him next. No more and no less. After you've shown him what he's asked for, take his temperature again.

When your prospect arrives at ten, simply ask for the signed order or credit card number.

The thermometer test takes the guesswork out of knowing how ready your prospect is to close.

The reverse close

Occasionally, someone will come in and announce up front that she is not going to book her event right now that she is just looking around at the possible restaurants in the area. This is a classic "shield" or defensive technique designed to give the prospect a clean way out if she doesn't hear exactly what she wants to hear. Now is the time for reverse psychology.

Thank her for coming in and offer to put her name on a waiting list. Explain to her that you have so many people who are interested in booking weddings right now that you can't possibly spend time with someone who is not ready to make a decision. Be polite but be firm; ask the prospect to pick a date for her tour a month from now.

For example:

I'm sorry, Ms. Garcia, but I have so many people scheduled for tours this month who are ready to decide that I will have to make an appointment for you next month. Tell me what's a good date for you and I'll be happy to add you to the list.

This never fails to change the prospect's mind. The moment she hears she *can't* take a tour, you have dissolved her shield. Suddenly she wants to be there. An interesting turn of events occurs at this point. Now the prospect is actually trying to sell you on letting her buy! A side effect of this close is that it automatically builds value and credibility into your restaurant. What kinds of restaurants have waiting lists? Good ones!

The Columbo close

Over the last thirty years, there have been hundreds of cop shows on television. Few TV detectives have been less glamorous in appearance than the seemingly bumbling Columbo. After interviewing a suspect, when he reached the door he would always turn back and ask if the suspect could just help him go over a detail one more time so he could understand.

> **Restaurant:** *Mr. Miller, I understand that you're not going to be booking your event with our restaurant but wonder if you would do me a favor.*

> **Prospect:** *Sure! [At this point they will drop their sales defenses because you have acknowledged that they said no. They are now more willing to help you to cushion the blow of them turning you down.]*

> **Restaurant:** *You see, I truly believe that our restaurant has the most incredible banquet package that I have ever seen…I feel so great about what I do that I just don't understand why I fail to get others as excited about the restaurant as I am. I would really appreciate it if you would tell me why I didn't communicate that same feeling to you so it will help me in the future. Can you tell me where I went wrong?*

At this point Mr. Miller will do one of two things: he will either tell you exactly why you didn't convince him, or he will reveal his hidden reason for inaction. In either case, this gives you an opportunity to provide him with additional information and ask him for a response on the new and improved proposition. In the process, it doesn't hurt that you have stroked Mr. Miller's ego and self-esteem by asking for his advice.

SUMMARY

Your sales presentation should be carefully scripted; however, you don't need any special gift of gab to be a legendary salesperson. You just need to involve your prospect and explain your benefits in a credible way.

Overcoming objections to your presentations is one of the most challenging parts of the sales process. Yet if you believe in your value, you will be helping people to see the benefits more clearly. As you learn to deal better with objections, you will also improve your qualifying and presenting. The sales system works together to make you more effective. Just remember, your benefits can overcome any objections for the right prospects. Look for them, find them, and help them see how your offer meets their needs.

There are almost an unlimited number of ways to close a sale and I've covered the most successful ones here. Try them out, say them out loud, and role-play them with your staff. Find the ones that seem most natural for you and put them into action at once to increase your banquet and event sales.

"I only drink Champagne on two occasions, when I am in love and when I am not."
— **Coco Chanel**

CHAPTER 21

Boosting Your Profits by Selling More Wine

With profit margins low on most meals, beverages from the bar, especially wine, are the key to boosting your profits. The wine list can be intimidating for some servers, and without confidence in selling wine, that may lead to lower wine sales overall than you would have had with confident servers.

Converting Servers to Sellers

The ability to sell takes a good server and turns them into a valuable asset. Train your servers to be sellers by teaching them the basics of wine selection and handling so they can select, present, open, and pour wine with confidence. If the server is shy or uncomfortable handling wine, they will be less likely to offer it. These add-on sales can double your profits

Sales Start with Confidence

In my youth I worked as a server in high-end steak house in the Palm Beach area. While I had a good amount of restaurant experience, I had little to none in a high-end place and had never really opened much wine. No one there ever asked me about my experience or showed me how to do it. It also seemed someone must have been storing it poorly because, in the first few bottles I opened, the corks broke although I managed to open them eventually, sweating profusely as I did.

As much as I wanted my tables' checks to grow, I really hoped my customers would drink beer rather than put me through the agony of opening wine. Then it happened: A table of eight ordered a very expensive bottle of wine. I had been practicing with the help of an older server, but once again the cork was dry and broke halfway out. The table all stopped talking and started watching me, I felt like a condemned man at a firing squad as I gently coaxed the cork from the bottle. I thought I had succeeded. As I poured the sample to the host out came the wine with no cork. Then just as I was breathing a sigh of review, a tiny piece fell into his glass. He immediately took his eyes from the glass to me. Everyone else turned towards me as if in slow motion. I was dying but thinking quickly, I gave a toothless smile and an open-handed gesture as I said, "Sir, it was a great year for wine, but a lousy year for cork." The rest of the table broke into spontaneous laughter, and he so grinned too and nodded to pour it out.

The point is, if your servers are not confident in selling wine they are going to avoid doing it. So step wine it to give them confidence. I can't tell you how many times I have asked a server for a recommendation only to be told, "I don't really drink wine, so I don't know."

If servers are new or haven't mastered the intricacies of your wine training, you should have a chart of what wines are recommended for each dish. Even if servers don't know anything about wine, they should at least be able to respond with something like, "Our chef recommends a sauvignon blanc or a rosé to go with the veal piccata."

1. Train Your Staff in Wine and Wine Sales

There is no substitute for actual tasting when it comes to learning about wine. Wine tasting should be part of new hire training and ongoing activity *for all waitstaff*. Servers don't have to taste every wine on the list; instead, train them in broader wine categories and focus on each, one at a time.

Set out 3 glasses and pour 3 examples of the same type of wine, such as 3 different Cabernet Sauvignons, each with a different finish. Help them understand the differences when tasted side by side and learn the characteristics of the grape. Consider doing this with major grape varieties such as Chardonnay, Pinot Noir, Sauvignon Blanc and Sparkling for a basic understanding of each. Keep it fun, encourage tasters to talk about what they're smelling and tasting.

2. Focus on General Wine Categories

It could be impossible for servers to memorize the detailed descriptions of every single wine. Instead of scaring them, train them on broader categories of wine. Come up with descriptions such as Big & Bold & Fruity, Bright & Crisp, etc., Then train them on which bottles fall into which categories. This allows them to ask a diner if they like their white wines bright and crisp, or their reds big and bold which provides for the opportunity to point them in the right direction and sell them a good bottle.

3. Give Some Basic Talking Points to Sell the Story

Rather than overwhelming servers with geography lessons, offer basic knowledge such as this Big Zinfandel is from California's, Lodi Valley. This dark and voluminous wine will definitely leave your senses quivering. A rich, burly wine with peppery spice and baked cherry pie aromas. Jammy and chewy with flavors of berry, plum, vanilla, herbs, and spice. Only a limited production is offered each year, and the price is very attractive.

It's astonishing how few restaurants provide any beverage training for servers: filling glasses to the top, topping up when not even half done because the waitress happens to be passing the table, etc. That training I leave to you.

Twelve Ways to Increase Wine Sales

1. **Use Conversational Tones**
   Instead of saying, "Would you like a glass of champagne to start?" say, "Maybe we should begin with a glass of champagne for you before ordering? Who doesn't like a little bubbly to get the party started?"

2. **Suggest parings**
   For example; "A nice bottle of champagne is not only a great start for the evening while you are looking at the menu, but it will go nicely with most of our appetizers as well." This thought gives dual purpose to the bottle making it more likely guest choose a bottle over a glass.

3. **Always assume everyone at the table wants wine.**
   Instead of asking if they'd like wine, ask whether they would prefer red or white.

4. **Propose Options in Three Different Price Ranges**
   Start by asking the host-guest what type of wine they like? Once they have answered that they prefer Cabernet Sauvignon or bold reds propose three bottles of wine in that category. Preferably at three different price points low, medium and high.

5. **Upsell**
   If the table orders two glasses, instead of a bottle always offer the full bottle. It's a better deal for the customer and less back and forwards to the bar so the waitstaff can focus on serving the table. Customers who order bottles also tend to order more food than those who drink by the glass.

6. **Offer Packages**
   If you sell wine by the glass, consider offering a pairing package of three glasses rather than one. Say a glass of champagne, a Pinot Noir and dessert wine together.

7. **Sales 101**
   When a bottle has been emptied, don't ask if they'd like another bottle, instead, ask if they'd like the same again or a different variety.

8. **Sell Wine by the Half Glass**
   Although it may seem counterintuitive, selling by the half glass can be another effective way to upsell. Selling half glasses is always a great way to boost sales at the beginning of a meal, at the end, or between courses and requires only a little bit of commitment on the guest's part. It's also a great way to introduce guests to wines that might be out of their comfort zone. They may not be willing to buy a $175 bottle, but for $20 they would sure like to see what it tastes like. Thus, increasing the chances, they might upgrade to a bottle in the future

9. **Offer More Half Bottles**
   Single diners are more prevalent than ever, and yet very few restaurants have a decent selection of half bottles, many have none at all. Not only are half bottles the perfect size for the single diner but they can also be used the second or third time around when a table wants more but it's obvious a full bottle will be too much.

10. **The More You Tell, the More You Sell**
    Just like sales copy, the more you know and share about the wine—where it's made and the people behind the vineyard—the better your story becomes. Better stories result in more sales.

11. **Pitch a liquid desert if they turn down your cheesecake**
    Many guests are already full by the time they finish their main course so they may not be very likely to order dessert. Pitch a dessert wine instead.

12. **Always keep pushing your staff to increase their wine knowledge.**
    Hold contests or offer rewards to make learning about the different geography, varieties and families of wine fun. Sales will increase with knowledge ever time!

How to Triple Your Dessert Sales

Dessert sales are the icing on the cake of every restaurant check, but few places do a good job of selling desert. The waiter says, "Anyone leave room for dessert?" hoping more than expecting that everyone says. "Yes" as that bumps his check up another $30 or more. But they don't. More typically, three people immediately decline, and the fourth says, "I'll have a look" without much enthusiasm. Eventually the order is for cheesecake and four forks.

Now let's look at how we could approach that same situation with a little more flare and salesmanship. Salesmanship that enhances rather than infringes on your guests' dining experience.

"Ladies and gentlemen, if I could have your attention for just a moment, please. The chef wanted me to let you know that he had fresh key limes flown in from Florida today, that he picked only the finest half dozen. Then, he used his Aunt Sally's secret recipe handed down now for three generations. He has baked from scratch what he believes will be the finest key lime pie you have ever tasted in your life. The only problem is, I think there are just three slices left. Shall I assume one of you would be willing to share?"

Now the question is not do you want dessert? The question is shall I assume one of you is willing to share?

Be rude not to, right?

1. Everyone loves a good story, it makes the food more enjoyable, valuable and desirable. Come up with stories that work for you.

2. How you ask a question makes a massive difference to your sales.

3. Don't offer the very same deserts as every other restaurant. Ditch the cheesecake for something more interesting!

Now you could come back with, "I have great news. I made a mistake. There were actually four left; no one has to share." But I leave that up to you. The fact is that stories sell food. The better the story the better the sales and that goes for everything, not just desserts.

SUMMARY

To maximize your wine sales, you must convert severs to sellers. The first step in doing this is to educate them and provide them with enough knowledge to gain confidence. Give them some basic stories to sell with. Always assume the table wants wine. Using conversational tones suggest pairings and offer packages. Consider selling more wine by the half bottle and the half glass and suggesting a liquid dessert. To sell more actual desserts, offer more specials and deliver them with a story. Always remember the more you tell the more you sell.

"Wine is bottled poetry."
— **Robert Louis Stevenson**

Andrew Wood

CHAPTER 22

Building a Referral Machine for Your Restaurant

Ask any good restaurant how they generate most of their business, and they will instantly and enthusiastically tell you they do it through word of mouth. However, if you ask them to explain their referral system to you, you are very likely to get a blank stare or a shrug.

I recently asked the owners of a high-end restaurant what type of referral systems they had in place. Both had the same answer: they didn't; referrals just happened. So does death, but it doesn't mean you should wait around for it!

Referrals are the best way to bring in new guests for three simple reasons. First, other people are doing the marketing for you, usually at no cost to you. Second, when other people promote you, they are seen as more objective and credible. Third, referrals are generally made in order to help prospects improve their quality of life. A prospect who comes to you referred by his family, friends, or neighbors is already leaning toward a purchase decision.

Referrals are the lifeblood of any restaurant. There is simply no quicker and less expensive way to build your customer base and increase your income than to double or triple your referral rate. It doesn't matter what type of restaurant you are running; referral business makes you more money than any other type of new business (not surprising as referrals cost little or nothing to get).

While some referrals will happen by accident, you cannot build a reliable marketing system on accidental events. You have to plan, measure, and implement a referral system that ensures two or three referrals from every single person with whom you come into contact.

In this chapter, you will discover:
- ✓ the difference between word of mouth and referrals,
- ✓ how to measure referral success,
- ✓ the psychology of referrals,
- ✓ the best time to ask,
- ✓ how to ask,
- ✓ who to ask,
- ✓ six ways to get referrals, and
- ✓ setting up an ambassador program.

YOU ALWAYS GET WORD OF MOUTH, BUT IS IT GOOD OR BAD?

Perhaps you hadn't thought about it, but you are always getting word of mouth, whether you ask for it or not. While the terms "word of mouth" and "referrals" are frequently used interchangeably, there is a difference. Referrals are specific attempts to help someone—either the person you refer to a business, or the business you refer to an individual, or both. Word of mouth can include a referral, but it can also include general comments. For instance, someone might say, "I hear that the scenery is great there."

You get the point. People talking are word of mouth. Sometimes it helps you and sometimes it doesn't. By combining a strong USP, a program to communicate to all your staff and guests, and a system for driving referrals, you can generate more and better word of mouth *and* more referrals.

REFERRAL GOALS

The age-old business adage that what gets measured gets done is just as true for referrals as for any other part of your business. Referrals are far too important a part of your marketing strategy to leave them to mere chance as most restaurants do. They must instead be sought from every customer, every client, every contact, and every supplier that does business with your restaurant. Furthermore, they must be sought out from all your personal relationships from your accountant to your dry cleaner.

The only way you can see whether your referral program is working is to set goals in each category and measure your progress against them monthly.

Depending on your restaurant, you should set monthly goals for referrals in the appropriate following areas:

- Group referrals
- Meeting referrals
- Wedding referrals
- Banquet referrals

THE PSYCHOLOGY OF REFERRALS

Start building your referral machine by first understanding the psychology of referrals. Giving referrals involves two contrary impulses. First, people like to give referrals because it allows them to help others at low cost to themselves. It makes them feel good about themselves and be a "hero" to others. Second, people worry about giving referrals because if something goes wrong they get the blame. Yet, if things go right, the thanks they get is usually small. Because of this ambivalence, it's easy to get some people to give referrals and hard to get others to. The same people may change their attitude over time, or be more comfortable giving referrals to some types of people than others. Clearly, your job is to encourage referrals and also to make it *safe* to give referrals to your restaurant.

People like to give referrals for three important reasons

1. Ego. When someone buys a new home, membership, car, or investment, he wants his friends and neighbors to be impressed. He wants them to know what a great deal he got. When was the last time someone who bought a new car told you what a schmuck he was for buying it? It simply doesn't happen, at least not in the first few weeks.

The same will be true for discovering a new restaurant, booking a meeting, banquet, or group event—once the meeting is booked, those people will naturally tell others in their circle that they booked or dined with you. Your job is to expand that circle and make it even more proactive.

2. Most people like to feel important; they like to be the center of attention or information. When the opportunity to take center stage arises by giving a referral, they are more than ready to step up to the plate and recommend a restaurant.

3. Birds of a feather flock together. People like their friends and neighbors to share and experience the same things they do.

WHEN IS THE BEST TIME TO ASK FOR A REFERRAL?

The short answer is: anytime. But ask often. Early in the relationship can be the best time. Asking for a referral is a good habit to get into when you talk with people. The second-best time to ask for a referral is as soon as you have developed a rapport with the prospect. He may not buy and you may never see him again so you should never let the prospect leave without asking for a referral. After someone has told you no is also a good time. Oftentimes a person who has just turned you down feels bad about having done so and will give you a referral to compensate.

The very best time to ask for a referral is right after you have completed a sale with a new customer. People who have just purchased from you are very open to helping you. Over 80 percent of all referrals happen within four to six weeks of acquiring a new customer. This is the time when excitement and top of the mind awareness are always at the highest level. After that period, people tend to fall into their regular routines and tend to forget to give referrals.

HOW TO ASK FOR REFERRALS

Many people are bashful or downright scared of asking for a referral. They don't want to seem pushy, desperate, or—heaven forbid—both. While I assure you that most people really do like giving referrals, you can make the process even more painless by reframing the way you ask for a referral. Plan your referral requests in advance so they flow smoothly and effortlessly from your mouth.

As mentioned earlier, *how* you ask for referrals can make a big difference. The most important point is that you have to develop a method that works for you, remembering that it takes a little practice before you'll feel completely comfortable asking for referrals.

There are many ways to ask for referrals. The way you ask will depend on your restaurant's specific offer, positioning, and your personality. Some people just **come right out and ask,** business-person to business-person like this:

> *Simone, just as you probably do in your business, we find we get most of our new customers from referrals by other customers. I'd appreciate it if you might pass along a couple of my cards to your colleagues.*

Notice that I am assuming that they know people who are a good fit rather than asking, "Do you know anyone?" This subtle difference creates very different results.

If you have established any degree of rapport during the sales process, your customer should at least be willing to pass on a card.

Another type of appeal is a **personal appeal:**

George, it would really help me if you could suggest two or three other people I could talk to about a meeting, banquet, or group event.

Notice that we set an expectation by asking for two or three other people.

You can use a **personal favor** approach:

Simone, I wonder if you could do me a favor. I'm looking to fill a couple of spots with events and I'd appreciate it if you could suggest some people who might be appropriate for me to approach.

If they give you names, ask if you can use their name as the referral source when approaching the new people.

You can provide tools to **make it easy** to give referrals. Here are some other examples of ways to ask for referrals. You should pick or develop ways that fit your own style and your position in the marketplace:

George, we're trying to build up our banquet business here at the restaurant. It would really help me if you could suggest a few groups you're a member of who might hold a banquet or event. Are you in any business groups, a car club, alumni organization or any other group that might hold a banquet event?

If the first answer is no, try a few probes with specific examples.

For instance:

- ✓ Are you a member of the local Chamber of Commerce?
- ✓ Do you have any kids in schools that have fundraisers?
- ✓ Do you work with any charities that raise money?

If this doesn't work, try for the names of other people who are better leads.

- ✓ Can you suggest someone else I can ask about group events?

- ✓ Who do you know who is a member of a local association?
- ✓ Who do you know who knows the most people? Who do you ask for a referral when you need a new contact?

WHOM TO ASK FOR REFERRALS

The short answer is, ask everyone you know or do business with for referrals.

Did you ask the UPS truck driver to buy today? I did. When I say everyone, I mean everyone. I include the mailman, the fire inspector, and the plumber. Hey, you won't know if you don't ask and everyone has friends who can afford to buy or is affiliated with a group that can use your restaurants facilities.

SIX GREAT WAYS TO GET REFERRALS

There are six key groups from whom you can gain referrals

1. Ask new clients to buy again. The reason we get referrals is so that we can sell more, right? Well, the first thing to consider before we ever work on the referrals to others is self-referrals: Can we sell anything else to the new guest in front of us right now?

Can they book another meeting, banquet or anniversary later in the year while we have all the paperwork together?

Can they lock in next year's golf group, little league banquet or reunion at this year's rates if they book now?

2. Ask new clients who else might benefit. Even if your most recent customer doesn't want to buy something else from you, it's almost certain that he knows someone in his line of work or situation who has similar needs. Everyone is an opinion leader—at least to a few people. A special few are opinion leaders to hundreds, or perhaps even thousands, of people.

3. Ask business suppliers for referrals. Remember, you and your restaurant make purchases. You buy lots of goods and services from others. You are a good customer to someone. That *someone* should be glad to give you referrals as a reward for the business you give him. They may belong to groups that have outings or charity events, including their own. At one restaurant where I was consulting, I had no sooner finished talking to the team when the chef ran back into the room to announce he had just booked a high-end banquet for fifty people with his food supplier. "Best of all," he said with a smile, "they do this every quarter!" In sales, just as in other areas of your life, you won't receive if you don't ask, so be sure to remind your suppliers that you are always in the market for new leads.

4. Don't forget personal suppliers. You bought a car locally, a home locally, and have relationships with dry cleaners, gardeners, and a host of other personal service companies. They have *your* business; have you asked them to help your business?

5. Get everyone on staff involved. Make it a clear policy that sales is *everyone's* job! Remind employees that "nothing happens until a sale is made" and that the restaurant's success and their paychecks depend on a constant stream of new business. You can also reward them for each referral or sale.

How about bartenders and waitstaff? They come into contact with hundreds of people a week and often have jobs at more than one place. They can be a huge source of referral business. The more people on your staff you get involved at a grass-roots level, the quicker your referrals will grow exponentially. Have everyone leverage his or her personal relationship by asking for referrals.

6. Catch bees with honey: Get referrals from your competitors. Most business owners would be surprised to learn that your competitors can often be a good source of referrals.

Sometimes you get a request for a wedding or banquet on a date you're full. Or you and the prospect simply don't hit it off—she's from Venus, you're from Mars. He wants a restaurant closer to home. Your restaurant isn't physically large enough. Or whatever. In these cases, instead of letting the prospect bounce around to three or four more people, take the proactive approach and refer them to someone who can help them. Then call that restaurant to fill them in about the prospect. When you give referrals, others should return them out of courtesy.

You can also set up a formal alliance whereby it's agreed in advance that all extra business gets referred. In one case, two of our clients in Orlando have this arrangement and give each other a 15 percent commission for the referral. Think about that—a day when your restaurant is full and you are able to generate more than 100 percent of revenue!

Setting up an Ambassador Program

Why take care of all referrals yourself when you can enlist the help of others? Develop your own ambassador program.

In short, your goal is to have a group of your customers reaching out to the community on your behalf to find more business. Look for people who want to have an official role in your success. Maybe they are retired and have time. Maybe they are in fields like insurance where they want a reason to meet more people. They are likely to be more outgoing.

Members can be assigned by age, geographic background, and skill so that similar people will relate to each other.

Ambassadors can specialize in group sales, events, or individual sales.

A formal rewards program should be set up to thank ambassadors based on their success in attracting new business.

Make them VIP Club members and treat them like royalty when they come in for a meal.

BUILDING YOUR REFERRAL MACHINE

With all your tools in hand, it's time to commit to the development of a referral habit that will pay untold dividends over the course of your business career. (Even if you're not in sales or marketing, the ability to generate business—to be a rainmaker—makes you more valuable in any position.)

The first thing you must do to build a referral machine is to make a serious commitment to gathering referrals and following them up. You can often double or triple your referrals by simply asking for them. Not sometimes, not when you feel like it, not when you are having a good day, not if you feel the prospect likes you, but every single contact in as many different ways as you can until you get what you need. In the book *Marketing Your Services: For People Who Hate to Sell*, the author (Rick Crandall) says that most people have a "prayer" referral system—they simply *hope* that someone will give them a referral. It takes more than two months of constant repetition to develop a habit, so give yourself more than a prayer of a chance for referrals—get started today!

Be specific when asking for referrals

Once you are given a referral, make every effort possible to get a little background on the person you will be dealing with. When I was selling my consulting services a few years ago, I asked each client to provide me with three referrals.

One client in Mississippi hit me right back with the names of three people.

The first was mildly interested.

The second told me that if this client was using me, then he certainly wouldn't.

The third started shouting at me on the phone at the mere mention of the client, and went on to tell me what he would do with the "son of a #@!#@" if he ever got hold of him.

I was completely confused and called the client back to ask him what was going on. He said he had simply referred people to me who he knew needed my services. He didn't know they had to like him!

Whenever you get a referral, try to find the connection between the person referring and the referral. Ask how Joe knows Harry. Ask how long Sally has been friends with Chelsea. Ask what line of work the prospect is in. The more information you have about the referral and the clearer you are about the relationship with the referrer, the better are your chances of a successful outcome.

CULTIVATE REFERRAL SOURCES

Some people don't give referrals, no matter what you do. Some people like to give referrals. It might be a manager of a sporting goods shop, a realtor, or the Chamber of Commerce who is a good referral source. When you find one, look for more who are similar. Most important, when you find a person who gives referrals, build the relationship. Keep in touch. Give them referrals back. Put them on your VIP list. Find out what they like. Treat them or their family and friends as special people.

SHOW YOUR GRATITUDE

Once you have received a referral, whether it works out to your advantage or not, make sure that you thank people. When a customer gives you a referral that results in a sale, make a big production out of the event. At the very least, you should send him a thank-you note or, failing that, at least an email. If the amount of money involved in closing the sale is substantial, consider sending the customer who gave you the referral a suitable gift for his assistance. A book on a subject that interests him or a bottle of his favorite wine will go a long way toward ensuring that this particular person will continue to refer good prospects to you.

REWARD WITH MONEY?

Some restaurants offer a financial inducement to encourage referrals, but these do not always work. Studies show that a large percentage of people feel uneasy about being paid for referring their friends, unless their friends benefit equally in the process. Coming up with a reward whereby both parties benefit is by far the most effective way to say thank you for a referral and to encourage more. Of course, many companies don't allow this, but it will be an option with the more entrepreneurial customers.

Ask again for referrals

Every time you thank a customer for a referral, you have the opportunity to repeat the cycle by asking for another referral. Always end each thank-you communication, whether it's an email, letter, or a phone call, by asking if the customer knows of anyone similar who might benefit from what you have to offer. Remember, the best time to get a referral is right after a sale. Strike while the iron is hot and ask for more names at once.

Make it easy to give referrals

The easier you make it for other people to promote your restaurant, the more they will do it. If a guest is happy, hand them a card and ask them to post a review on Trip Advisor, Yelp, Facebook, Google, or whichever review site your restaurant needs a boost on. Email them a thank-you, follow up with a nice video attachment, and suggest they share it with their friends. Hand them a small brochure at checkout and suggest they give it to a friend.

The law of large numbers

The more people you know, the more referrals you get. Now that's a pretty simple concept, but far too many people fail to take advantage of this simple fact. Join the club or association in your town that will bring you into contact with the largest number of prospective contacts.

Okay, so there are already ten people in your field involved in the chamber who are more established than you are, so now what? Well, before you take the next step, consider this: more than half of them never go to a meeting anyway. Of the half that go, they only go once a year or spend their time in aimless socializing rather than building relationships. As Woody Allen said, "Ninety percent of success is just showing up." If you still feel there is too much competition in the local chapters of whatever organizations you have considered, try a jump to left field and change the game. Join a related organization rather than the most obvious. Join the chamber in the next town over, or instead of the realtors' association join the builders' association or the mortgage association.

Word of mouth is the lifeblood of any restaurant. And you receive good words a whole lot more predictably and effectively when you develop and follow a system so that good leads don't just slip through the cracks.

LOOK FOR OPINION LEADERS; THEY ARE EVERYWHERE

In Joe Girard's remarkable book *How to Sell Anything to Anyone*, he talks about the "250 rule." Basically, this states that everyone knows at least 250 people, and each of them knows another 250. Get the idea?

I know many more than 250 people, and I conduct seminars and give lectures to thousands across the country. What if the person to whom you are selling something is in the same position as I am, coming into contact with thousands of new people every year? What appears to be an individual, isolated sale could turn into hundreds of sales. Ask questions after each sale to find out what you can about your customer's sphere of influence.

SALES-CYCLE LEADS

Certain products have sales cycles, for example state and government meetings may be on a cycle where they move around and will only return to the same restaurant once every five years by mandate. Being aware of your product's life cycle gives you the edge in knowing when a previous customer will be ready for another purchase. Keep an active file in your customer-relationship management system that lets you know a specific number of months in advance when these previous customers will be at their hottest to book.

But let me give you an even simpler example. Everyone has a birthday. You could approach a frequent guest's spouse a month or so in advance in advance and suggest a party at your restaurant. Perhaps even a surprise party? If you're not sure of the timing, follow the first rule of referrals: ask early and often!

Social Proof

Social sites like Yelp, Trip Advisor, Facebook and Google play a big part in some guests' decisions to visit your restaurant yet many people pay little attention to them. For example, more than half the restaurants in many cities have not even claimed their business on Yelp. You must claim your business in order to respond to reviews.

Make no mistake about it, customers will freely speak their minds and publish their opinions about your business whether they are fair or not. And unfortunately, it seems the angry customer wants to tell many more people than a satisfied customer. We all love the positive reviews, but how should you handle the negative ones?

Five Steps to Dealing with Negative Reviews

1. Check your reviews daily. You do not want negative reviews to go unanswered.

2. Take action at once on negative reviews. The worst thing you can do with a negative review is ignore it. Some review sites like Yelp allow you to start by sending the reviewer a private message.

3. Don't argue with the customer; instead, acknowledge their issue. "I understand you were upset about the slow service on Thursday night."

4. Explain your side of the story: "Unfortunately service was slow on the day of your visit. We had three servers out that day without notice, which is highly unusual."

5. Apologize if appropriate and offer to put right or make up the best you can. "I can only apologize and offer to make it right on your next visit."

Fighting Back on Yelp

While the above is sage advice, I don't always agree you should follow it, and there are a growing number of frustrated restaurant owners who don't. While not following standard protocol does come with greater risks, if you stick to the facts and write the post carefully, the vast majority of potential customers will side with you and ignore the review. This example is from Meghan Lee, owner of the Heirloom restaurant in Delaware.

Her response on Yelp was "Unlike your review, YOU DID, in fact, dine at Heirloom on the 27th. In fact, I have the itemized receipt, credit card slip and authorization code to prove it. In addition to your 'disappointing dining review,' you not only ate at Heirloom, but you and your friends also created a HUGE scene at my bar...You were asked by the women, by my manager, by myself, by the bartenders, and by other bar guests to stop filming the women — as it made them uncomfortable and [was] inappropriate as well as it being downright creepy. So, Jay, you can take your bogus review, your perverted actions and your narcissistic manners and NEVER come back into this building again.

Tip for you — respect women. Sincerely, Meghan, owner."

Lee also stated that Jay's actions were captured on two video cameras in her restaurant and that he could view the footage if he desired. Lee stated, in article in *Delaware online,* that she was not going to let anyone walk over her highly acclaimed restaurant or staff and that she routinely bites back at unfair or bogus reviews.

Mark Nery, co-owner of Onefold in Denver, a 38-seat breakfast and lunch spot, doesn't take bad reviews lying down either.

"You didn't like our food the second time, that's cool... We make everything from scratch so of course we will have some inconsistency. The uncool part was how you acted towards our staff who were more than accommodating to you, they happily refunded the drinks you didn't like and listened to all of your complaints and tried to make it better. However, after all that you didn't even leave a tip, it's not their fault you didn't like the food. So if you were thinking that you 'might give us another shot' do us favor and not."

Here's another

"...not recommending this place to your friends is a purely hypothetical situation. First you will probably need friends then second you will have to be likable enough for them to visit you in Denver. I hope we can survive without your theoretical friends visiting our establishment."

While he admits that if he feels a customer has a legitimate complaint, he'll private message the customer and try and deal with it but he's not going to take rude or untrue reviews lying down.

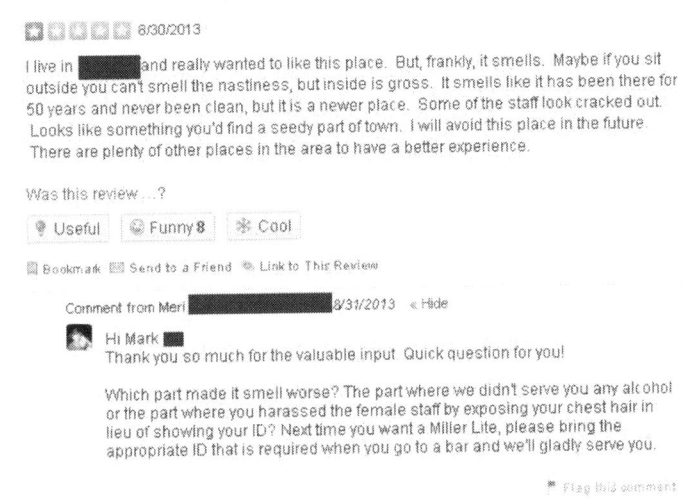

In another case a restaurant owner asked every one of his customers to write a great review but only give him one-star, hundreds did, thus making a mockery of the star system.

I might even go "Basil Fawlty" on them if they were really obnoxious which usually embarrasses them so much, they take the review down. It's risky but in my experience it usually works.

For example, take a review something like this.

"The servers were sullen. The food took too long and came out cold. To save the hassle I ate it, then they refused to take it off my bill." **Mark**

The Basil Fawlty response, played by John Cleese is the fictional owner of Fawlty Towers, in the cult British, TV show, would be something like this:

"Mark really sorry for your poor experience. I'll admit the servers were all a bit sullen on Friday and service was slow for all our guests. Our chef was killed in a car crash on his way to work around 4pm, so we were a bit short staffed and everyone was a little stunned. His wife, our assistant chef was cooking in the kitchen and a bit off her game. I insisted she go home but she didn't want to let our guests down on a Friday night. A real team player that one. Gutted that our tragedy ruined your meal." **Sid**

Perhaps the best solution is a balance of using the standard method most of the time but fighting back occasionally just to let people know you won't be bullied?

SUMMARY

There is no quicker or less expensive way to increase your business than to build a referral system rather than leave it to chance as most restaurants do. Your system must be structured and measured. Then your staff must be trained and rewarded for following it. No less important is the recognition and rewarding of those who are doing the referring.

Another form of referrals comes in the form of social proof. Ask all your good customers to leave reviews on Yelp, Trip Advisor, Facebook, Google and other sites. Thank people for their positive reviews and deal with negative ones quickly. For the most part you should follow the five-step formula for these. There are times however when fighting back just makes more sense.

"The food was terrible and, my, what small portions." — **Woody Allen**

CHAPTER 23

Developing Legendary Service and a Guest-Friendly Culture

One of the most overlooked parts of marketing at any business is service! While a reputation can be built, enhanced, and even achieved with marketing, at some point your reputation is going to be put to the test. You may be the fastest gun in the West on all the wanted posters, but when the other guy draws, reputation doesn't count for much unless you really are fast! When you can back up your reputation with legendary service, you immediately vault yourself to the top echelon in your field. Great service drives repeat business, referrals, and long-term relationships with groups and guests.

There is a lot of talk about providing great service in the restaurant business, about making your guests feel special. We all want it yet so few places deliver it! In fact, when you ask the managers what good service is, you won't get a very straight answer. Instead, you will get a bunch of vague platitudes about being friendly and "taking care of our customers' needs." All very nice, but how often can you truthfully say that your service is not just good, but exceptional? Not just exceptional, but outrageously great?

In this chapter, you will discover:

✓ how to define great service,

- ✓ how to determine what a customer is worth to you,
- ✓ why customers leave,
- ✓ the ten commandments of customer service, and
- ✓ whether or not your restaurant's policies are really customer friendly.

WHAT IS YOUR REPUTATION?

How are reputations for service, good or bad, formed in the minds of the public? How much of any person's or restaurant's reputation is true and how much is hype? In the minds of your customers and prospects, perception is reality. Your reputation is based on word of mouth and observations. It may be accurate, or it may not be.

If we see someone stepping out of a limousine in front of a ritzy restaurant, we automatically assume that the person is rich, successful, and perhaps even powerful or famous. If we see that a company's stock is rising, we assume the company must be doing well; if it's falling, we assume the company must be doing poorly. If other people tell us a particular restaurant is good or bad, we are inclined to believe them. The fact that our taste may be totally different from theirs doesn't really enter into it; a good reputation is good and a bad reputation is bad. Most people won't take the time or effort to confirm either way; instead they will just accept what they hear or read as the truth right up until something happens to change their minds (this is especially true of online reviews).

WHAT MAKES YOU THINK YOUR SERVICE IS GREAT?

The hype, the posturing, the positioning, marketing, the promotions, and the advertising must take a back seat to good old-fashioned service. Ask yourself these questions:

- ✓ Can you deliver the goods?
- ✓ Can you back up the position you've claimed?

✓ Are you who you think you are?

Everyone *says* they give good service. And everyone probably *means* to offer customers a great experience. But most have no system in place with standards, measurement, and rewards.

Great service is partly intangibles. It's people who treat you like a real person, not as an indistinguishable unit passing through their restaurant. It's a friendly tone of voice and good body language. It's a personal connection, not a "professionally friendly" employee. It's personal recognition.

Unfortunately, it's all too easy to come up with examples of bad service even when dealing with "quality" businesses. Here are three examples where, as a customer, I expected a big service response. Instead, I received, well...

Breakfast of blunders

On a recent trip to Ireland, I decided to have breakfast in the hotel's coffee shop. There were five items on the breakfast menu. I ordered a Danish and coffee, my friend a cocoa. No Danish. No problem. I ordered a scone. No scones. No problem—what do you have? The waitress left, then returned and suggested a croissant (not one of the five menu items). I gladly ordered it and was duly served a fresh croissant accompanied by one of those little individual strawberry jam pots. As I opened the jam pot, my friend and I both burst out laughing! The jam was half-eaten. By this time, soured on the service, I just dug in and didn't even bother to mention it!

We all have stories similar to these, about people and businesses from whom we thought we would get superior service, but didn't. Fortunately, there is the other end of the service spectrum.

OUTRAGEOUSLY GOOD SERVICE

I was staying the Vital-Hotel Meiser in Germany near the beautiful town of **Dinkelsbuhl**. The owner happened by my dinner table and asked me about me stay. I told him it was great and that I had chosen his hotel several times. My only complaint was that unlike US and UK hotels there was no way to make coffee or tea in the room. He said that, yes, he had heard this, but it was not normal in German hotels. None the less when I got back to my room after dinner there was a large Keurig coffee machine on my table… Nice!

I was staying at a large property in Thailand with three separate resorts. The manger himself escorted my wife and me to our room. Later that night we told him on our way out that we were going to have dinner at the steak house, a five-minute walk away. The maître'd was waiting for us with a smile and took us to table with our name on it though we had not made a reservation. Best of all, as soon as we walked in the piano player started playing American classics like Sinatra, a very different genre from what we had heard him playing before physically entering the room. Top notch service! The food was great too!

Whose Problem Is It Anyway?

I was a 20-year old waiter in West Palm Beach, Florida, back when many people smoked. A guy came in with his wife and asked me to get him a packet of cigarettes. He handed me two dollars, and I got change from the bar to use in the cigarette machine. The machine did not have the brand he was looking for, and I want back to tell him. He looked at me like I was dumb as a rock, raised his eyebrow and said, "Is that my problem?"

I quickly got the hint and looked around the restaurant. It was early not busy, so I went over to Felix, the other waiter and told him to watch my two tables for a few minutes. I then ran 300 yards down to the 7/11 store to get the brand he wanted. I came back sweating, with the Marlboro's open on a plate with one cigarette protruding from the packet, and a Bic lighter next to it. He nodded and gave a slight smile. The lesson he taught me that night was worth far more than the outrageously large tip he left me. $100 on a $60 tab!

It was the first of many runs I would make to 7/11 on the same mission. I would, of course, be sure to mention it. "Sorry, it took me so long, sir. We did not have the brand you were looking for, so I ran down to the 7/11 to get them for you." The result was always the same, a delighted customer and a much larger tip!

My wife and I were celebrating our anniversary at a fancy restaurant in Laguna Beach. She wanted dessert but was not impressed with the unusual offerings of cheesecake and carrot cake. She said, "You know, what I would love is some chocolates." The waiter apparently overheard because shortly after bringing our coffee he appeared with a plate of six Godiva chocolates. "I overheard the lady asking for chocolates. Would this do?" He asked politely.

Damn right it would do and however he got them and whatever it cost me, it didn't matter!

Going the extra mile does not work out every time, but close enough not to matter!

YOU NEED TO KNOW WHAT A CUSTOMER IS WORTH TO YOU!

We talked earlier about what a customer is worth to you but it's worth brining up again in the context of service. Knowing this information not only helps determine how much money you should spend on advertising and marketing to get a customer, but also how much time, money, and effort you should spend on trying to *keep* a customer. If your customers spend only a few dollars a year, then you certainly can't send them a hamper full of goodies at Christmas time. If, however your customers spend thousands of dollars with you, then it might well be worth the extra goodwill!

I remember, back in the mid-Eighties, reading Carl Sewell's book *Customers for Life*. At that time he found that the average Cadillac buyer at his dealership would spend over $375,000 with him over the years as long as he kept them happy! It must be triple that today.

- ✓ Take a look at the best 20 percent of your guests—what did they spend with you last year?
- ✓ Take a look at your bottom 20 percent—what did they spend with you?
- ✓ After throwing out the bottom 5 percent and top 5 percent that might throw off the scales, what is your average guest worth to your restaurant?

You might be surprised by how much your best guests spend with you in a year. (And you probably haven't counted the referral business they bring in.) Now, project that number over five years, ten years, or perhaps even longer.

For example, I use a local limo service at least once a month to go to the airport and back at a cost of $100 plus tip per trip. This means that if I continue to use them, I will be worth well over $6000 in business to them in the next five years and over to $12,000 over the next ten years when you take inflation into account.

As a good customer I ought to rate the occasional upgrade from a town car to their stretch limo. I should make their Christmas card list and maybe get a small token gift once in a while. Going the extra mile and spending $25 to $50 a year on me is going to be well worth the cost and will be far cheaper than finding a new client to replace me!

The value of a guest cannot, and should not, be measured only in terms of dollars spent. There are other intangible measures of a client's worth that are equally important in terms of building your business. For example, I have several clients who don't do a great deal of business with me but account for a large portion of my referrals. They are always telling others how my business has helped them. Their worth in terms of referral business adds up to far more than the dollars they spend.

Other clients are worth far more than the books show because of their marquee value or brand names. I just picked up the marketing account for a large and prestigious resort. Although the dollars involved are small, having their name on my list of clients will undoubtedly produce more business for me. You will encounter the same sorts of situations. Certain people or companies with whom you do business will add to other people's positive perceptions of your restaurant. That makes those customers special!

Going through this process and figuring out just what your customers are worth, both tangibly and intangibly, on an annual basis, can go a long way to helping you focus your efforts on the customers who most deserve your attention.

CUSTOMER SERVICE IS EVERYONE'S JOB

A fact that often goes unnoticed by executives is that, despite the best advertising, media relations, and all the good intentions in the world, reputations are won and lost on the front lines. An airline is not judged by the quality of its pilots or management, but by its flight attendants and its ticketing agents. I do not use a certain major airline because their ticket lady called me an idiot when I asked her to sign me up for their frequent flyer program and she found that my travel agent had already done it. Then she told me to make sure I had the second number removed when I got off the plane in Dallas. Despite my better judgment, I asked her to do it for me. She refused, saying she only had thirty minutes before the flight took off and she had to deal with other passengers.

Now, you might be thinking that maybe this ticket agent was just having a really bad day, but the following week when my Delta flight was cancelled due to an equipment problem, I found myself once again standing in line with this same agent at the counter. This time, it was the person in front of me who suffered her wrath. I just smiled and never flew Delta again! A car dealership is not judged by the models it sells, but by its salespeople and customer service staff in the shop.

The point is that your staff has your success in their hands. Do you pay them minimum wage, give them no training, and yet expect great results? Or do you put your staff first so they, in turn, will put your customers first?

WHY GUESTS DON'T COME BACK

It is easy to forget that the people we serve can leave at any time. If they leave with an unsolved problem, they are liable to tell a whole bunch of people about that problem. According to the best studies, here is a breakdown of why people stop doing business with any particular person or company. The greatest percentage of loss can be avoided if you train your staff well.

- ✓ 1% get injured, ill, or die.
- ✓ 2% just disappear or get lost in the shuffle.
- ✓ 4% move away from the area.
- ✓ 6% change activities because of friends.
- ✓ 9% leave because of cost.
- ✓ 10% of people just love to change.
- ✓ 68% of customers leave because of indifference to them or their child.

Let's take a moment to look at that last statistic. Almost two thirds of all lost customers leave because of perceived indifference.

THE TEN COMMANDMENTS OF GUEST SERVICE

Guests these days have plenty of options, and plenty of others vying for their time and money. Make the most of your opportunities by following the ten commandments of customer service!

1. Stay close to the wants and needs of your guests. Ask them for honest and critical opinions on your operation. Do not argue or try to defend your position, just shut up and listen. Use follow-up surveys, telephone interviews, and the feedback you get on Trip Advisor, Yelp, Facebook and other social media to generate ways to improve your service. Almost every innovation most restaurants have made over the years has been born out of a guest's suggestion for improvement.

Ask your guests questions like:

- ✓ How do you think we could improve the appearance of our restaurant?
- ✓ Do our hours of operation suit your lifestyle?
- ✓ What specific improvements or additions could we make to serve you better?

Just the fact that you ask their opinions will make your customers feel more special. If you implement a customer's idea, that customer could be yours for life!

Get a consultant to help you make amazing discoveries

In addition to direct customer feedback, another invaluable tool is to get a different pair of eyes examining your business, even if from a totally unrelated sector. You are never the best person to judge your own operation. Quite simply, you can't see the forest for the trees. You need to have an outside person come in and point out obvious things that you can't see.

Solicit opinions from friends, colleagues, and peers and, if all else fails, a consultant. Invite them to ask dumb questions about your greeting procedure, signage, décor, follow up, and your service. By encouraging them to do so, you will often discover areas that could be improved. You will make amazing discoveries such as that your restaurant smells funny, that what you think is a clean bathroom doesn't cut it when you ask a woman. You might discover that you confuse your clients with too many menu choices. You might find you are charging too little for some of your items, as is often the case when I consult with a business. Not all of this feedback will be useful, of course, but it really does pay huge dividends to have outside people look at your operation and open your eyes to what is going on around you.

2. Existing guests are more important than ones you don't have yet.

Don't treat new guests or prospects better than old guests. It is very easy to fall into this trap and it's a surefire recipe for the destruction of your reputation and your business. For example, it's not unusual for a business, in an attempt to gain more customers, to cut prices for new customers to attract business while charging existing customers more money. All the explanations in the world, even if they are heard or read, are not going to change the perception of the established guest that he is getting a raw deal.

A great way to make sure you are doing your best is to always act like your guest has just told you he or she is considering another restaurant as their "go to" place. What would you do differently to try and keep that diner from leaving? Well, first of all, you would likely try to find out what was wrong. But let's suppose there is nothing in particular, or at least nothing the guest is willing to share with you—then what?

You should develop a system to aid in getting guests back on track. Here are some possible steps you could take:

- ✓ Ask everyone on staff what they know about the guest. (They may have shared some problem with the bartender.)
- ✓ Give him personal attention. Take time to chat about his interests (which you should have in your database).
- ✓ Get him involved in an event that is in the future— preferably one that might help lock him in.

In short, you need to go out of your way to do anything in your power to see that he doesn't quit!

Of course, you know as well as I do that most guests, event planners or group leaders do not give a warning before riding off into the sunset never to be seen again. There is a solution, though: Treat each and every client as though they were going to quit each and every month, and you will soon see a dramatic improvement in your customer service and retention.

3. Follow up on all the things you say you will do, or don't say anything.

One of the simplest ways to insure good service is to schedule a follow-up call at the very same time you resolve to fix a problem or respond to a request. Murphy's law pretty much guarantees that if a diner has a problem that you resolve to fix, something will also go wrong with the planned fix, adding insult to injury. The best way to ensure that such events don't permanently damage your reputation is to outline the proposed action, then immediately schedule a follow-up call to ensure that such action has taken place.

When fixing problems or responding to requests, you must always have a fail-safe system to ensure that the actual requests, however simple, were carried out. In fact, nothing damages a reputation more than a few simple requests not carried to their successful conclusion. People then start to wonder: If the owner or manager can't take care of such a little thing, how will larger problems be managed?

4. Remember and use guests' names and other information.

As mentioned earlier, remembering someone's name is one of the sincerest compliments you can pay a person. It builds their self-esteem; it lets them know you think they are important and they have made an impression on you. The sound of a person's name, pronounced correctly, is one of the nicest sounds in the world, at least to that person.

Staff should be trained to remember and use people's names. Some people are just better at this than others. Don't put the inept ones in customer contact positions.

On an episode of the TV show *Undercover Boss,* the CEO of 7/11 visited a store in Shirley, New York, to find out why it was one of the chain's top coffee-selling stores in the nation, selling 2500 cups of coffee a day. That's a lot of coffee in a town whose population is less than 30,000. Dolores had made the coffee and served customers there for 18 years and knew almost all of her customers by name. People would come in for coffee and a good morning smile from Dolores. The CEO said, "That's why we're selling 2,500 cups of coffee. Not because we have great coffee, but because we have Dolores there."

When a diner is greeted by name, it starts their experience in your restaurant off on a positive note.

It is vital when you engage in a conversation, or are introduced to someone, to remember his or her name. The fastest way to lose any rapport that you are building is to forget the name and have to ask it again. It has been shown that calling someone by their name, first or last, dramatically increases the bonding and communication. Other people feel as though they know you if you call them by their names.

Some people are good with names. Almost everyone at the pinnacle of success is excellent. People like former President Harry Truman could call literally thousands of people, from senators to scullery maids, by their first names. Can you imagine the feeling of joy and satisfaction you would get by having the president of the United States call you by your first name? Can you imagine the lengths a simple attendant might go to please when the president took the trouble to remember his or her name? The answer is clear. If you really try to improve your retention of people's names, you will soon discover the astonishing power of this simple act.

The simple effort of correctly pronouncing a person's name is a hundred times more powerful when the name has its origins in a foreign country. Learn how to correctly say a particularly difficult Greek name, or Japanese name, and you may be the only person they have ever met who has made the effort. That makes for a powerful bonding in your relationship that will have very deep roots. The person can't help but like and respect you when you alone have gone to the trouble of learning to pronounce his or her name correctly.

Unfortunately, not everyone has the natural ability to instantly put a name to a face. To remember names or other data the first time you hear them, you must pay attention. Be really mentally alert when you are introduced to a new person. Listen to their name closely and repeat it several times in your head. Ask them to repeat it if you are unsure you heard them correctly. Ask them to pronounce it for you if it is unusual. Echo the name back to them in a way that encourages correction if necessary. "Nice to meet you, Darin..." Or you can echo the name to simply acknowledge and confirm that you have understood. Use their name as often as you can in the first few minutes you talk to them. This will help reinforce the name in your memory.

Some memory techniques suggest that you look at the face and link a facial feature with the sound of the name. This could be something like, "Roberta, for her rosy cheeks," or "Stan, for a strong jaw." The idea is to be looking at a facial feature and linking their name with that feature. This technique greatly improves your ability to retain a name.

Another technique is to link this new person to a person you know well. For example, if I meet a "Ron," I link it to my good friend Ron. I find something that is similar between the new Ron and the familiar friend Ron. In this way, your mind links the two names and individuals together, making it easier to remember the name. These types of techniques will greatly assist you in recalling and remembering the names and faces of new people. This will also help you in bonding to these people quickly, which will make meeting new people fun and rewarding.

When a greeter or server uses a customer's name, it makes the customer feel like they're special, not just another customer. The same thing is accomplished by recalling something about that customer:

- Would you like to start off with your usual Coors Light?
- The last time you were in, you were about to leave for New York. Did you have a good trip?
- Do you want your usual medium rare hamburger and onion rings today, or should I bring you a menu?
- I see you're no longer using a cane. Your back must be better!
- Your favorite booth is currently occupied, but the adjacent one is available.

5. Give personal attention.

Many business relationships today come down to just that—relationships. The deeper you understand your guests' wants, needs, prejudices, and personal interests, above and beyond the actual dining transactions, the greater the chance you have of serving them for the long haul. Simple touches like birthday cards, Christmas cards, and anniversary cards go a lot further than the dollars you spend on advertising. Make notes of their favorite beverages, cigars, and foods. In fact, developing a customer profile in a database is a must for legendary service.

The profile I use has over 50 questions about my clients ("partners") that over time, through various conversations, I fill in. It contains information like where they were born, where they went to school, what their parents did, what sports they like, what teams they support, which cars they drive, what religion they are, how many children they have, and so forth. Some of these things I ask point blank; others my clients tell me over time in the natural flow of conversation. All of this information is deeply valuable in building a relationship and turning conversations toward their areas of interest rather than mine.

Remember, everyone in the world has this great big badge on his or her chest which reads "MAKE ME FEEL IMPORTANT." Succeed in that endeavor and you will succeed in everything. No matter what else is going on, at least smile, nod, or wave whenever someone meets your eye.

6. Make employees—all employees—service oriented.

The best way to get all employees in a service mode is simply to tell every new employee that their number one job, regardless of position or job description, is customer service. Let them know that if they cannot answer a question or help a customer, they are to help that customer locate someone else who can. Employees, like everyone else, will rise to the level of your expectations only if they are given those expectations. Set yourself up for service success by making customer service everyone's job!

7. Be accessible.

When customers want to reach your restaurant, they want to do it now! Few things are more irritating than calling a restaurant and getting voice mail automatically. When people call to book a table, they want immediate confirmation. If they have to call back, they may decide to try elsewhere.

If callers are trying to reach you personally, tell your receptionist when you will be returning calls, so that the person waiting for the call can continue with his daily life. Nothing irritates me (and most other people) more than being told I will be called right back only to be hanging by the phone for two hours waiting for the call.

Provide real people to your website's visitors

You are going to think I am making this up, but I assure you I am not. Recently I had a general manager call me and yell at me because I put his contact information on his restaurant's web site. He told me in no uncertain terms that he did not want his guests emailing him at all hours of the day. In fact, he didn't want them to email him at all! Don't play hide-and-seek with your guests and potential guests. Include your name, phone number, email address, and street address, to show that you are a real person and value service. A mark of the company with poor service is that it doesn't have any contact information displayed on its site, or hides it so no one can find it. (Another sign is that they don't answer their email!) Show your website visitors that you care by including your contact number and the times you wish to be called. Offer a feedback email section to get guests' opinions on your food and service. It's better they tell you there's a problem than telling all of their friends!

8. Never tell your customers about your problems or the restaurant's; they don't care.

Often, especially in situations where an employee like a bartender spends a lot of time with a particular guest, the guest may ask questions or probe about the restaurant's business information or problems with a guest. There is the temptation for the employee to cross the boundary and give out information. Train employees to answer questions with vague replies like, "It varies a lot," or "My manager can better answer that. Shall I call her over?"

Various people may try to get information from you directly. In reality, they are not interested in your problems. Do not be conned into sharing with them. Find out everything you can about your guests, while saying little or nothing about yourself. As the Chinese say, "Keep the tiger behind the bamboo!"

9. Be consistent in all your actions.

Simple, consistent actions build reputations. It is through your simple actions that you can build your customer service. And if you combine several simple actions together you can take giant leaps over your competition as you build your reputation.

After each visit to the dentist, my dentist called my house that evening to make sure I felt all right. Not only that, but when he referred me to surgery with another physician, he found out when the surgery was scheduled and called me that night to see how it had gone, even though he was not personally involved. When my child was born, he sent me a bottle of wine with his label on it. Now this is someone whom I only saw every six months, yet he acted as if he was almost part of the family. The result was simple: Even when I moved my business over fifty miles away, I still drove to his office. He had backed up his reputation with service!

10. Always smile!

Body language is something that's not often considered as part of service but is important. It not only affects your customers; it affects your other employees. Many high-end restaurants won't hire servers who don't make positive eye contact in the interview. If someone can't sit straight, stand straight, and walk around with a smile, it's a problem that will grow like cancer. Tell staff that one of the surest ways of giving good service (and therefore getting good tips) is to project the type of attitude you expect to get back. They need to pay careful attention to your body language, posture, and facial expressions. They should always look as if they are having the time of your life, no matter what is going on around them! Research shows that emotions are contagious. Diners will be happier when the staff is happier.

ARE YOU DOING YOUR BEST?

A question I often ask in my seminars is, "Are you good at what you do?" To which—surprise, surprise—most people answer with the most resounding YES of the day. Then I ask them if, in fact, they are settling for being good when they could be GREAT! Usually it gets a little quiet around that time. In today's competitive climate, good is the standard—if you aren't good, you won't be around for very long. But how much more could you accomplish in building your reputation for service (and your income) if, instead of just being good, you actually were GREAT!

You must build your reputation first with your employees, then with your customers, then with the broader community of all prospects.

CUSTOMER SERVICE GOALS FOR THE SUPERIOR BUSINESS

I devised the following customer service goals that, with a little amendment, you might find useful in applying to your particular restaurant.

- Collect information about customer preferences and habits and use this information to personalize relationships and services.
- Keep our present guests.
- Keep our diners delighted, not just satisfied, with our services.
- Ensure that our guests always have reason to speak well of our business and employees.
- Help our present guests help us attract new guests and keep them happy as well.
- Maintain excellent communication with our guests at all times and greet clients by name.
- Treat our employees well so they'll treat our customers the same way.
- Realize that all guest complaints give us a chance to improve. Act quickly and fairly to resolve all complaints.

- Make every single employee responsive to customer service.
- Be known as a restaurant that has superior guest service and retention.

QUANTIFYING SUPERIOR SERVICE

Goals like the ones above are a great place to start when it comes to improving service, but what exactly is great service? Ask that question of most people and their answers will be, "I can't quite describe it, but I know it when I get it!" Great service is like good taste; it varies with the eye of the beholder. Despite this, you must specify what great service is.

A major reason that poor service happens is because in most business and restaurants, great service is not *quantified*. It may be talked about, talked about, and talked about again, but rarely is it taken to the next step and measured in a host of different ways. As you no doubt already know from other areas of your business, what gets measured is what gets done.

With that thought in mind, I suggest that you sit down with your staff and identify as many areas as you can in which service is given.

For example:
- ✓ Answering the phone: How many rings are acceptable?
- ✓ How often will you send follow-up cards, thank you cards, or reminders?
- ✓ How quickly will you resolve any billing problems?
- ✓ How and when will you thank people for their referrals?
- ✓ What level do you want to keep your number of monthly complaints below?
- ✓ How clean will the restaurants be? The restrooms?

By specifically quantifying how you intend to measure performance, you will take a quantum jump in your ability to achieve higher levels of service performance.

Policy must back up your position

A key factor many forget is that once a reputation enhancement plan is in place, policies must allow your employees to carry out their mission without conflict. You cannot build a reputation for service and then not set a good example yourself. If your employees don't believe you are committed to great service, you can be sure no one else will! For example, you can't create a friendly atmosphere if signage all over the property tells you WHAT YOU CAN'T DO!

Review all polices regularly, eliminate as many negative or guest unfriendly ones once as possible. Provide front-line employees with discretion and training to solve common problems on the spot.

SUMMARY

Backing up your reputation with the real McCoy is essential for the long-term establishment of your legendary reputation. When it comes to service, it is the frontline people and the little things that can make or break your reputation.

Understand why guests leaves and what their most common complaints are, then take action to address them. Stay close to your guests and always solicit feedback on how you are doing and how you might improve. Remember that existing customers are always more valuable than guests you don't have yet.

Follow up on everything you say you will do, and check that it's been done. Make an extra effort to remember all your guests' names and give them the special attention that everyone craves. Make sure your employees are trained and that they understand that, no matter what their positions, customer service is everyone's job.

Always be accessible or give clear instructions on when and where you can be reached. Never discuss any of your problems with guests and instruct staff to do the same; they don't care. Constantly re-evaluate polices to make them more customer friendly and remove all negative signage.

Continually question whether you are doing your best to set customer service goals and, most important of all, quantify superior service. Once you decide what you will do to create great service, back up your goals and policies by giving those who work for you the power, authority, and moral guidance to provide superior service.

Last, but not least, always be consistent in your actions and don't forget to smile!

The words of Henry David Thoreau ring just as true today in the new millennium as they did when he first spoke them, "What you do speaks so loud I cannot hear what you are saying."

"Life is uncertain. Eat dessert first."
—Ernestine Ulmer

Epilogue

The restaurant business is changing fast. Your traditional income streams are being attacked from all sides. You must maximize your marketing at every level to stay ahead of the competition. Start by choosing a unique selling proposition for your restaurant. Back this up by using the "One Strategy" (making ONE thing at every touchpoint of your restaurant memorable to your guests—so memorable that they market for you) and creating "Kodak moments" for your guests at every touchpoint. This will turn your guests into your own social media marketing army.

Use your website to sell not just to provide information. Use real sales copy, stories, testimonials and calls to action. Prospective guests will read copy if it's interesting and Google will read it either way, which helps your SEO rankings.

He with the biggest database wins, so do everything you can to build yours and not just your email database. Build your Facebook fan base, you Instagram followers, your LinkedIn contacts and grow whatever other social media you use. The more eyes that see your marketing, the more effective it will be. Constantly be growing your own "media empire."

Use landing pages and targeted Facebook ads to rapidly expand your lists. Be creative with your emails. Don't bombard your guests with boring corporate-speak or discount offer after discount offer. Engage, educate and entertain your guests with your social media posts and your emails. Offer fun and value in your emails and your open rates will remain high while minimizing your unsubscribe rates. If you do this, you can email far more often than you do now. No matter what anyone tells you, the more you mail the more you make!

Print ads, brochures, flyers and direct mail still have their place but you must use them strategically and they must be creative. Creating brochures, ads or flyers that look and sound the same as all your competitors will not get you anywhere. If you can't stand out don't do it!

The more specialized your marketing, the more successful it will be. Sort your email lists into as many specific segments as possible (for example, millennials, seniors, wine lovers, and market activities and events to those most likely to respond.

Train your people how to sell. I have seen a few simple scripts at the front desk lead to amazing gains in revenue. Formal sales training in the back of the house can make or break a restaurant. Turn your servers into sellers! Educate them in the basics of wine and storytelling, for all good storytellers are great salespeople.

Referrals should drive your banquet and events business, but they should not be left to chance. Social proof is also an indirect form of referrals or not! Ask your good customers to post reviews on Yelp, Trip Advisor, Facebook and Google. Deal with negative reviews quickly and professionally using the five-step formula I provided. On occasion, you must take the offensive. Do not be afraid of doing so; call out the fakers, freeloaders and the trolls. Your real customers will support your efforts

Make sure you quantify your service at every level—if you don't, there is really no telling how good or bad it really is. Review your rules and restrictions to make sure they are as guest friendly as possible.

Try to make incremental improvements in each one of these key areas we have discussed, and your business is sure to grow. I'd wish you good luck but if you follow the advice in these pages you won't need it!

Have a Legendary Year,
Andrew Wood

ABOUT ANDREW WOOD

Andrew Wood is the CEO of Legendary Marketing, a Tampa/Orlando based ad agency. He is the world's leading expert on golf, resort, destination, and real estate marketing - although his successes go far beyond these core industries.

Author of over 20 books including: *Selling -Out Sell Everyone! The Golf Marketing Bible, Cunningly Clever Marketing, Cunningly Clever Entrepreneur, Making Your Business the One They Choose, Legendary Leadership* and *Legendary Advice!*

Andrew has spoken to thousands of audiences worldwide and was the top ranked speaker at 97.7% of the events where he has spoken.

A pioneer in internet marketing his creative talent, out of the box ideas, copywriting skills and marketing strategy are at the core of his expertise. He is regarded as one of the top marketing minds in the world for his ability to craft a winning strategy, generating leads and increase income!

Andrew offers expert business consulting services. For more information please contact him direct using his phone number below.

Contact: Andrew Wood, Direct @ 1 352-266-2099
www.AndrewWoodinc.com

OTHER BOOKS BY THE AUTHOR...

Other Books by Andrew Wood

Fame – How to Build an Iconic Personal Brand in Any Industry

No One Gets Out Alive – How to Create a Life Well Lived

Cunningly Clever Entrepreneur

Legendary Advice—101 Proven Strategies to Increase Your Income, Wealth & Lifestyle

Legendary Achievement—How to Maximize Your True Potential & Live the Life of Your Dreams

Cunningly Clever Marketing

Your Million Dollar Laptop

Legendary Selling

Legendary Leadership

Making Your Business the One They Choose

The Traits of Champions (with Brian Tracy)

The Joy of Golf

The Golf Marketing Bible

The Hotel & Resort Marketing Bible

The Golf Sales Bible

How to Make $150,000 a Year Teaching Golf

Desperately Seeking Members (as Harvey S. McKlintock)

Andrew Wood

Made in the USA
Columbia, SC
12 February 2024